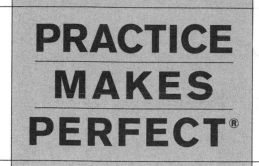

PRACTICE MAKES PERFECT®

German Problem Solver

Ed Swick

New York   Chicago   San Francisco   Lisbon   London   Madrid   Mexico City
Milan   New Delhi   San Juan   Seoul   Singapore   Sydney   Toronto

The McGraw·Hill Companies

Copyright © 2013 by The McGraw-Hill Companies, Inc. All rights reserved. Printed in
the United States of America. Except as permitted under the United States Copyright
Act of 1976, no part of this publication may be reproduced or distributed in any form
or by any means, or stored in a database or retrieval system, without the prior written
permission of the publisher.

1 2 3 4 5 6 7 8 9 10 11 12 13 14 15   QDB/QDB   1 0 9 8 7 6 5 4 3

ISBN   978-0-07-179115-1
MHID   0-07-179115-9

e-ISBN   978-0-07-179116-8
e-MHID   0-07-179116-7

Library of Congress Control Number 2012947474

McGraw-Hill, the McGraw-Hill Publishing logo, Practice Makes Perfect, and related
trade dress are trademarks or registered trademarks of The McGraw-Hill Companies
and/or its affiliates in the United States and other countries and may not be used
without written permission. All other trademarks are the property of their respective
owners. The McGraw-Hill Companies is not associated with any product or vendor
mentioned in this book.

McGraw-Hill products are available at special quantity discounts to use as premiums
and sales promotions or for use in corporate training programs. To contact a
representative, please e-mail us at bulksales@mcgraw-hill.com.

This book is printed on acid-free paper.

Also by Ed Swick

Practice Makes Perfect: German Vocabulary
Practice Makes Perfect: Complete German Grammar
Practice Makes Perfect: German Pronouns and Prepositions
Practice Makes Perfect: German Sentence Builder
German Grammar Drills

Contents

Preface

This book is aptly named a *problem solver*. Unlike other approaches to the German language, this book does not look at all aspects of German grammar and structure; rather, it isolates those things in the language that English speakers find problematic. It then describes them, analyzes the complexities that cause consternation, and provides explanations and examples of how the problem areas work.

There are nineteen chapters in the book that delve into nineteen specific areas of difficulty. After these areas have been described, explained, and illustrated, they are placed in a wide variety of exercises, in which the reader can manipulate the problem areas and become more familiar with how they function and thereby take control of them. If a particular subject still seems difficult after working through a chapter, the reader should simply repeat the chapter and practice with the exercises again.

German irregular verbs are a special problem for English speakers, even though the English language has numerous irregular verbs that are similar to German verbs. To make working with German irregular verbs more convenient, the reader will find an appendix comprising a list of all irregular verbs in German. This appendix shows the verb in its infinitive form, with any present tense irregularity, in its past tense, in its participial form, and as a subjunctive II conjugation. This resource will prove to be essential for working with verbs in this book.

The twentieth chapter of the book does not discuss a specific problem area or describe any particular linguistic difficulty in German. Instead, it is a miniature linguistic laboratory that the reader can use to practice all aspects of the language simultaneously. German, like any language, is not a random series of conjugations, declensions, and usages of vocabulary. It is a combination of all those things that make communication in the language comprehensible and accurate. Therefore, in the twentieth chapter the reader will be writing creatively and not just practicing with isolated concepts. The exercises are not for grammatical or vocabulary practice; rather, they are a forum for the reader to apply his or her knowledge of German in a personal way. Of course, there will be some guidelines for this type of creative writing, but generally the reader will have ample opportunities to experiment in writing.

This series of books is intentionally called *Practice Makes Perfect* because that idea is basic to learning and mastering a new language. **Übung macht den Meister.**

Acknowledgment

I would like to express my gratitude to my friend Stefan Feyen for his generous help and suggestions.

Determining gender and forming plurals

Many who are learning German struggle with the seemingly illogical approach that the language takes when determining gender. This is particularly true for English speakers, who are accustomed to a simple method for assigning gender to a noun: If the noun refers to a male, it's masculine. If it refers to a female, it's feminine. And if it refers to an inanimate object, the noun is neuter. There are a few exceptions, but for the most part, gender in the English language is determined by the obvious sexual gender of a person or the fact that an object is inanimate.

In small measure, German often considers males and females as masculine and feminine nouns, respectively. This is easy for an English speaker to understand. But it is the other ways of assigning gender to a noun that cause consternation. There often seems to be no rhyme or reason for why a noun is assigned a certain gender. But that is only what it *seems*. Let's look at the various patterns to German gender, which will help make sense of why a noun is considered masculine, feminine, or neuter.

Knowing the right gender of a noun is important for speaking and writing correctly in German. If the wrong gender is used in a sentence, the speaker or writer will still be understood, but the sentence will seem awkward or sometimes even silly. Let's use a couple examples in English, in which the wrong pronoun is used. This is similar to what a German understands when the wrong article is used. The gender is wrong, but the message is understood.

> Question: "Is your mother at home?"
>
> Answer: "No, he's at work right now."
>
> Question: "Did your brother leave for school yet?"
>
> Answer: "No, it's taking a shower."

There is no harm in making a gender error, but concentrating on the patterns that can help determine gender will aid you in increasing your accuracy in German.

First, let's look at those masculine and feminine nouns that are of these two respective genders, because these nouns describe males and females. For example:

Masculine nouns

der Mann	*man, husband*
der Junge	*boy*
der Onkel	*uncle*
der Sohn	*son*
der Neffe	*nephew*

der Vater	*father*
der Löwe	*lion*
der Stier	*bull*

Feminine nouns

die Frau	*woman, wife*
die Tante	*aunt*
die Tochter	*daughter*
die Schwester	*sister*
die Nichte	*niece*
die Mutter	*mother*
die Löwin	*lioness*
die Kuh	*cow*

ÜBUNG

1·1

In the blank provided, write the correct article for the gender of the given noun. For example:

der Mann *man*

1. _____ Großvater   *grandfather*

2. _____ Großmutter   *grandmother*

3. _____ Bruder   *brother*

4. _____ Henne   *hen*

5. _____ Hahn   *rooster*

6. _____ Hirsch   *stag*

7. _____ Stute   *mare*

8. _____ Schwager   *brother-in-law*

9. _____ Schwiegermutter   *mother-in-law*

10. _____ Stieftochter   *stepdaughter*

Neuter nouns are not exclusively inanimate objects in German. Many are, such as the following:

Neuter nouns

das Haus	*house*
das Dorf	*village*
das Buch	*book*
das Restaurant	*restaurant*
das Tischtuch	*tablecloth*

But other neuter nouns can refer to people, animals, and plants. Often these nouns are neuter because they have one of the neuter suffixes, **-chen** or **-lein**, which are used to form a diminutive. For example:

das Mädchen	*girl*
das Röslein	*little rose*
das Kind	*child*
das Pferd	*horse*
das Schwein	*pig, swine*

ÜBUNG
1·2

In the blank provided, write the correct article for the gender of the given noun. For example:

<u>der</u> Mann *man*

1. _____ Schwägerin — *sister-in-law*
2. _____ Hemd — *shirt*
3. _____ Brüderchen — *little brother*
4. _____ Bruthenne — *sitting hen*
5. _____ Urgroßvater — *great-grandfather*
6. _____ Dach — *roof*
7. _____ Bier — *beer*
8. _____ Fräulein — *miss, little woman*
9. _____ Sau — *sow*
10. _____ Feuerwehrmann — *fireman*

Now let's look at some patterns that are helpful in determining the gender of a noun. It's important to understand that these patterns are only *helpful* in coming up with the correct gender of a noun. German has many exceptions, and in some cases a noun can have two genders. The patterns are only general guidelines that indicate what the gender of a noun is *most likely* to be.

Patterns that identify masculine nouns

1. Many nouns that end in **-el**, **-en**, or **-er** tend to be masculine: **der Onkel** (*uncle*), **der Garten** (*garden*), **der Lehrer** (*teacher*).

2. Many nouns that are formed from the stem of a verb or from its past tense or past participle tend to be masculine. For example:

VERB	STEM	MASCULINE NOUN	
besuchen	besuch	der Besuch	*visit*
gehen	gegangen (*participle*)	der Gang	*walk, gait*

(*continued*)

VERB	STEM	MASCULINE NOUN	
schlafen	schlaf	der Schlaf	*sleep*
schlagen	schlag	der Schlag	*blow, punch*
schmelzen	schmelz	der Schmelz	*glaze*
sitzen (saß)	sass (*past tense*)	der Satz	*sentence*
sitzen	sitz	der Sitz	*seat*
sprechen	gesprochen (*participle*)	der Spruch	*motto, adage*
verstehen	verstand (*past tense*)	der Verstand	*understanding*

3. Nouns that end in **-ich** or **-ig** tend to be masculine: **der Teppich** (*carpet*), **der Käfig** (*cage*).

4. Nouns that end in **-ling** or **-us** are masculine: **der Jüngling** (*boy*), **der Kommunismus** (*communism*).

5. Several nouns that end in **-e** and refer to males are masculine: **der Löwe** (*lion*), **der Matrose** (*sailor*), **der Knabe** (*boy, lad*).

Patterns that identify feminine nouns

1. Nouns that are the feminine counterpart of a masculine noun, particularly a profession, end in **-in** and are always feminine.

MASCULINE	FEMININE	
der Arzt	die Ärztin	*doctor, physician*
der Chef	die Chefin	*boss*
der Kanzler	die Kanzlerin	*chancellor*
der Lehrer	die Lehrerin	*teacher*
der Schauspieler	die Schauspielerin	*actress*

2. Nouns that end in **-heit** and **-keit** are feminine: **die Gesundheit** (*health*), **die Einsamkeit** (*loneliness*).

3. Nouns that end in **-ung** and **-schaft** are feminine: **die Lösung** (*solution*), **die Landschaft** (*landscape*).

4. Nouns that end in **-ion** and **-tät** are feminine: **die Position** (*position*), **die Universität** (*university*).

5. Many nouns that end in **-e** tend to be feminine. For example:

die Bluse	*blouse*
die Frage	*question*
die Lampe	*lamp*
die Landkarte	*map*
die Schule	*school*

6. Nouns that end in **-ik** tend to be feminine: **die Kritik** (*criticism*), **die Statistik** (*statistics*).

7. Nouns that end in **-ur** tend to be feminine: **die Natur** (*nature*).

8. Nouns that end in **-ei** are feminine: **die Schweinerei** (*mess*).

9. Nouns that end in **-kunft** are feminine: **die Auskunft** (*information*).

10. A few nouns end in **-a**. They are mostly foreign words, and some are considered feminine nouns. These need to be contrasted with the few neuter nouns that end in **-a**. The two groups can *sometimes* be distinguished by their plural formations. Feminine nouns form their plural with an **-s** ending. Neuter nouns sometimes form their plural by changing **-a** to **-en** but also sometimes to an **-s**. For example:

FEMININE		NEUTER	
die Kamera, die Kameras	*camera*	das Sofa, die Sofas	*sofa*
die Mama, die Mamas	*mama*	das Drama, die Dramen	*drama*

ÜBUNG
1·3

In the blank provided, write the correct article for the gender of the given noun. For example:

der Mann (*man*)

1. _____ Zeitung (*newspaper*)
2. _____ Versuch (*attempt*)
3. _____ Krankheit (*illness*)
4. _____ Computer (*computer*)
5. _____ DVD-Spieler (*DVD player*)
6. _____ Ausstellung (*exhibition*)
7. _____ Musik (*music*)
8. _____ Mantel (*coat*)
9. _____ Höhe (*height*)
10. _____ Gescheitheit (*cleverness*)
11. _____ Gesellschaft (*society*)
12. _____ Wagen (*car*)
13. _____ Bruch (*break*)
14. _____ Situation (*situation*)
15. _____ Krankenschwester (*nurse*)

16. _____ Hausfrau (*housewife*)
17. _____ Künstlerin (*artist*)
18. _____ Frühling (*spring*)
19. _____ Blitz (*lightning*)
20. _____ Qualität (*quality*)
21. _____ Kollege (*colleague*)
22. _____ Rettich (*radish*)
23. _____ Brunnen (*well*)
24. _____ Brüderlein (*little brother*)
25. _____ Freiheit (*freedom*)
26. _____ Katze (*cat*)
27. _____ Sportler (*athlete*)
28. _____ Kamera (*camera*)
29. _____ Sicherheit (*safety*)
30. _____ Gärtnerin (*gardner*)

Patterns that identify neuter nouns

1. Infinitives are often used as nouns. When that is so, the noun is neuter. For example: das **Einkommen** (*income*), **das Haben** (*credit*).

2. Nouns that end in **-um** or **-tum** are most frequently neuter: **das Studium** (*studies*), **das Königtum** (*kingdom*).

3. In many cases, nouns with the prefix **Ge-** are neuter. Although most nouns with the prefix are neuter, the prefix can occur with other genders. For example:

NEUTER		OTHER GENDER	
das Gespräch	*conversation*	die Gestalt	*form, build*
das Gesicht	*face*	der Geschmack	*taste*
das Gesetz	*law*	die Geschichte	*history*
das Geschehen	*happening*	der Geruch	*smell*
das Geschäft	*business*	die Geschwindigkeit	*speed*
das Gewicht	*weight*	der Gestank	*stench*
das Geschrei	*screaming*	die Gewalt	*power*
das Getränk	*drink*	der Gewinn	*profit*

4. Words that end in **-o** are foreign words and tend to be neuter: **das Auto** (*car*).

ÜBUNG
1·4

In the blank provided, write the correct article for the gender of the given noun. For example:

der Mann (*man*)

1. _____ König (*king*)

2. _____ Rechnen (*arithmetic*)

3. _____ Getreide (*grain*)

4. _____ Übung (*exercise*)

5. _____ Kino (*movie theater*)

6. _____ Schädel (*skull*)

7. _____ Summen (*humming*)

8. _____ Behörde (*authority*)

9. _____ Erniedrigung (*humiliation*)

10. _____ Gymnasium (*prep school*)

11. _____ Lotto (*lottery*)

12. _____ Eigentum (*property*)

13. _____ Fluss (*river*)

14. _____ Straße (*street*)

15. _____ Literatur (*literature*)

16. _____ Ankunft (*arrival*)

17. _____ Managerin (*manager*)

18. _____ Büchlein (*little book*)

19. _____ Foto (*photo*)

20. _____ Klarheit (*clarity*)

21. _____ Vertrag (*contract*)

22. _____ Gelächter (*laughter*)

23. _____ Wissen (*knowledge*)

24. _____ Gehorsamkeit (*obedience*)

25. _____ Spielerei (*playing around*)

26. _____ Deckel (*top, lid*)

27. _____ Häuptling (*chief*)

28. _____ Datum (*date*)

29. _____ Besen (*broom*)

30. _____ Unterkunft (*accommodation, lodging*)

Prefixes

Only on rare occasion will the addition of a prefix on a noun change its gender. For the most part, prefixes—whether separable or inseparable or a noun—do not change the gender of a noun. For example:

der Spruch	*motto*
der Anspruch	*claim*
die Lage	*situation*
die Beilage	*supplement*
das Buch	*book*
das Handbuch	*handbook*

A rare exception would be:

die Kenntnis	*knowledge*
das Bekenntnis	*confession*

ÜBUNG
1·5

In the blank provided, write the correct article for the gender of the given noun. For example:

der Mann (*man*)

1. _____ Beifall (*applause*)
2. _____ Übertragung (*transmission*)
3. _____ Vermittler (*mediator*)
4. _____ Aussprache (*pronunciation*)
5. _____ Gegensatz (*opposite*)
6. _____ Enttäuschung (*disappointment*)
7. _____ Abstieg (*descent, decline*)
8. _____ Ertrag (*yield*)
9. _____ Durchflug (*transit, flight through*)
10. _____ Widerstand (*resistance*)
11. _____ Waffenschmuggel (*gun-running*)
12. _____ Untergang (*setting, downfall*)
13. _____ Bemühen (*effort*)
14. _____ Fürbitte (*intercession*)
15. _____ Vorsorge (*precautions*)
16. _____ Umtausch (*exchange*)
17. _____ Pinselstrich (*brushstroke*)
18. _____ Nachfolge (*succession*)
19. _____ Mitfahrer (*fellow passenger*)
20. _____ Kursbuch (*timetable*)

Plurals

The plural ending that is so familiar to English speakers is **-s**. This plural ending also exists in German but to a much smaller degree. It only occurs with foreign words, primarily those that end in a vowel. For example:

die Kamera, die Kameras	*cameras*
das Kino, die Kinos	*movie theaters*

English is derived in great part from Anglo-Saxon German, and therefore many old English words form their plural in the Anglo-Saxon way. These words do not end in -s, and the plural forms are called *irregular*. For example:

SINGULAR	PLURAL	SINGULAR	PLURAL
man	men	child	children
mouse	mice	goose	geese

Over the centuries, words such as those illustrated have changed only slightly and still retain some of the old approach to forming plurals. German still forms plurals in this traditional way. That should be recognized to understand and *accept* how Germans change a singular word to a plural word. It's different from English, yet it conforms to our own very small, English/Anglo-Saxon tradition. Let's look at plurals from the standpoint of gender, because it is within each gender that certain patterns evolve.

Masculine plurals

Masculine nouns that end in **-el**, **-en**, and **-er** do not have a suffix that has to be added in the plural. Instead, the plural article (**die**) is used, and often an umlaut is added to the noun. For example:

SINGULAR	PLURAL	
der Onkel	die Onkel	*uncles*
der Garten	die Gärten	*gardens*
der Bruder	die Brüder	*brothers*

If a masculine noun is composed of one syllable or one syllable plus a prefix, it tends to form its plural with an **-e** ending and often an umlaut. For example:

SINGULAR	PLURAL	
der Satz	die Sätze	*sentences*
der Vertrag	die Verträge	*contracts*
der Fahrstuhl	die Fahrstühle	*elevators*

There are two notable exceptions to this rule, namely, **der Mann** and **der Herr**. They form their plurals in an irregular way: **der Mann, die Männer** (*men*); **der Herr, die Herren** (*gentlemen*).

Masculine nouns that come from a foreign source and have the accent on the last syllable tend to form the plural with an **-en** ending. For example:

SINGULAR	PLURAL	
der Soldat	die Soldaten	*soldiers*
der Präsident	die Präsidenten	*presidents*
der Komponist	die Komponisten	*composers*

In the blank provided, write the correct plural form of the given noun. For example:

der Mann (*man*) *die Männer*

1. der Elefant (*elephant*) _____

2. der Junge (*boy*) _____

3. der Wagen (*car*) _____

4. der Lehrer (*teacher*) _____

5. der Pilot (*pilot*) _____

6. der Absatz (*heel*) _____

7. der Fluss (*river*) _____

8. der Löwe (*lion*) _____

9. der Diplomat (*diplomat*) _____

10. der Tänzer (*dancer*) _____

11. der Bleistift (*pencil*) _____

12. der Tisch (*table*) _____

13. der Schädel (*skull*) _____

14. der Boden (*floor*) _____

15. der Pinsel (*paintbrush*) _____

Feminine plurals

Feminine nouns that end in **-e** form their plural with an **-n** ending. Feminine nouns that end in **-in** form their plural with an **-nen** ending. For example:

die Lampe, die Lampen	*lamps*	die Lehrerin, die Lehrerinnen	*teachers*
die Frage, die Fragen	*questions*	die Chefin, die Chefinnen	*bosses*

The plural ending **-en** is used with feminine nouns that end in **-heit**, **-keit**, **-ung**, **-schaft**, **-ion**, **-tät**, **-ik**, **-ur**, and **-ei**. For example:

die Einheiten	*unities*	die Grausamkeiten	*cruelties*
die Zeitungen	*newspapers*	die Wirtschaften	*economies*
die Situationen	*situations*	die Universitäten	*universities*
die Statistiken	*statistics*	die Naturen	*natures*
die Schweinereien	*messes*		

Feminine nouns that end in **-kunft** form their plural by the addition of an umlaut and the ending **-e**. For example: **die Auskünfte** (*information*).

Two feminine nouns have their own distinct plural formation: **die Mutter, die Mütter** (*mothers*); **die Tochter, die Töchter** (*daughters*).

Neuter plurals

Many monosyllabic neuter nouns form their plural by adding an umlaut and/or the ending **-er** to the noun. For example:

das Buch	die Bücher	*books*
das Kind	die Kinder	*children*

In the plural, neuter nouns that are infinitives have no plural ending: **die Einkommen** (*incomes*). But neuter nouns ending in **-um** change this ending to **-ien**: **das Studium, die Studien** (*studies*); **das Gymnasium, die Gymnasien** (*prep schools*).

Neuter nouns ending in **-tum** form their plural by the addition of an umlaut and the ending **-er**: **das Königtum, die Königtümer** (*kingdoms*).

Nouns with a **Ge-** prefix change to the plural in a variety of ways. There is no pattern that is signaled by the prefix **Ge-**. Instead, the base word is often the means by which the plural form is determined. For example, **das Gesetz** is the stem of the verb **setzen**. Verb stems are most often masculine, and their plural formation is formed by the suffix **-e**. This is, therefore, the plural of the prefixed noun: **die Gesetze** (*laws*). But some nouns in the category seem to follow no pattern at all. Let's look at some examples:

SINGULAR		PLURAL
das Gespräch	*conversation*	die Gespräche (*verb stem*)
das Geschehen	*happening*	die Geschehen (*infinitive*)
das Geschäft	*business*	die Geschäfte (*verb stem*)
das Gewehr	*rifle*	die Gewehre (*verb stem*)
das Gespenst	*ghost*	die Gespenster
das Gewicht	*weight*	die Gewichte
das Gesicht	*face*	die Gesichter

Foreign words ending in **-o** add the suffix **-s** to form the plural: **das Kino, die Kinos** (*movie theaters*).

ÜBUNG
1·7

In the blank provided, write the correct plural form of the given noun. For example:

das Kind (*child*) *die Kinder*

1. das Haus (*house*) _____

2. das Gelächter (*laughter*) _____

3. die Landung (*landing*) _____

4. das Gewitter (*storm*) _____

5. der Vater (*father*)   _____

6. das Land (*country*)   _____

7. das Radio (*radio*)   _____

8. die Endung (*ending*)   _____

9. das Harmonium (*harmonium*)   _____

10. das Gebiet (*region*)   _____

11. die Tochter (*daughter*)   _____

12. das Buch (*book*)   _____

13. die Gefolgschaft (*allegiance*)   _____

14. die Konstitution (*constitution*)   _____

15. der Junggeselle (*bachelor*)   _____

·2· Haben, sein, and werden

Perhaps the three most important verbs in the German language are **haben**, **sein**, and **werden**. Their functions in the language go far beyond their basic meanings. Therefore, this chapter will look at them closely and describe them fully, because using them accurately is essential for speaking and writing German well.

Haben and sein

Let's look at **haben** and **sein** first. They have meanings quite distinct from one another: **haben** (*to have*), **sein** (*to be*). Yet in a very special function, they are used identically: in the perfect tenses. To begin with, let's look at their conjugations in various tenses:

PRESENT	PAST	PRESENT PERFECT	FUTURE
ich habe *have*	hatte *had*	habe gehabt *have had*	werde haben *will have*
du hast *have*	hattest	hast gehabt	wirst haben
er hat *has*	hatte	hat gehabt *has had*	wird haben
wir haben *have*	hatten	haben gehabt	werden haben
ihr habt *have*	hattet	habt gehabt	werdet haben
Sie, sie haben *have*	hatten	haben gehabt	werden haben
ich bin *am*	war *was*	bin gewesen *have been*	werde sein *will be*
du bist *are*	warst *were*	bist gewesen	wirst sein
er ist *is*	war *was*	ist gewesen *has been*	wird sein
wir sind *are*	waren *were*	sind gewesen	werden sein
ihr seid *are*	wart *were*	seid gewesen	werdet sein
Sie, sie sind *are*	waren *were*	sind gewesen	werden sein

If a noun is the subject of a sentence, use the third-person singular conjugation of **haben** or **sein** with a singular noun and the third-person plural conjugation with a plural noun. For example:

Der Mann **hat** kein Geld.	*The man has no money.* (er **hat** = third-person singular)
Der Mann **ist** sehr alt.	*The man is very old.* (er **ist** = third-person singular)
Die Kinder **haben** Hunger.	*The children are hungry.* (sie **haben** = third-person plural)
Die Kinder **sind** krank.	*The children are sick.* (sie **sind** = third-person plural)

However, the replacement for the pronoun **wir** will be a noun combined with **ich**. For example:

> **wir** haben—**mein Freund und ich** haben
> **wir** sind—**die Kinder und ich** sind

ÜBUNG
2·1

Rewrite each sentence in the past and present perfect tenses. For example:

Er hat keine Zeit. *He has no time.*

Er hatte keine Zeit.

Er hat keine Zeit gehabt.

1. Wir haben neue Bücher (*new books*).

   _____

   _____

2. Sie ist meine Freundin (*my girlfriend*).

   _____

   _____

3. Meine Töchter sind Tänzerinnen (*dancers*).

   _____

   _____

4. Erik und Gudrun haben ein Geschenk für dich (*a gift for you*).

   _____

   _____

5. Ich bin kein Fußballspieler (*soccer player*).

   _____

   _____

6. Seid ihr in den USA (*in the USA*)?

_____

_____

7. Hast du keinen Bleistift?

_____

_____

8. Wo (*where*) sind Sie?

_____

_____

9. Habt ihr keine Handschuhe (*no gloves*)?

_____

_____

10. Meine Geschwister (*brothers and sisters*) sind zu Hause (*at home*).

_____

_____

11. Ich habe nur ein altes Kleid (*only an old dress*).

_____

_____

12. Du bist ein guter Freund (*a good friend*).

_____

_____

13. Seid ihr in der Hauptstadt (*in the capital city*)?

_____

_____

14. Haben Sie eine Eintrittskarte (*ticket*)?

_____

_____

15. Unsere Lehrerin ist freundlich (*kind*).

_____

_____

In the blank provided, rewrite each sentence, changing the subject pronoun to any appropriate noun or noun phrase. For example:

Er ist mein Freund. *Martin ist mein Freund.*

1. Sind sie Ausländer (*foreigners*)?

_____

2. Wir haben keinen Regenschirm (*no umbrella*).

_____

3. Ist er ein Freund von dir (*of yours*)?

_____

4. Sie war in der Bibliothek (*library*).

_____

5. Er hat nur zehn Euro (*ten euros*) gehabt.

_____

6. War es sehr alt?

_____

7. Sie sind interessanter (*more interesting*) als die anderen Bücher (*than the other books*).

_____

8. Wir sind in der Hauptstadt gewesen.

_____

9. Sie hatte kein Geld.

_____

10. Er war ziemlich (*rather*) krank.

_____

11. Es ist auf dem Tisch.

_____

12. Wir hatten keine Zeit dafür (*for that*).

_____

13. Sind sie im alten Dom (*cathedral*) gewesen?

_____

14. Sie haben vier Eintrittskarten gehabt.

_____

15. Er hatte meinen Regenschirm.

_____

16. Sie ist im Krankenhaus (*hospital*) gewesen.

_____

17. Es hatte keinen Zweck (*served no purpose*).

_____

18. Wir waren Schulkameraden (*classmates*).

_____

19. Sie haben Durst gehabt (*were thirsty*).

_____

20. Ist er Sportler (*athlete*) gewesen?

_____

The present perfect and the past perfect tenses

The present perfect tense of transitive verbs (verbs that can have a direct object) is composed of the present tense conjugation of **haben** and a past participle: **ich habe gesagt** (*I have said*), **ich habe gesungen** (*I have sung*). Since English uses the simple past more frequently in casual conversation, the translation of the example sentences more likely would be *I said* and *I sang*.

Past participles in German are either regular or irregular. The stem of a verb in a regular participle is preceded by the prefix **ge-** and followed by the suffix **-t**. For example:

INFINITIVE		STEM	REGULAR PARTICIPLE
sagen	*to say*	sag	**ge**sagt
machen	*to do, make*	mach	**ge**macht
hören	*to hear* ·	hör	**ge**hört
kaufen	*to buy*	kauf	**ge**kauft
suchen	*to look for*	such	**ge**sucht

ÜBUNG
2·3

Rewrite each sentence in the regular present perfect tense.

1. Er braucht (*needs*) einen Bleistift.

_____

2. Ich suche meinen Bruder.

_____

3. Herr Schmidt lehrt (*teaches*) Mathematik (*math*).

_____

4. Was lernt (*learn*) ihr?

_____

5. Die Jungen kaufen ein paar CDs.

_____

6. Meine Eltern (*parents*) hören Radio.

_____

7. Was sagt der Bürgermeister (*mayor*)?

_____

8. Es stört (*disturbs*) mich nicht.

_____

9. Gudrun stellt die Blumen (*puts the flowers*) auf den Tisch.

_____

10. Die Mädchen spielen gern Schach (*like to play chess*).

_____

Irregular participles have a **ge-** prefix but tend to end with **-en** instead of **-t**. And the stem of the participle varies and does not always conform to the stem of the infinitive. For example:

INFINITIVE		STEM	IRREGULAR PARTICIPLE
singen	*to sing*	sung	**ge**sung**en**
halten	*to hold*	halt	**ge**halt**en**
schlagen	*to hit*	schlag	**ge**schlag**en**
brechen	*to break*	broch	**ge**broch**en**
schreiben	*to write*	schrieb	**ge**schrieb**en**

One of the keys to knowing which auxiliary (**haben** or **sein**) to use with a participle is the existence of a direct object in a sentence. The direct object is a signal that the auxiliary will be **haben**. For example:

Sie hat **ein schönes Lied** gesungen.	*She sang **a pretty song**.*
Er hat **sein Wort** gehalten.	*He kept **his word**.*
Warum hast du **den Hund** geschlagen?	*Why did you hit **the dog**?*
Ich habe **die Vase** gebrochen.	*I broke **the vase**.*
Hast du **den Brief** geschrieben?	*Did you write **the letter**?*

The past perfect tense is identical to the present perfect tense except for the auxiliary, which appears in the past tense (**hatte**). This tense indicates an action begun and completed in the past. For example:

Er **hatte** sein Wort gehalten.	*He **had** kept his word.*
Ich **hatte** die Vase gebrochen.	*I **had** broken the vase.*

Refer to the Appendix for a list of irregular verbs, which can aid you in completing the exercises.

ÜBUNG
2·4

Rewrite each sentence in the irregular present perfect and the past perfect tenses.

1. Mein Vater schreibt einen Roman (*novel*).

   _____

   _____

2. Liest (*read*) du die Zeitung?

   _____

   _____

3. Meine Schwester findet die alte Bluse.

   _____

   _____

4. Sonja trägt (*wears*) ein rotes Kleid (*red dress*).

   _____

   _____

5. Sie fangen den Ball (*catch the ball*) nicht.

   _____

   _____

6. Ich sehe (*see*) einen alten Freund.

   _____

   _____

7. Der Mann stiehlt ihre Tasche (*steals her purse*).

   _____

   _____

8. Mein Sohn nimmt die Fahrkarten (*takes the tickets*).

   _____

   _____

9. Er brät ein paar Würstchen (*roasted a couple sausages*).

_____

_____

10. Karl und ich finden fünfzig Euro (*find fifty euros*).

_____

_____

If there can be no direct object in a sentence, the sentence is most likely *intransitive*. German intransitive verbs often show a *change in a state of being*, for example, **sterben** (*to die*), **werden** (*to become*), **wachsen** (*to grow*). These verbs use **sein** as their auxiliary. Verbs that show a motion from one place to another also use **sein** as their auxiliary, for example, **gehen** (*to go*), **fliegen** (*to fly*), **reisen** (*to travel*). This category of verbs can be either irregular in their formation of participles or regular. But in all cases they use **sein** as their auxiliary. For example:

INFINITIVE		STEM	THIRD-PERSON AUXILIARY AND PARTICIPLE
reisen	*to travel*	reis	er ist gereist
fahren	*to drive*	fahr	er ist gefahren
kommen	*to come*	komm	er ist gekommen
bleiben	*to stay*	blieb	er ist geblieben
sterben	*to die*	storb	er ist gestorben

Both the present perfect and past perfect tenses exist with verbs that take **sein**. For example:

Er ist nach Hause gefahren.	*He drove home.*
Er war nach Hause gefahren.	*He had driven home.*
Wir sind in Berlin geblieben.	*We stayed in Berlin.*
Wir waren in Berlin geblieben.	*We had stayed in Berlin.*
Ich bin mit dem Bus gereist.	*I traveled by bus.*
Ich war mit dem Bus gereist.	*I had traveled by bus.*

ÜBUNG
2·5

Rewrite each sentence in the present perfect tense. Be careful! A few verbs are regular.

1. Die Kinder gehen zur Schule (*to school*).

_____

2. Die Touristen eilen ins Restaurant (*hurry into the restaurant*).

_____

3. Der junge Mann fällt ins Wasser (*falls into the water*).

   _____

4. Bleibst du in der Schweiz (*in Switzerland*)?

   _____

5. Niemand folgt uns (*no one follows us*).

   _____

6. Wann (*when*) fliegen sie nach Deutschland (*fly to Germany*)?

   _____

7. Wann seid ihr in Heidelberg?

   _____

8. Sonja läuft so schnell (*runs so fast*).

   _____

9. Viele (*many*) Touristen reisen nach Frankreich (*France*).

   _____

10. Warum (*why*) stirbt die Frau?

    _____

Werden

Werden is another important verb that has four unique functions. They are:

1. When standing alone, **werden** means *to become* or *get*:

   Es **wird** kalt.   *It becomes cold.*

2. When followed by an infinitive, it forms the future tense:

   Er wird Deutsch **lernen**.   *He will learn German.*

3. When followed by a past participle and auxiliary, it forms the future perfect tense:

   Sie werden das Geld **gefunden haben**.   *They will have found the money.*

4. The passive voice is formed by **werden** and a past participle (the passive voice will be discussed in detail in Chapter 15):

   Es wird **gebaut**.   *It is being built.*

Rewrite each sentence in the missing tenses.

1. PRESENT **Es wird ziemlich heiß (*hot*).**

   PAST _____

   PRESENT PERFECT _____

   PAST PERFECT _____

   FUTURE _____

2. PRESENT _____

   PAST **Meine Eltern fuhren in die Stadt (*to the city*).**

   PRESENT PERFECT _____

   PAST PERFECT _____

   FUTURE _____

3. PRESENT _____

   PAST _____

   PRESENT PERFECT **Der Diplomat ist nach Madrid geflogen.**

   PAST PERFECT _____

   FUTURE _____

4. PRESENT _____

   PAST _____

   PRESENT PERFECT _____

   PAST PERFECT **Der Koch hatte einen schönen Kuchen gebacken (*baked a nice cake*).**

   FUTURE _____

5. PRESENT _____

   PAST _____

   PRESENT PERFECT _____

   PAST PERFECT _____

   FUTURE **Meine Familie wird zu Hause (*at home*) bleiben.**

The future perfect tense is used with regular or irregular verbs and verbs that require either **haben** or **sein** as their auxiliary. For example:

Bis zehn Uhr wird er den Brief geschrieben haben. *He will have written the letter by ten o'clock.*

Sie wird bis Montag nach Hause gekommen sein. *She will have come home by Monday.*

ÜBUNG
2·7

The following sentences appear in various tenses. Rewrite each one in the future perfect tense. For example:

Er hat das Geld gefunden.
Er wird das Geld gefunden haben.

1. Meine Eltern kaufen eine Wohnung (*apartment*) in der Stadt.

   _____

2. Die Ausländer reisten in die Schweiz.

   _____

3. Ich bin endlich wieder gesund (*finally healthy again*) geworden.

   _____

4. Erik und ich hatten den Dieb (*thief*) gefangen.

   _____

5. Wirst du mexikanisch essen gehen (*go eat in a Mexican restaurant*)?

   _____

The verbs **haben**, **sein**, and **werden** also occur with a variety of idioms and special phrases. No matter the meaning of the idiom or special phrase, the conjugations already illustrated will still apply. Let's look at some sample idioms and phrases:

Hunger/Durst haben	*to be hungry/thirsty*
Angst haben	*to be afraid*
Pech haben	*to have bad luck*
Es war einmal…	*Once upon a time . . .*
Wie ist es…?	*How about . . . ?*
Kann sein.	*Could be.*
Was willst du einmal werden?	*What do you want to be (when you grow up)?*
Es wird dunkel.	*It's turning dark.*
Es wird höchste Zeit!	*It's high time!*

Change the underlined word or words in each sentence to any appropriate word or phrase.

1. Die Kinder haben Hunger.

   _____

2. Warum hat sie Angst?

   _____

3. Der arme (*poor*) Mann hat oft (*often*) Pech.

   _____

4. Wie ist es mit einer Amerikareise (*a trip to America*)?

   _____

5. Es wird sehr dunkel.

   _____

·3· Declensions with **der**-words and **ein**-words

German adjective endings too often cause a problem for students of the language. Admittedly, there are complications that do not exist in English, but using the correct endings in the various cases is not an insurmountable task. Distinct patterns can help make using adjective endings more simple and accurate.

When considering declensions, it is important to distinguish between socalled der-words and ein-words. This is particularly important in the nominative case and in the accusative case of feminine and neuter nouns. Let's look at the derwords first.

Der-words

Naturally, the definite articles (**der, die, das**) are **der**-words. In addition, there are also:

MASCULINE	FEMININE	NEUTER	
dieser	diese	dieses	*this*
jener	jene	jenes	*that*
jeder	jede	jedes	*each*
welcher	welche	welches	*which*
solcher	solche	solches	*such (a)*

When an adjective follows a **der**-word in the nominative case, the adjective ending is always **-e**. It is also always **-e** in the accusative case of feminine and neuter nouns. For example:

	MASCULINE	FEMININE	NEUTER
nom.	der gute Mann	die gute Frau	das gute Kind
acc.		die gute Frau	das gute Kind

Notice that gender is inferred in the **der**-word by the final letter in the definite articles (**-r, -e, -s**), and the adjective ending is the *neutral* **-e**. This occurs with all the **der**-words. For example:

	MASCULINE	FEMININE	NEUTER
nom.	dieser gute Mann	jene gute Frau	jedes gute Kind
acc.		welche gute Frau	dieses gute Kind

24

With **der**-words, the adjective ending is always **-en** in the masculine accusative, throughout the dative and genitive, and in all cases of plural nouns. For example:

	MASCULINE	FEMININE	NEUTER	PLURAL
nom.	dieser gute Mann	welche gute Frau	jedes gute Kind	jene guten Kinder
acc.	diesen gut**en** Mann	welche gute Frau	jedes gute Kind	jene gut**en** Kinder
dat.	diesem gut**en** Mann	welcher gut**en** Frau	jedem gut**en** Kind	jenen guten Kinder**n**
gen.	dieses gut**en** Mannes	welcher gut**en** Frau	jedes gut**en** Kindes	jener guten Kinder

That means that with **der**-words there are only two adjective endings to worry about: **-e** and **-en**. Note: In the dative plural, nouns always end in **-n** except plurals formed with an **-s**.

Let's quickly review how the four cases are used:

- Nominative: the subject of a sentence or its predicate nominative
  Der Lehrer ist hier. Herr Braun ist **der Lehrer**.
- Accusative: the direct object in a sentence, the object of an accusative preposition, or an expression of time
  Kennst du **den Lehrer**? Ich habe ein Buch für **den Lehrer**. Ich war **den ganzen Tag** zu Hause.
- Dative: the indirect object, the object of a dative verb, or the object of a dative preposition
  Ich gab **dem Lehrer** ein Geschenk. Wir helfen **dem Lehrer**. Sie spricht mit **dem Lehrer**.
- Genitive: a possessive or the object of a genitive preposition
  Das ist das Haus **des Lehrers**. Anstatt **des Lehrers** kam der Direktor ins Klassenzimmer.

ÜBUNG 3·1

*In the blanks provided, fill in the missing **der**-word and adjective endings. For example:*

Tina spricht mit d_em_ alt_en_ Herrn.

1. Ist dies_____ jung_____ Matrose (*sailor*) ein Freund von Ihnen?

2. Erik hat mit dies_____ nett_____ Frauen (*nice women*) getanzt.

3. Mein Vater wird jen_____ blau_____ Wagen kaufen.

4. Ich kann (*can*) d_____ neu_____ Chefin nicht glauben (*believe*).

5. Welch_____ frisch_____ Brot (*fresh bread*) hat sie gebacken?

6. Der Lehrer erzählte (*told*) von jed_____ amerikanisch_____ Wildwestfilm (*western*).

7. D_____ neu_____ Student wird dies_____ weiß_____ Hemden bügeln (*iron white shirts*).

8. Tanja singt in d_____ neu_____ Kleinkinderchor (*little children's choir*).

9. Sind das d_____ alt_____ Ringe (*rings*) dies_____ Frau?

10. Karl wird d_____ lang_____ Nagel (*nail*) in die Wand (*into the wall*) schlagen.

11. Jen_____ schön_____ Studentin war gestern in Paris.

12. Ist dies_____ klein_____ Kind Ihr Sohn?

13. In welch_____ groß_____ Krankenhaus (*big hospital*) arbeitet (*works*) dein Onkel?

14. Während d_____ ganz_____ Winter_____ (*whole winter*) wohne ich in den Bergen (*live in the mountains*).

15. Ich habe dies_____ schön_____ Ansichtskarte (*postcard*) bekommen.

16. D_____ Mädchen haben an jen_____ klein_____ Fenster (*window*) gesessen.

17. Wer hat dies_____ interessant_____ Ausflug (*interesting excursion*) arrangiert?

18. Erik sprach mit jen_____ alt_____ Leute_____.

19. Sie hat dies_____ alt_____ Kirche besucht (*visited*).

20. Ich stelle die Vase auf d_____ neu_____ Klavier (*piano*).

Three more **der**-words are **mancher** (*many a*), **derselbe** (*the same*), and **derjenige** (*the very one*). In the cases of **derselbe** and **derjenige** you will note that the neutral ending **-e** is already attached to the **der**-words. However, those endings change just as if they were ordinary adjectives. Let's look at the declension of all three:

MASCULINE	MANCHER	DERSELBE	DERJENIGE	NOUN
nom.	mancher gute	derselbe	derjenige	Mann
acc.	manchen gut**en**	denselb**en**	denjenig**en**	Mann
dat.	manchem gut**en**	demselb**en**	demjenig**en**	Mann
gen.	manches gut**en**	desselb**en**	desjenig**en**	Mannes

FEMININE	MANCHER	DERSELBE	DERJENIGE	NOUN
nom.	manche junge	dieselbe	diejenige	Frau
acc.	manche junge	dieselbe	diejenige	Frau
dat.	mancher jung**en**	derselb**en**	derjenig**en**	Frau
gen.	mancher jung**en**	derselb**en**	derjenig**en**	Frau

NEUTER	MANCHER	DERSELBE	DERJENIGE	NOUN
nom.	manches nette	dasselbe	dasjenige	Kind
acc.	manches nette	dasselbe	dasjenige	Kind
dat.	manchem nett**en**	demselb**en**	demselb**en**	Kind
gen.	manches nett**en**	desselb**en**	desselb**en**	Kindes

PLURAL	MANCHER	DERSELBE	DERJENIGE	NOUN
nom.	manche gut**en**	dieselb**en**	diejenig**en**	Kinder
acc.	manche gut**en**	dieselb**en**	diejenig**en**	Kinder
dat.	manchen gut**en**	denselb**en**	denjenig**en**	Kindern
gen.	mancher gut**en**	derselb**en**	derjenig**en**	Kinder

Two other **der**-words are used only with plural nouns: **alle** (*all*) and **beide** (*both*). The adjective ending -**en** is always used with them. **Alle** and **beide** are declined like **mancher** in the plural as just illustrated.

Derjenige is most frequently used when followed by a relative clause but is always declined as a **der**-word. Let's look at a sample sentence:

Mein Bruder besuchte **denjenigen** Mann, der mein Wagen reparieren wird.

*My brother visited **the very** man who is going to repair my car.*

ÜBUNG
3·2

*In the blanks provided, fill in the missing **der**-word and adjective endings. For example:*

Tina spricht mit d<u>em</u>selb<u>en</u> alt<u>en</u> Herrn.

1. Manch_____ schwarz_____ Katze (*black cat*) bringt Pech.

2. Manch_____ Kind hat Angst vor dem Weihnachtsmann (*Santa Claus*).

3. Ich habe d_____selb_____ Hut (*hat*) gekauft.

4. D_____selb_____ Leute beklagen sich (*complain*) immer.

5. Sie ist immer d_____jenig_____, der niemand helfen will (*wants to help*).

6. Er ist der Sohn d_____jenig_____, die in dem großen Haus dort drüben (*over there*) wohnen.

7. Manch_____ Leut_____ gefällt (*like*) der Film nicht.

8. Jeden Tag (*every day*) sitzt er unter d_____selb_____ Baum (*tree*).

9. Der Bauer (*farmer*) schickt all_____ fett_____ Gänse (*fat geese*) zum Markt (*to market*).

10. Sie hat mit beid_____ Brüder_____ gesprochen.

Ein-words

Ein-words consist of the indefinite article (**ein**), the possessive adjectives [**mein** (*my*), **dein** (*your*), **sein** (*his*), **ihr** (*her*), **unser** (*our*), **euer** (*your*), **Ihr** (*your*), **ihr** (*their*)], and **kein**. Unlike the **der**-words, **ein**-words infer the gender of a noun in the adjective in the nominative case and in the accusative case of feminine and neuter nouns. For example:

	MASCULINE	FEMININE	NEUTER
nom.	ein gut**er** Mann	meine gut**e** Frau	unser gut**es** Kind
acc.		seine gut**e** Frau	Ihr gut**es** Kind

In all other instances of declension with **ein**-words, the adjective ending will again be **-en**. For example:

	MASCULINE	FEMININE	NEUTER	PLURAL
nom.	kein guter Mann	eine gute Frau	mein gutes Kind	eure gut**en** Kinder
acc.	keinen gut**en** Mann	eine gute Frau	mein gutes Kind	eure gut**en** Kinder
dat.	keinem gut**en** Mann	einer gut**en** Frau	meinem gut**en** Kind	euren gut**en** Kindern
gen.	keines gut**en** Mannes	einer gut**en** Frau	meines gut**en** Kindes	eurer gut**en** Kinder

So what may appear at first glance as a complicated structure of adjective endings is really just the application of three adjective endings: the inferred gender (**-r**, **-e**, **-s**), **-e**, and **-en**.

ÜBUNG
3·3

*In the blanks provided, fill in the missing **ein**-word and adjective endings. For example:*

Tina spricht mit ihr*em* alt*en* Freund.

1. Der Kutscher (*coachman*) schlägt sein_____ arm_____ Pferd (*poor horse*).

2. Das Mädchen hat ein_____ lang_____ Gedicht (*long poem*) gelernt.

3. Der Lehrer suchte sein_____ jünger_____ (*younger*) Sohn.

4. Wo sind Ihr_____ ausländisch_____ Gäste?

5. Die Dame verkaufte ihr_____ alt_____ Pelzmantel (*fur coat*).

6. Unser_____ klein_____ Garten ist von ein_____ groß_____ Zaun (*fence*) umgeben (*surrounded*).

7. Ich kenne kein_____ süßer_____ Äpfel (*sweeter apples*) als diese.

8. In ein_____ groß_____ Stadt (*city*) gibt es viele Geschäfte (*many stores*).

9. Mein_____ Schwester spült ihr_____ neu_____ Tassen ab (*washes up cups*).

10. Er misst die Größe (*measures the size*) ein_____ klein_____ Garten_____ aus.

*In the blanks provided, fill in the missing **der**-word or **ein**-word and adjective endings. For example:*

Tina spricht mit ihr*em* alt*en* Freund.

1. D_____ groß_____ Tor (*gate*) der Stadt wurde geschlossen (*was closed*).

2. Die Schulden (*debts*) mein_____ tot_____ Vater_____ (*dead father*) sind ein_____ Belastung (*burden*).

3. Was für Möbel (*what kind of furniture*) stehen in jed_____ modern_____ Wohnung?

4. Warum haben Sie Ihr_____ neu_____ Wagen verkauft?

5. Ihr_____ jünger_____ Kind ist nur zwei Jahre alt (*two years old*).

6. Wir werden mit d_____ nächst_____ Straßenbahn (*next streetcar*) fahren.

7. Mein Bruder will ihr_____ neu_____ Roman lesen.

8. Mein_____ krank_____ Onkel wohnt in ein_____ Vorort (*suburb*) von Berlin.

9. Habt ihr mit eur_____ best_____ Freundinnen gesprochen?

10. Welch_____ braun_____ Hut willst du kaufen?

Breaking the pattern

Der-words also go by the name *determiners*. Other determiners can be followed by adjectives, but this group of determiners breaks the patterns that go with **der**-words and **ein**-words. These determiners are:

einige	*some*
mehrere	*several*
sämtliche	*all*
viele	*many*
wenige	*few*

They have the same endings as the **der**-words. And the adjectives that accompany them also have *the very same endings* as **der**-words. However, these determiners are used only with plural nouns. For example:

nom.	einige junge Frauen	viele neue Tische
acc.	einige junge Frauen	viele neue Tische
dat.	einigen jungen Frauen	vielen neuen Tischen
gen.	einiger junger Frauen	vieler neuer Tische

Unpreceded adjectives

In some cases, there is no article or determiner in front of an adjective. This can occur in two instances:

1. The plural of a noun that is introduced by an *indefinite article* remains indefinite when it is not preceded by a determiner:

ein junger Mann *a young man*	junge Männer *young men*
eine rote Blume *a red flower*	rote Blumen *red flowers*

2. A general, nonspecific statement:

Kaltes Wasser ist erfrischend.	*Cold water is refreshing.*
Kleine Kinder spielen gern.	*Little children like to play.*

Let's look at the declension of this type of structure:

	MASCULINE	FEMININE	NEUTER	PLURAL
	hot tea	*cold milk*	*good weather*	*nice people*
nom.	heißer Tee	kalte Milch	gutes Wetter	nette Leute
acc.	heißen Tee	kalte Milch	gutes Wetter	nette Leute
dat.	heißem Tee	kalter Milch	gutem Wetter	netten Leuten
gen.	heißen Tees	kalter Milch	guten Wetters	netter Leute

ÜBUNG
3·5

In the blanks provided, complete the determiners and fill in the missing adjective endings. For example:

Viele junge Leute stehen vor dem Rathaus.

1. Ich mag (*like*) kalt_____ Bier.

2. Mein_____ Mutter wird mit einig_____ Nachbar_____ tanzen.

3. Trinken Sie kein_____ Weißwein (*white wine*)?

4. Wenig_____ arm_____ Jungen können Schach spielen.

5. Meine Mutter hat immer krank_____ Leute_____ geholfen.

6. Frau Bauer will mehrer_____ schön_____ Bilder (*pictures*) verkaufen.

7. Ich habe nichts gegen kalt_____ Suppe.

8. Nicht all_____ deutsch_____ Autos sind teuer.

9. D_____ neu_____ Uniformen sämtlich_____ Schüler (*pupils*) sind dunkelblau (*dark blue*).

10. Ist das Ihr erst_____ (*first*) Gedicht?

11. Warum trinkst du kalt_____ Tee?

12. Viel_____ neu_____ Arbeiter (*workers*) werden entlassen (*fired*).

13. Ich denke oft an mein_____ alt_____ Schulkameraden in Paris.

14. Dies_____ unartig_____ (*naughty*) Kinder werden von ihr_____ Vater bestraft (*punished*).

15. Welch_____ deutsch_____ Bücher hast du gelesen?

Complete each sentence with the phrases provided in parentheses. For example:

Er bekommt _____.

(ein neuer Hut) *einen neuen Hut*

Wegen _____ ging Thomas sofort ins Bett (*immediately to bed*).

1. (die schwere Arbeit [*job*]) _____

2. (ein gefährliches Gewitter [*dangerous storm*]) _____

3. (seine lange Krankheit [*illness*]) _____

Der Vater _____ ist erfreut (*pleased*).

4. (der fleißige [*diligent*] Schüler) _____

5. (dieses nette Mädchen) _____

6. (eine junge Tänzerin) _____

Meine Tante trinkt nicht gern _____.

7. (kalter Kaffee) _____

8. (warmes Bier) _____

9. (heiße Milch) _____

Haben Sie _____?

10. (keine amerikanische Zeitung) _____

11. (einige russische Briefmarken [*stamps*]) _____

12. (mein neuer Regenmantel [*raincoat*]) _____

Viele haben gegen _____ gekämpft (*fought*).

13. (seine gefährliche Politik [*politics*]) _____

14. (laute [*loud*] Musik) _____

15. (ihre ewigen Feinde [*eternal enemies*]) _____

Wir werden _____ dorthin (*to there*) reisen.

16. (nächster Montag [*Monday*]) _____

17. (mit diesem Zug [*train*]) _____

18. (dieser Freitag [*Friday*]) _____

Viele Studenten arbeiten in _____.

19. (diese große Bibliothek) _____

20. (verschiedene Hörsäle [*various lecture halls*]) _____

21. (jener Park) _____

Singen _____ Volkslieder (*folk songs*)?

22. (viele alte Leute) _____

23. (alle ausländischen Studenten) _____

Jetzt haben sie _____ unter Kontrolle (*now under control*).

24. (diese gefährliche Lage [*situation*]) _____

25. (mehrere Aufstände [*uprisings*]) _____

Pronoun choice by gender ·4·

Gender plays a far bigger role in German than it does in English. In German, gender goes beyond sexual gender, and as discussed in Chapter 1, both males and objects can be masculine, both females and objects can be feminine, and both people and objects can be neuter. Conforming to those gender distinctions is essential for speaking and writing German correctly. It has already been pointed out that making an error in the choice of gender will not prohibit communication. But making the right gender choice avoids awkward and even funny statements.

Selecting the correct pronoun to replace a noun in a sentence requires an understanding of the role gender plays in regard to German pronouns. The pronouns that replace nouns in German may seem strange at times to English speakers, but with practice and experience, the German approach becomes natural and comfortable to use. First, let's look at the German personal pronouns in the nominative case:

GERMAN	ENGLISH
ich	*I*
du	*you (singular informal)*
er	*he, it*
sie	*she, it*
es	*it, he, she*
wir	*we*
ihr	*you (plural informal)*
Sie	*you (singular or plural formal)*
sie	*they*
wer	*who*
was	*what*
man	*one*

When pronouns are the subject used with a verb, the verb must have certain endings appropriate for each pronoun. For example:

	MACHEN *TO MAKE/DO*	HABEN *TO HAVE*
ich	mache	habe
du	machst	hast
er	macht	hat
sie *s.*	macht	hat

(continued)

33

	MACHEN *TO MAKE/DO*	HABEN *TO HAVE*
er	macht	hat
es	macht	hat
wir	machen	haben
ihr	macht	habt
Sie	machen	haben
sie *pl.*	machen	haben
wer	macht	hat
was	macht	hat
man	macht	hat

Verbs can be regular or irregular, and the conjugations are adjusted slightly for the differences required of certain verbs. But in general, the preceding conjugations are used with all verbs.

In a conjugation, gender does not affect a conjugation in any way. Indeed, pronouns and gender need to be used carefully only in the third-person singular (**er**, **sie**, **es** *s.*) and third-person plural (**sie** *pl.*). The other pronouns are not affected by gender.

If a masculine noun is replaced by a pronoun, it must be replaced by the masculine pronoun **er**. If the noun is a person, **er** is translated as *he*; if it is an object, **er** is translated as *it*. For example:

Karl ist mein Freund.	*Karl is my friend.*
Er ist mein Freund.	***He** is my friend.*
Der Sportler ist sehr stark.	*The athlete is very strong.*
Er ist sehr stark.	***He** is very strong.*
Der Tisch war zu alt.	*The table was too old.*
Er war zu alt.	***It** was too old.*
Wo ist der VW?	*Where is the VW?*
Wo ist **er**?	*Where is **it**?*

This means that a sentence can have two translations, depending on what the pronoun replacement stands for. For example:

Ist dein Vater in der Garage?	*Is your father in the garage?*
Ist **er** in der Garage?	*Is **he** in the garage?*
Ist der Wagen in der Garage?	*Is the car in the garage?*
Ist **er** in der Garage?	*Is **it** in the garage?*

The feminine pronoun **sie** works in the same way: the pronoun can be translated as *she* or *it*, depending upon whether it is the replacement for a noun that is a person or an object. For example:

Meine Schwester ist Lehrerin.	*My sister is a teacher.*
Sie ist Lehrerin.	***She** is a teacher.*
Die Schule war neunzig Jahre alt.	*The school was ninety years old.*
Sie war neunzig Jahre alt.	***It** was ninety years old.*

The neuter pronoun **es** also follows the same pattern.

Das Mädchen wohnt dort drüben.	*The girl lives over there.*
Es wohnt dort drüben.	***She** lives over there.*
Sein Brüderlein ist krank.	*His little brother is sick.*
Es ist krank.	***He** is sick.*
Das Haus ist klein.	*The house is little.*
Es ist klein.	***It** is little.*

ÜBUNG
4·1

In the blank provided, write the pronoun that correctly replaces the noun or noun phrase in bold. For example:

Wo war **das Haus**? *es*

1. **Seine Idee** (*idea*) war sehr gut. _____

2. **Meine Freundin** geht auf eine Party. _____

3. Wie alt ist **das Kind**? _____

4. **Ihr Vater** will Politiker werden (*become a politician*). _____

5. **Peter** fing den Ball nicht. _____

6. **Der alte Dom** ist sehr interessant. _____

7. **Maria** hat kein Fahrrad (*bicycle*). _____

8. Ist **ihr Auto** kaputt (*broken*)? _____

9. **Dieser Blumenstrauß** duftet so schön (*smells so nice*). _____

10. **Ein Fluss** kann gefährlich sein. _____

11. **Ein Stück Kreide** (*piece of chalk*) liegt auf dem Boden (*lies on the floor*). _____

12. **Diese Lampe** gehörte (*belonged to*) meiner Großmutter. _____

13. Wo arbeitet **dieses Mädchen**? _____

14. Fährt **dieser Zug** nach München? _____

15. **Sein Fahrrad** steht hinter der Garage (*behind the garage*). _____

The third-person plural pronoun is always **sie** *pl.* (*they*) and replaces any plural noun. No differences are made for masculine, feminine, or neuter, nor for persons or objects. For example:

Die Männer sitzen am Tisch.	*The men sit at the table.*
Sie sitzen am Tisch.	***They** sit at the table.*
Die Bücher sind auf dem Tisch.	*The books are on the table.*
Sie sind auf dem Tisch.	***They** are on the table.*

There is no problem distinguishing between **sie** *s.* and **sie** *pl.* The former requires a singular verb and the latter a plural verb when they are the subject of a sentence.

Sie ist im Garten.   ***She/It*** *is in the garden.*
Sie sind im Garten.   ***They*** *are in the garden.*

Rewrite each sentence by changing the singular subject noun or noun phrase to a pronoun. Then rewrite the sentence by changing the noun to a plural noun. After that, rewrite the sentence with the appropriate pronoun replacement for the plural noun. For example:

Der Mann ist alt.

Er ist alt.

Die Männer sind alt.

Sie sind alt.

1. Mein Bruder bekommt einen Brief.

   _____

   _____

   _____

2. Ein Glas stand auf dem Tisch.

   _____

   _____

   _____

3. Die Touristin spricht gut Deutsch.

   _____

   _____

   _____

4. Warum ist diese Flasche zerbrochen (*bottle broken*)?

   _____

   _____

   _____

5. Der Zug kommt um elf Uhr (*at eleven o'clock*).

   _____

   _____

   _____

Pronouns and declensions

When the third-person pronouns are declined in other cases, they still must conform to the gender and number of the noun they replace. Let's look at how all the pronouns are declined:

NOM.	ACC.	DAT.	ENGLISH
ich	mich	mir	*I*
du	dich	dir	*you (singular informal)*
er	ihn	ihm	*he, it*
sie	sie	ihr	*she, it*
es	es	ihm	*it, he, she*
wir	uns	uns	*we*
ihr	euch	euch	*you (plural informal)*
Sie	Sie	Ihnen	*you (singular or plural formal)*
sie	sie	ihnen	*they*
wer	wen	wem	*who*
was	was	N/A	*what*
man	einen	einem	*one*

Again, only the third-person pronouns can act as replacements for nouns in all the cases. For example:

nom.	Herr Brau ist zu Hause. **Er** ist zu Hause.	*He is at home.*
acc.	Ich kenne Herrn Braun. Ich kenne **ihn**.	*I know him.*
dat.	Er glaubt Herrn Braun nicht. Er glaubt **ihm** nicht.	*He doesn't believe him.*

Possessive adjectives

When a noun shows possession and is in the genitive case, a third-person possessive adjective is used as its replacement, instead of a third-person pronoun. The possessive adjectives are **mein** (*my*), **dein** (*your*), **sein** (*his*), **ihr** (*her*), **sein** (*its*), **unser** (*our*), **euer** (*your*), **Ihr** (*your*), **ihr** (*their*), and **wessen** (*whose*). Let's look at some examples:

Der Bruder der alten Frau wohnt in der Stadt.	*The old woman's brother lives in the city.*
Ihr Bruder wohnt in der Stadt.	*Her brother lives in the city.*
Karls Mutter kaufte einen Wagen.	*Karl's mother bought a car.*
Seine Mutter kaufte einen Wagen.	*His mother bought a car.*

If a first- or second-person possessive adjective is used in the genitive case phrase, it is the gender of the noun and not of the possessive adjective that always determines the gender of the possessive adjective replacement. For example:

das Haus ihres Bruders   *her brother's house*

In this phrase, *her* is third person and refers to a female, and *brother* is masculine. It is the genitive case *brother* that determines the kind of possessive adjective that will replace it. This phrase becomes:

sein Haus   *his house* (**sein** = masculine = *brother*)

The case of the noun modified becomes the case of the possessive adjective. For example:

nom.	Das Haus meines Bruders ist klein.	*My brother's house is little.*
	Sein Haus ist klein.	
acc.	Die Kinder laufen ins Haus ihres Bruders.	*The children run into her brother's house.*
	Die Kinder laufen in sein Haus.	
dat.	Ich wohne im Haus seines Bruders.	*I live in his brother's house.*
	Ich wohne in seinem Haus.	

ÜBUNG
4·3

Rewrite each sentence by changing the genitive case noun to the correct possessive adjective. For example:

Er kennt die Schwester des Mannes.

Er kennt seine Schwester.

1. Wann ist die Party der Mädchen?

   _____

2. Willst du die Bluse seiner Tochter tragen?

   _____

3. Er spricht mit den Eltern eines Professors.

   _____

4. Er hat die Adresse meiner Freundinnen.

   _____

5. Sie kam ohne die Ringe ihres Bruders.

   _____

6. Ich kaufte den Stoff (*fabric*) deiner Schneiderin (*seamstress*).

   _____

7. Sie spielen im Keller (*basement*) des Lehrers.

   _____

8. Er hat die Zeitung des Arztes gelesen.

   _____

9. Er erzählt von den Kindern meiner Chefin.

   _____

10. Wo ist die Bettdecke (*blanket*) Ihres Kindes?

    _____

Wer and was

The interrogative pronouns **wer** and **was** are third-person pronouns, and they replace nouns in order to ask a question. In this instance, the only consideration made is whether a noun is animate or inanimate. If it is animate, use **wer**. If it is inanimate, use **was**. For example:

Der Lehrer wohnt in dieser Straße.	*The teacher lives on this street.*
Wer wohnt in dieser Straße?	***Who** lives on this street?*
Das neue Haus ist groß.	*The new house is big.*
Was ist groß?	***What** is big?*

Be careful! **Wer** can be used in other cases and in the possessive. Let's look at some examples:

Der Mann kauft einen VW.	*The man buys a VW.*
Wer kauft einen VW?	***Who** buys a VW?*
Wir sehen den Mann.	*We see the man.*
Wen sehen wir?	***Whom** do we see?*
Sie sprechen mit dem Mann.	*They speak with the man.*
Mit **wem** sprechen sie?	*With **whom** do they speak?*
Das ist das Auto des Mannes.	*That is the man's car.*
Wessen Auto ist das?	***Whose** car is that?*

ÜBUNG
4·4

*Write a question with **wer** or **was** based upon the noun or phrase in bold print. For example:*

Er besucht **den Lehrer**.

Wen besucht er?

1. Thomas arbeitet mit **einigen Freunden von mir**.

   _____

2. Der Junge hat **ein Stück Kreide**.

   _____

3. **Der Ring des Mädchens** ist aus Gold (*made of gold*).

   _____

4. Ich habe **es** gekauft.

   _____

5. **Die Kinder** laufen in den kleinen Garten.

   _____

6. Wir haben **unsere Nachbarn** kennen gelernt (*became acquainted with neighbors*).

_____

7. Es gibt (*there is*) **ein gutes Restaurant** in dieser Straße.

_____

8. **Ihre** Geschwister sind in die Schweiz gereist.

_____

9. Dieser Wildwestfilm gefällt **uns** nicht.

_____

10. **Sie** haben ein paar Briefe bekommen.

_____

When a question is asked with **was** preceded by a preposition, a special structure formed with **wo(r)-** is used. For example:

Er kam mit einem schönen Blumenstrauß.	*He came with a beautiful bouquet.*
Womit kam er?	*What did he come with?*

If the preposition begins with a vowel, the prefix is **wor-**: **worin**, **woran**. Let's look at a few more examples of how a question with **was** and a preposition is formed:

vom Bahnhof	**wovon?**	*from the railroad station/from what?*
an der Tür	**woran?**	*at the door/at what?*
durch das Fenster	**wodurch?**	*through the window/through what?*

ÜBUNG
4·5

Form a question with **wo(r)-** with the prepositional phrase in each sentence. For example:

Er steht an der Tür.
Woran steht er?

1. Wir müssen auf den Zug warten.

_____

2. Katrin freute sich (*was glad*) über das Geschenk.

_____

3. Erik weiß nichts (*knows nothing*) von deinen Problemen.

_____

4. Mein Sohn interessiert sich für Sport.

_____

5. Ich habe den Ring im Koffer gefunden.

_____

6. Tina hat oft nach dem Krieg gefragt (*about the war*).

_____

7. Der Hund wird unter dem Esstisch schlafen (*sleep under the dining room table*).

_____

8. Der Schaffner hat um (*conductor asked for*) unsere Fahrkarten gebeten.

_____

9. Frau Benz fährt mit dem Zug nach Hause.

_____

10. Er lief durch die Kirche.

_____

 # Special masculine nouns

The declension of masculine nouns was discussed in Chapter 3. In this chapter, this discussion must be continued, because three categories of masculine nouns do not follow the regular patterns of declension. Those regular patterns are:

nom.	der Lehrer	ein Mann	dieser Tisch
acc.	den Lehrer	einen Mann	diesen Tisch
dat.	dem Lehrer	einem Mann	diesem Tisch
gen.	des Lehrers	eines Mannes	dieses Tisches

Whether accompanied by a **der**-word or an **ein**-word, masculine nouns add no ending except in the genitive (**des Mann̲e̲s**). If a word is monosyllabic or ends in a sibilant sound, masculine nouns tend to add **-es** in the genitive case. If the noun is polysyllabic, it tends to end in **-s**.

Masculine nouns that end in -e

Some masculine nouns end in the vowel **-e**. Many beginners to the language often jump to the conclusion that these are feminine nouns, because so many feminine nouns in German end in **-e**. Despite this final vowel in the noun, certain ones are, indeed, masculine. And they require a special declension that *adds an* **-n** to the noun in all the cases except the nominative. This pattern also occurs with adjectives used as nouns, but adjectives used as nouns conform to the rules associated with **der**-words and **ein**-words in the nominative. Let's look at some examples:

	NOUN	ADJECTIVE USED AS NOUN	
nom.	der/ein Löwe (*lion*)	der Deutsche	ein Deutsche**r**
acc.	den/einen Löwe**n**	den Deutsche**n**	einen Deutsche**n**
dat.	dem/einem Löwe**n**	dem Deutsche**n**	einem Deutsche**n**
gen.	des/eines Löwe**n**	des Deutsche**n**	eines Deutsche**n**

You will notice that the genitive case of such nouns does not require the addition of an **-s** ending.

Complete the declension of each of the following masculine nouns.

1. nom. der Matrose (*sailor*)

   acc. _____

   dat. _____

   gen. _____

2. nom. dieser Kunde (*customer*)

   acc. _____

   dat. _____

   gen. _____

3. nom. jeder Junge (*boy*)

   acc. _____

   dat. _____

   gen. _____

4. nom. der Knabe (*boy, chap*)

   acc. _____

   dat. _____

   gen. _____

Complete each sentence with the word or phrase in parentheses. For example:

(der Matrose)

Ich kenne *den Matrosen* nicht.

Der Matrose ist ein Freund von mir.

Be careful to distinguish between nouns and adjectives used as nouns.

1. (der neue Kollege [*colleague*])

   Kennen Sie _____?

   _____ kommt aus Bonn.

   Ich möchte (*would like*) mit _____ sprechen.

   Das sind die Kinder _____.

   Frau Bauer hat ein Geschenk für _____.

2. (dieser Riese [*giant*])

   _____ wohnt in den Bergen.

   Ich habe _____ nie gesehen.

   Warum sind die Leute gegen _____?

   Die Hütte (*hut*) _____ ist sehr groß.

   Alle fragen nach _____.

3. (ihr Gatte [*male spouse*])

   Sie tanzt gern mit _____.

Wir werden _____ besuchen.

_____ ist Polizist in der Stadt.

Das Auto _____ ist wieder kaputt.

Der Mann an der Ecke (*corner*) ist _____.

4. (mein Verwandter [*relative*])

_____ will nach Österreich ziehen (*move*).

Lars möchte _____ kennen lernen.

Ich muss bei _____ wohnen.

Ich komme wieder ohne _____.

Die neue Wohnung _____ war im Stadtzentrum (*downtown*).

5. (ein Franzoser [*Frenchman*])

Das Leben (*life*) _____ ist oft sehr lustig (*fun*).

_____ hat mir dieses Buch gegeben.

Sie spielte Schach mit _____.

Erik möchte _____ fotografieren (*photograph*).

Wir wurden durch _____ benachrichtigt (*informed by*).

A few more high-frequency adjectives that are used as masculine nouns are **der Alte/ein Alter** (*old man*); **der Beamte/ein Beamter** (*official, bureaucrat*); **der Fremde/ein Fremder** (*stranger*).

Several masculine nouns that end in **-e** break the declensional pattern illustrated here and add an **-s** in the genitive case. For example:

nom.	der Name (*name*)	der Glaube (*belief*)
acc.	den Namen	den Glauben
dat.	dem Namen	dem Glauben
gen.	des Namen**s**	des Glauben**s**

Other masculine nouns that follow this pattern are **der Buchstabe** (*letter*), **der Funke** (*spark*), **der Gedanke** (*thought*), and **der Friede** (*peace*). (The more contemporary word for *peace* is **der Frieden**.)

Although **das Herz** (*heart*) is not a masculine noun, it should be mentioned here that it is irregular and follows the same pattern in the dative and genitive cases as a noun such as **der Name**:

nom.	das Herz
acc.	das Herz
dat.	dem Herzen
gen.	des Herzens

Complete each sentence with the word or phrase in parentheses. For example:

(mein Name)

Mein Name ist Werner.

Ich kann *meinen Namen* schreiben.

1. (dieser Buchstabe)

    Kannst du _____ lesen?

    Ist _____ F oder P?

    Er hat das Wort (*word*) ohne _____ geschrieben.

    Der Name _____ ist Ypsilon.

    Welcher Buchstabe soll vor _____ stehen?

2. (ein Fremder)

    Warum hat sie mit _____ gesprochen?

    _____ steht vor dem Fenster.

    Sie sorgt sich um _____.

    Wir sollen _____ in der Stunde der Not (*in a time of need*)
    helfen.

    Brauchen wir die Hilfe (*aid*) _____?

3. (Funke)

    Die Lok (*locomotive*) sprühte viele _____.

    Dieser Angriff (*attack*) war der _____ der Revolution.

    Geht von _____ Gefahr aus?

    Die kleinen Kinder erschraken vor dem _____.

    Ein _____ ist nicht immer gefährlich (*dangerous*).

Don't be fooled by the masculine noun **der Käse** (*cheese*). It follows the regular masculine declensional pattern.

nom.	der Käse
acc.	den Käse
dat.	dem Käse
gen.	des Käses

Traditional declensions

Another category of masculine nouns also requires an -(e)n ending in its declension. Some call this a *weak* declension. This declension occurs because it has come down through the ages as a tradition to decline certain nouns in this way. Let's look at a couple of nouns in this category:

nom.	der Herr (*gentleman*)	der Graf (*count*)
acc.	den Herr**n**	den Graf**en**
dat.	dem Herr**n**	dem Graf**en**
gen.	des Herr**n**	des Graf**en**

Other *traditional* nouns that follow this pattern are **der Prinz** (*prince*); **der Mensch** (*man, human*); **der Bär** (*bear*); **der Bauer** (*farmer*); **der Nachbar** (*neighbor*); **der Fürst** (*prince*); and **der Held** (*hero*).

ÜBUNG
5·4

Complete each sentence with the phrase in parentheses.

1. (der große Bär)

   Martin hatte Angst vor _____.

   Tina hat nach _____ gefragt.

2. (ein englischer Prinz)

   Ist dieser Herr _____?

   Kennen Sie _____?

3. (ein sehr guter Mensch)

   Wir haben _____ eingeladen (*invited*).

   Die alte Frau denkt an _____ von ihrer Vergangenheit (*past*).

4. (der alte Bauer)

   Hat _____ seinen Garten gepflegt?

   Außer _____ hat niemand mir geholfen.

5. (unser Nachbar)

   Die Kinder _____ waren sehr unartig (*naughty*).

   Ich möchte _____ vorstellen (*introduce*).

6. (der hübsche [*handsome*] Fürst)

   Sie ist ganz verliebt (*quite in love*) in _____.

   Das Pferd _____ ist ein Schimmel (*white horse*).

7. (der junge Held)

   Alle wollten _____ kennen lernen.

   Der Kanzler hat _____ gratuliert.

Foreign words

German is very accepting of foreign words, and most people use them with ease. Many are masculine words, and when these words have the *accent on the last syllable*, they tend to require an **-en** ending in the accusative, dative, and genitive cases. For example:

nom.	der Soldát (*soldier*)	ein Elefánt (*elephant*)
acc.	den Soldat**en**	einen Elefant**en**
dat.	dem Soldat**en**	einem Elefant**en**
gen.	des Soldat**en**	eines Elefant**en**

Other words that fit into this category are **der Student**, **der Pianist**, **der Komponist**, **der Präsident**, and **der Diplomat**. The list of words in this group is quite long.

ÜBUNG
5·5

Complete the declension for each of the following nouns.

1. nom. der Student

   acc. _____

   dat. _____

   gen. _____

2. nom. ein Pianist

   acc. _____

   dat. _____

   gen. _____

3. nom. unser amerikanischer Präsident

   acc. _____

   dat. _____

   gen. _____

4. nom. kein ehrlicher Diplomat

   acc. _____

   dat. _____

   gen. _____

ÜBUNG
5·6

Write the following nouns in the nominative case with the definite article.

1. Junge _____

2. Matrose _____

3. Mantel _____

4. Lampe _____

5. Mensch _____

*Write the following nouns in the nominative case with **kein**.*

6. Beamte _____

7. Bauer _____

8. Tourist _____

9. Name _____

10. Idiot _____

Write the following nouns in the accusative case with the indefinite article.

11. Herr _____

12. Gedanke _____

13. Glaube _____

14. Aristokrat _____

15. Architekt _____

*Write the following nouns in the dative case with **dieser**.*

16. Journalist _____

17. Lehrerin _____

18. Nachbar _____

19. Dirigent (*orchestra conductor*) _____

20. Deutscher _____

*Write the following nouns in the genitive case with **welch**.*

21. Graf _____

22. Name _____

23. Held _____

24. Demokrat _____

25. Kapitalist _____

26. Buchstabe _____

27. Junge _____

28. Mädchen _____

29. Student _____

30. Herz _____

Conjunctions
and word order

6

German word order is relatively strict when it comes to the position of the subject and the verb in a sentence. When a sentence begins with the subject, the verb follows the subject.

subject   verb
Der Lehrer besucht einen alten Freund.   *The teacher visits an old friend.*

But if something other than the subject begins the sentence (e.g., an adverb, a prepositional phrase, or a clause), the verb precedes the subject.

adverb
Heute besucht der Lehrer einen alten Freund.

prepositional phrase
Nach dem Konzert besucht der Lehrer einen alten Freund.

clause
Wenn er in Berlin ist, besucht der Lehrer einen alten Freund.

But these simple rules are altered slightly when a conjunction is added to the scheme. There are three types of conjunctions:

1. Conjunctions that do not change the order of the subject and verb in a sentence: **aber** (*but*); **denn** (*because*); **oder** (*or*); **und** (*and*); and **sondern** (*but, rather*).

2. Conjunctions that cause the conjugated verb to be the last element in a clause, for example: **dass** (*that*); **ob** (*whether, if*); and **weil** (*because*).

3. Interrogative words used as conjunctions, for example: **wann** (*when*), **wie** (*how*), **wo** (*where*), and **warum** (*why*).

Coordinating conjunctions

Aber, denn, oder, und, and **sondern** are called *coordinating conjunctions*. They combine two sentences into one, but in the process have no effect on word order. The position of the subject and verb in the original two sentences remains the same when combined by such conjunctions.

Original sentences
Sie bleibt zu Hause. Ihr Bruder ist in Hamburg.

Combined with aber

Sie bleibt zu Hause, **aber** ihr Bruder ist in Hamburg.

*She stays home, **but** her brother is in Hamburg.*

If the subject and verb in a sentence have switched positions due to some preceding element, that word order remains. For example:

adverb   **verb subject**

Sie bleibt zu Hause, **aber** <u>diese Woche</u> <u>ist</u> <u>ihr Bruder</u> in Hamburg.

*She stays home, **but** this week her brother is in Hamburg.*

Let's look at some further examples of how these conjunctions are used:

Stefan arbeitet nicht im Garten, **denn** es regnet.

*Stefan isn't working in the garden, **because** it's raining.*

Bleiben Sie in Deutschland, **oder** besuchen Sie Verwandte im Ausland?

*Are you staying in Germany, **or** are you going to visit relatives overseas?*

Die Kinder schlafen, **und** die Eltern sehen fern.

*The children are sleeping, **and** the parents are watching television.*

Herr Benz arbeitet nicht bei dieser Firma, **sondern** er arbeitet bei einer Bank in der Stadt.

*Mr. Benz doesn't work at this company, **but** rather he works at a bank in the city.*

Note that **sondern** is used after a sentence that contains a negative: **Herr Benz arbeitet <u>nicht</u> bei dieser Firma.**

If the subjects of the two sentences to be combined by **aber** or **und** are identical, the subject of the second sentence can be omitted.

Er sitzt im Garten, aber **er** hört mich nicht rufen.

*He's sitting in the garden, but **he** doesn't hear me calling.*

Er sitzt im Garten aber hört mich nicht rufen.

He's sitting in the garden but doesn't hear me calling.

ÜBUNG
6·1

*Combine each pair of sentences with **aber**. For example:*

Sie will nach Paris fahren. Sie hat kein Auto.

Sie will nach Paris fahren, aber sie hat kein Auto.

1. Er versucht (*tries*) das Gedicht zu lernen. Er versteht es gar nicht.

_____

2. Du bist zwar mein Freund. Ich kann dir nicht damit helfen.

_____

3. Der Soldat war schwer verwundet (*badly wounded*). Die Ärztin gab die Hoffnung nicht auf (*did not give up hope*).

_____

*Combine each pair of sentences with **denn**.*

4. Ich will nicht wandern (*hiking*) gehen. Es ist zu regnerisch (*rainy*).

   _____

5. Mein Sohn kann nicht im Garten spielen. Es ist sehr kalt geworden.

   _____

6. Thomas ist sehr müde. Er hat den ganzen Tag gearbeitet.

   _____

*Combine each pair of sentences with **oder**.*

7. Reist ihr nach Amerika? Bleibt ihr zu Hause?

   _____

8. Lars muss gehorchen (*obey*). Er hat die Folgen selbst zu tragen (*bear the consequences himself*).

9. Heute könnt ihr hier spielen. Ihr könnt zum Stadtpark gehen.

   _____

*Combine each pair of sentences with **sondern**.*

10. Mein Vater spricht nicht nur Deutsch. Er kann auch Spanisch und Englisch.

    _____

11. Angelika spielt nicht nur Tennis. Sie spielt auch Fußball und Golf.

    _____

12. Wir haben nicht ferngesehen. Wir sind ins Kino gegangen.

    _____

*Combine each pair of sentences with **und**.*

13. Professor Schneider kommt morgen an. Er kann bis Mittwoch bei mir bleiben.

    _____

14. Ich spiele Klavier. Mein Bruder spielt Flöte (*flute*).

    _____

15. Meine Tante liest die Zeitung. Mein Onkel schläft auf dem Sofa.

    _____

Complete each sentence with any appropriate clause. For example:

Der Mann ist schnell gefahren, aber *er ist spät angekommen.*

1. Tina spielt Flöte (*flute*), und _____.

2. Ich kann nicht in die Stadt fahren, sondern _____.

3. Er versteht kein Wort Deutsch, denn _____.

4. Herr Schneider macht viele Überstunden (*overtime*), aber _____.

5. Kaufen Sie einen kleinen Wagen, oder _____?

6. Erhardt kam um elf Uhr an und _____.

7. Das Kind hat noch Fieber, aber _____.

8. Ich will kein Bier bestellen (*order*), sondern _____.

9. Sabine fliegt nach Frankfurt, denn _____.

10. Wohnen deine Verwandten noch in Bonn, oder _____?

Subordinating conjunctions

Subordinating conjunctions make up the largest group of conjunctions. The most familiar of them are **dass** (*that*); **weil** (*because*); **wenn** (*when, if*); and **ob** (*whether, if*). But there are many other important subordinating conjunctions. Some of these are:

als	*when (in the past tense)*
als ob	*as if*
bis	*until*
da	*since*
damit	*so that*
falls	*in case*
obwohl	*although*
seit(dem)	*since*
sobald	*as soon as*
soviel	*as far as*
während	*while*

The clause that is introduced by a subordinating conjunction requires a new position for the conjugated verb in that clause: the verb will stand at the end of the clause. For example:

Ich weiß, **dass** der Wirt nicht zu Hause **ist**.	*I know that the landlord is not at home.*
Sie besuchte mich, **als** sie in Berlin **war**.	*She visited me when she was in Berlin.*
Er nimmt einen Regenschirm mit, **falls** es **regnet**.	*He takes along an umbrella in case it rains.*
Sie ist spät zur Schule gekommen, **weil** ihr Wecker kaputt **ist**.	*She came to school late because her alarm clock is broken.*

Complete each sentence with the clauses in parentheses.

1. Sie fragt, ob _____.

   (Ist seine Tochter wieder gesund [*healthy*]?)

   _____

   (Kann das kleine Kind wirklich Geige [*violin*] spielen?)

   _____

2. Er lief zu seinem Vater, sobald _____.

   (Er sah den Fremden vor der Tür stehen.)

   _____

   (Er fand das Goldstück [*goldpiece*].)

   _____

3. Er verreist nach Rom, da _____.

   (Es ist wärmer [*warmer*] im Winter in Italien.)

   _____

   (Er hat jetzt viel Freizeit [*free time*].)

   _____

4. Lars lernte Klavier spielen, während _____.

   (Er wohnte bei seiner Tante.)

   _____

   (Er besuchte das Konservatorium [*music conservatory*] in München.)

   _____

5. Ich gehe oft Ski laufen (*skiing*), wenn _____.

   (Ich bin in den Bergen.)

   _____

   (Ich verbringe [*spend*] den Winter in Norwegen [*Norway*].)

   _____

Just as in English, a subordinating clause in German can either follow or precede its accompanying clause. Consider this example:

Sie ist eine sehr nette Frau, **obwohl sie sehr reich ist**.

She is a nice woman, although she is very rich.

Obwohl sie sehr reich ist, ist sie eine sehr nette Frau.

Although she is very rich, she is a very nice woman.

You will notice in the second example that the verb precedes the subject in the second clause, because something other than the subject began the sentence: the subordinating clause.

ÜBUNG
6·4

Complete each sentence with any appropriate clause. For example:

Martin fragt, ob *ich in die Stadt fahren will.*

1. Karin will nicht Karten spielen, weil _____.

2. Die Jungen wollen heute klettern (*climbing*) gehen, obwohl _____.

3. Ich wusste nicht, dass _____.

4. Während _____, wohnte sie in einem Studentenheim (*dormitory*).

5. Da _____, musste er einen neuen Job finden.

6. Seitdem _____, habe ich viele neue Leute kennen gelernt.

7. Als _____, ist mein Bruder jeden Abend in die Oper (*opera*) gegangen.

8. Ich bereite das Abendessen vor (*prepare supper*), wenn _____.

9. Soviel _____, wird der Chef ihn entlassen.

10. Wir werden nach Madrid reisen, sobald _____.

11. Ich warte an der Ecke (*corner*), bis _____.

12. Frau Bauer gab dem Mann fünf Euro, damit _____.

13. Falls _____, trägt sie einen warmen Mantel (*wears a warm coat*).

14. Der Journalist berichtet (*reports*), dass _____.

15. Herr Körner unterrichtet (*teaches*) Mathe, während _____.

Interrogative words as conjunctions

Interrogative words are used to form questions. They usually specify an element in a sentence that will determine the kind of interrogative used. If that element is a person, a *who* question will be asked. If that element is a period of time, a *when* question will be asked. Let's first look at a couple examples in English. The specified element in each sentence is set in bold.

STATEMENT	QUESTION
Mr. Brown recently bought a car.	**Who** recently bought a car?
Mr. Brown **recently** bought a car.	**When** did Mr. Brown buy a car?
Mr. Brown recently bought **a car**.	**What** did Mr. Brown recently buy?

It works the same way in German:

STATEMENT	QUESTION
Herr Braun hat neulich einen Wagen gekauft.	**Wer** hat neulich einen Wagen gekauft?
Herr Braun hat **neulich** einen Wagen gekauft.	**Wann** hat Herr Braun einen Wagen gekauft?
Herr Braun hat neulich **einen Wagen** gekauft.	**Was** hat Herr Braun neulich gekauft?

These interrogative words and many others can also act as conjunctions. They combine two clauses into one sentence, and the rules for the position of the verb in such sentences are the same as previously stated for other subordinating conjunctions. When used as a conjunction, these words do not necessarily introduce a question. That is determined by the accompanying clause and not by the subordinating clause. For example:

Statement

Ich weiß, was Herr Braun gekauft hat.   *I know what Mr. Brown bought.*

Question

Wissen Sie, was Herr Braun gekauft hat?   *Do you know what Mr. Brown bought?*

Let's look at the list of interrogative words that can be used as subordinating conjunctions:

wann	*when*
warum	*why*
was	*what*
wer, wen, wem, wessen	*who, whom, whose*
wo	*where*
woher	*from where*
wohin	*(to) where*

Wie (*how*) is, of course, also an interrogative word that can be used as a conjunction. But it can be combined with other words to form variations of **wie**. For example:

wie alt	*how old*
wie groß	*how big*
wie hoch	*how high*
wie lange	*how long*
wie oft	*how often*
wie viel(e)	*how much/many*

All these interrogative words function just like **wer**, **was**, and **wann** as subordinating conjunctions.

Complete each sentence with the questions in parentheses. Use the interrogative words as subordinating conjunctions. For example:

Ich weiß, _____.

(Wer hat den Wagen gekauft?)

Ich weiß, wer den Wagen gekauft hat.

1. Der Richter (*judge*) fragt ihn, _____.

   (Wo wohnt seine Frau jetzt?)

   _____

   (Wie lange bleibt er in der Hauptstadt [*capital*]?)

   _____

   (Mit wem ist er nach Polen [*Poland*] gefahren?)

   _____

2. Ich hatte keine Ahnung (*had no idea*), _____.

   (Wohin sind die Kinder gegangen?)

   _____

   (Wessen Bücher hat der Mann gestohlen [*stolen*]?)

   _____

   (Für wen musste die junge Frau arbeiten?)

   _____

3. Können Sie mir sagen, _____?

   (Wie alt ist die kranke Frau?)

   _____

   (Wie oft fährt der Zug nach Bremen?)

   _____

   (Wie viele Zeitungen haben Sie schon verkauft?)

   _____

4. Er erklärte, _____.

   (Warum ist er so böse [*angry*] geworden?)

   _____

   (Woher hat er diese Bilder bekommen?)

   _____

   (Wie schnell kann der Rennwagen [*racing car*] fahren?)

   _____

5. Weißt du, _____?

   (Wen wird der Polizist verhaften [*arrest*]?)

   _____

   (Wie viel Geld hat der reiche Herr?)

   _____

   (Von wem hat Gudrun dieses Geschenk bekommen?)

   _____

7

Mancher and solcher

Mancher (*many a*) and **solcher** (*such a*) are symbolic of a small number of determiners that can be used in more than one way. The varied usage can cause some confusion because for the most part, the meaning is the same despite the form in which the determiner is used. This chapter will deal with clearing up any problems that occur with these determiners.

Mancher

Mancher is used in four ways:

1. It is declined as a **der**-word with singular nouns and means *many a*: **mancher alte Mann** (*many an old man*), **mit mancher netten Frau** (*with many a nice woman*).

2. It is declined as a **der**-word with plural nouns and can be translated as *some*. It is also often translated in the singular as *many a*: **manche interessanten Bücher** (*some interesting books, many an interesting book*); **von manchen reichen Leuten** (*from some rich people, from many a rich person*).

3. It is not declined and appears without any ending. The adjective that follows it is declined as an unpreceded adjective (see Chapter 3) and is translated as *many a*: **manch armer Mann** (*many a poor man*), **manch gutes Kind** (*many a good child*).

4. It is not declined and appears without any ending. It is followed by the indefinite article (**ein**) as well as an adjective, both of which follow the normal declensional pattern of **ein**-words. It is translated as *many a*: **manch ein Beamter** (*many an official*), **manch eine hübsche Dame** (*many a beautiful lady*).

ÜBUNG

7·1

Decline each nominative case phrase in the other three cases.

1. nom. mancher gute Kerl (*fellow*)

    acc. _____

    dat. _____

    gen. _____

2. nom. manch eine kranke Frau

   acc. _____

   dat. _____

   gen. _____

3. nom. manch reicher Mann

   acc. _____

   dat. _____

   gen. _____

4. nom. manch schöne Stunden

   acc. _____

   dat. _____

   gen. _____

5. nom. manche weinenden (*crying*) Kinder

   acc. _____

   dat. _____

   gen. _____

6. nom. manches alte Haus

   acc. _____

   dat. _____

   gen. _____

7. nom. mancher gute Film

   acc. _____

   dat. _____

   gen. _____

8. nom. manch ein Verkäufer (*salesman*)

   acc. _____

   dat. _____

   gen. _____

9. nom. manch starke (*strong*) Männer

   acc. _____

   dat. _____

   gen. _____

10. nom. manche neue Lehrerin

acc. _____

dat. _____

gen. _____

Rewrite each sentence with the phrases provided in parentheses. For example:

Er hat _____ kennen gelernt.

(mancher gute Sportler)

Er hat manchen guten Sportler kennen gelernt.

1. _____ liest seinen neuen Roman.

(mancher Student)

_____

(manche neue Angestellte [*employee*])

_____

(manches kluge [*smart*] Kind)

_____

(manche ausländischen Touristen)

_____

(mancher Mann)

_____

2. Mit der Hilfe _____ haben wir den Mann gerettet (*rescued*).

(mancher tapfere [*brave*] Matrose)

_____

(manche zitternden [*trembling*] Mädchen)

_____

(manch ein müder Feuerwehrmann [*fireman*])

_____

(manches Kind)

_____

(manch verängstigte [*frightened*] Leute)

_____

(manche Polizisten)

_____

3. Ich habe _____ gefragt.

   (manch eine Studentin)

   _____

   (mancher junge Arzt)

   _____

   (manch ein alter Herr)

   _____

   (manche enttäuschten [*disappointed*] Diplomaten)

   _____

   (manche Professorin)

   _____

4. Erik hat es mit _____ diskutiert (*discussed*).

   (mancher Journalist)

   _____

   (manche ausländischen Akademiker)

   _____

   (mancher verwundete Soldat)

   _____

   (manch eine Amerikanerin)

   _____

   (manches naive Mädchen)

   _____

Solcher

Solcher is used in the following four ways:

1. It is most often declined as a **der**-word with plural nouns and means *such* or *like that*: **solche fremden Leute** (*such strange people, strange people like that*); **von solchen unartigen Jungen** (*from such naughty boys, from naughty boys like that*).

2. It is declined as a **der**-word with singular nouns and means *such a*: **solcher alte Mann** (*such an old man*), **solches Wetter** (*such weather*).

3. It follows **ein** and declines as an adjective and means *such a*: **eine solche Frau** (*such a woman*), **mit einem solchen Problem** (*with such a problem*).

4. It is not declined and appears without any ending. The adjective that follows it is declined as an unpreceded adjective (see Chapter 3) and is translated as *such*: **solch schlechtes Wetter** (*such bad weather*), **bei solch freundlichen Verwandten** (*at the home of such kind relatives*).

So ein is often used in spoken German and means *such a*. It follows the declensional pattern of other **ein**-words. For example:

Sie haben **so ein** großes Haus gekauft.	*They bought **such a** big house.*
Er spielt mit **so einer** kleinen Katze.	*He's playing with **such a** little cat.*

ÜBUNG
7·3

Decline each nominative case phrase in the other three cases.

1. nom. solcher gute Kerl

   acc. _____

   dat. _____

   gen. _____

2. nom. solche netten Leute

   acc. _____

   dat. _____

   gen. _____

3. nom. ein solcher Komponist

   acc. _____

   dat. _____

   gen. _____

4. nom. solch ein langes Schiff (*ship*)

   acc. _____

   dat. _____

   gen. _____

5. nom. solch dumme Sätze

   acc. _____

   dat. _____

   gen. _____

6. nom. solches interessante Buch

   acc. _____

   dat. _____

   gen. _____

7. nom. solches schlechte Problem

   acc. _____

   dat. _____

   gen. _____

8. nom. solch hübsche Tänzerin

   acc. _____

   dat. _____

   gen. _____

9. nom. solche hübschen Tänzerinnen

   acc. _____

   dat. _____

   gen. _____

10. nom. solch eine schöne Blume

    acc. _____

    dat. _____

    gen. _____

Rewrite each sentence with the phrases provided in parentheses. For example:

Er hat _____ kennen gelernt.

(solche guten Sportler)

Er hat solche guten Sportler kennen gelernt.

1. Lars hat _____ gesehen.

   (so ein großer Garten)

   _____

   (ein solches Bild)

   _____

   (so ein kleines Haus)

   _____

   (solches alte Theater)

   _____

   (solcher große Lastwagen [*truck*])

   _____

2. Alle sprechen von _____.

   (solch herrliches [*marvelous*] Wetter)

   _____

   (solcher dumme Roman)

   _____

   (ein solches Drama)

   _____

   (solche glücklichen [*happy*] Tage)

   _____

   (so ein furchtbares Gewitter [*terrible storm*])

   _____

Welcher

Just as **mancher** and **solcher** can be used without an ending to mean *many a* and *such (a)*, **welch** is often used in a similar way. Compare the following phrases:

nominative

manch netter Mann	*many a nice man*
solch gutes Wetter	*such good weather*
welch buntes Papier	***what** colorful paper*

accusative

manch netten Mann
solch gutes Wetter
welch buntes Papier

dative

manch nettem Mann
solch gutem Wetter
welch buntem Papier

genitive

manch netten Mannes
solch guten Wetters
welch bunten Papiers

Was für ein

The determiner **welcher**, as illustrated in Chapter 3, asks *which* or *what* of the noun it modifies: **welcher Roman** (*which novel*), **welches Schiff** (*what ship*). The interrogative word **was** also asks *what* but is a pronoun and not a modifier. **Was** is frequently part of a useful phrase: **was für ein** (*what kind of*).

There is sometimes confusion about how to use **was für ein** because the accusative preposition **für** is part of the phrase. The fact is that **für** does not require the use of the accusative case following this phrase. Consider this three-word phrase as a special **ein**-word. Indeed, the phrase functions exactly as the indefinite article **ein**. When **was für ein** modifies a plural, **ein** is omitted, which is exactly what occurs when the indefinite article **ein** stands alone. Compare these phrases, and note that only the word **ein** has any endings:

SINGULAR		PLURAL	
ein Mann	*a man*	Männer	*men*
was für ein Mann	*what kind of man*	was für Männer	*what kind of men*
eine Frau	*a woman*	Frauen	*women*
was für eine Frau	*what kind of woman*	was für Frauen	*what kind of women*

ÜBUNG

7·5

Decline each nominative case phrase in the other three cases.

1. nom. welch schöner Tag

   acc. _____

   dat. _____

   gen. _____

2. nom. welch glückliche Stunden

    acc. _____

    dat. _____

    gen. _____

3. nom. was für eine Wohnung

    acc. _____

    dat. _____

    gen. _____

4. nom. was für ein Esstisch (*dining table*)

    acc. _____

    dat. _____

    gen. _____

5. nom. was für ein Flugzeug (*airplane*)

    acc. _____

    dat. _____

    gen. _____

Numerals

When numerals precede an adjective, the adjective ending conforms to the pattern of unpreceded adjectives. This occurs with all numbers except *one*, and all numbers greater than *one* are accompanied by a plural. For example:

	EIN ONE (AN EIN-WORD)	VIER FOUR	NEUNZIG NINETY
nom.	ein kleiner Hut	vier kleine Hüte	neunzig kleine Hüte
acc.	einen kleinen Hut	vier kleine Hüte	neunzig kleine Hüte
dat.	einem kleinen Hut	vier kleinen Hüten	neunzig kleinen Hüten
gen.	eines kleinen Hutes	vier kleiner Hüte	neunzig kleiner Hüte

Besides numerals, words that describe quantities do not decline and are followed by adjectives that follow the pattern of unpreceded adjectives. Words that describe quantities are: **ein paar** (*a couple*); **etwas** (*some*); **mehr** (*more*); **viel** (*much, a lot of*); and **wenig** (*little*) (opposite of *much*). For example:

nom.	mehr frisches Brot (*more fresh bread*)
acc.	mehr frisches Brot
dat.	mehr frischem Brot
gen.	mehr frischen Brotes

The words **etwas**, **viel**, and **wenig** are used most often with singular nouns (**etwas Geld** [*some money*], **viel Geld** [*much/a lot of money*], **wenig Geld** [*less money*]). **Mehr** can be used with either singular or plural nouns (**mehr Geld** [*more money*], **mehr Bücher** [*more books*]). **Ein paar** always modifies plural nouns (**ein paar Flaschen** [*a couple bottles*]). In all cases, adjectives that accompany the nouns are treated as unpreceded adjectives.

7·6

Decline each nominative case phrase in the other three cases.

1. nom. mehr heißer Kaffee

   acc. _____

   dat. _____

   gen. _____

2. nom. viel schwierige (*difficult*) Arbeit

   acc. _____

   dat. _____

   gen. _____

3. nom. etwas warme Milch

   acc. _____

   dat. _____

   gen. _____

4. nom. wenig freie Zeit

   acc. _____

   dat. _____

   gen. _____

5. nom. ein paar englische Zeitungen

   acc. _____

   dat. _____

   gen. _____

6. nom. zehn neue Schlipse (*ties*)

   acc. _____

   dat. _____

   gen. _____

7. nom. einundvierzig kleine Vögel (*birds*)

    acc. _____

    dat. _____

    gen. _____

8. nom. ein großer Koffer (*suitcase*)

    acc. _____

    dat. _____

    gen. _____

9. nom. mehr neue Angestellte (*employees*)

    acc. _____

    dat. _____

    gen. _____

10. nom. ein paar deutsche Briefmarken (*stamps*)

    acc. _____

    dat. _____

    gen. _____

The determiners **viele** and **wenige** modify plural nouns and mean, respectively, *many* and *few*. They were taken up in detail in Chapter 3 and have a special declension that *breaks the pattern* of unpreceded adjectives, because the adjectives are preceded by **viele** or **wenige**.

nom.	viele neue Häuser (*many new houses*)
acc.	viele neue Häuser
dat.	vielen neuen Häusern
gen.	vieler neuer Häuser

Circle the letter of the word or phrase that best completes each sentence.

1. _____ Bücher dürfen die Kinder nicht lesen.
    a. Welch   b. Solche   c. Etwas   d. Manch

2. _____ Wagen möchten Sie kaufen?
    a. Was für ein   b. Was für eine   c. Was für einen   d. Was für einem

3. Erik hat _____ Boot (*boat*) gekauft.
    a. so ein   b. etwas   c. einen solchen   d. welche

4. Manch _____ Mann hat eine Sünde begangen (commited a sin).
   a. gute   b. guter   c. guten   d. gut

5. Eine _____ Prüfung (test) wäre zu schwierig für mich.
   a. welche   b. viele   c. viel   d. solche

6. _____ herrliches Wetter!
   a. Was   b. Manches   c. Solche   d. Welch

7. Ich kann _____ langes Gedicht nicht lernen.
   a. ein solch   b. etwas   c. manche   d. eines

8. Mein Großvater hat _____ Freizeit.
   a. mancher   b. ein paar   c. was für ein   d. viel

9. _____ Touristen verstehen Deutsch.
   a. Wenige   b. Manche   c. Was für   d. Ein paar
      amerikanische   amerikanische   amerikanisches   amerikanischen

10. Warum wollt ihr _____ großes Haus haben?
    a. so ein   b. solches   c. manche   d. mehr

11. Sabine hat auch _____ Rock genäht.
    a. ein paar schöne b. wenige neue   c. einen solchen   d. etwas

12. In _____ Bett musst du schlafen (sleep)?
    a. was für einem   b. manchen guten c. solches alte   d. wenigen kleinen

13. Hat sie _____ Worte zu ihm gesagt?
    a. was für   b. etwas   c. manches   d. solche bösen
                                         freundliche

14. Geben Sie mir bitte _____ Tee!
    a. etwas   b. wenige   c. manch   d. welchem

15. Warum trägst du _____ schweren (heavy) Koffer?
    a. solch ein   b. so einen   c. ein solcher   d. was für einen

Comparative, superlative, and irregularities

Comparative

Except for a few irregular formations, the German comparative is relatively easy to use and easy to understand for English speakers, because it follows a pattern quite similar to the English comparative. The suffix **-er** is added to an adjective or adverb to form the German comparative. For example:

POSITIVE	COMPARATIVE	ENGLISH
leicht	leichter	*lighter, easier*
nett	netter	*nicer*
schön	schöner	*prettier*
schwer	schwerer	*harder, heavier*
langweilig	langweiliger	*more boring*

In one category of adjectives and adverbs, English and German differ in the formation of the comparative. If English words have several syllables or the words come from a foreign source (usually Latin), the comparative is not formed with a suffix. Instead, the adjective or adverb is preceded by the comparative word *more*. German, however, uses the suffix **-er** no matter how long the adjective or adverb might be. For example:

POSITIVE	COMPARATIVE	ENGLISH
erfrischend	erfrischender	*more refreshing*
furchtbar	furchtbarer	*more terrible*
interessant	interessanter	*more interesting*
kompliziert	komplizierter	*more complicated*
lächerlich	lächerlicher	*more ridiculous*

ÜBUNG
8·1

In the blanks provided, write the comparative of the adjective provided and the English translation of that comparative. For example:

neu *neuer newer*

1. schlecht _____ _____

70

2. schnell   _____   _____

3. langsam   _____   _____

4. klein   _____   _____

5. weit   _____   _____

6. dick   _____   _____

7. bunt   _____   _____

8. praktisch   _____   _____

9. künstlich   _____   _____

10. verantwortlich   _____   _____

When a comparative is used as an adverb, just like its positive form, it has no ending:

Er läuft schnell. Er läuft schneller.	*He runs fast. He runs faster.*
Sie sprechen laut. Sie sprechen lauter.	*They speak loudly. They speak louder/more loudly.*

Comparative adjectives follow the declensional patterns of other adjectives. The comparative adjectives must conform to the number, case, and gender of the noun they modify. Only predicate adjectives in the comparative require no endings. For example:

Predicate adjectives

Heute wird es heißer.	*It is getting hotter today.*
Dein Sohn ist kleiner.	*Your son is smaller.*

Declined adjectives

Die nett**ere** Frau ist unser**e** Lehrerin.	*The nicer woman is our teacher.*
Er spricht mit den faul**eren** Jungen.	*He speaks with the lazier boys.*

The comparative forms are called *comparative* because they generally are used to compare two people or things. The word **als** (*than*) is used to draw that comparison. For example:

Mein Haus ist kleiner **als** dein Haus.	*My house is smaller **than** your house.*
Sie läuft langsamer **als** ihre Schwester.	*She runs slower **than** her sister.*

ÜBUNG
8·2

Fill in the blank with the missing word or ending.

1. Mein Vater möchte ein kleiner_____ Haus kaufen.

2. Ist diese Fahne (flag) bunt_____ als unsere Fahne?

3. Ihre Familie wohnt in der neuer_____ Wohnung.

4. War diese Übung leichter _____ die erste Übung?

5. Mein Großvater hat weiß_____ Haare (*hair*) als meine Großmutter.

6. Die S-Bahn (*city railway*) fährt schnell_____ als die Straßenbahn.

7. Ist der rote Wagen neu_____?

8. Sie kann die schwerer_____ Frage nicht beantworten (*answer*).

9. Erik tanzte mit den netter_____ Mädchen.

10. Ein kleiner_____ Hund schläft unter dem breiter_____ Tisch.

Many adjectives of one syllable that have an umlaut vowel add an umlaut in the comparative. For example:

POSITIVE	COMPARATIVE	ENGLISH
alt	älter	*older*
arm	ärmer	*poorer*
dumm	dümmer	*dumber, more stupid*
hart	härter	*harder*
jung	jünger	*younger*
kalt	kälter	*colder*
klug	klüger	*smarter, more clever*
krank	kränker	*sicker*
kurz	kürzer	*shorter*
lang	länger	*longer*
schwach	schwächer	*weaker*
stark	stärker	*stronger*
warm	wärmer	*warmer*

Although this formation of comparative adjectives and adverbs requires an umlaut, the regular rules for declensions still apply. For example:

Predicate adjective	Dein Onkel ist viel älter.	*Your uncle is much older.*
Declined adjective	Kennen Sie den jüngeren Lehrer?	*Do you know the younger teacher?*
Adverb	Sie spielt Tennis klüger als ihr Bruder.	*She plays tennis smarter than her brother.*

ÜBUNG
8·3

Rewrite the adjectives and adverbs in bold in the comparative. For example:

Er hilft dem **kleinen** Kind. *kleineren*

1. Dieser Roman ist **interessant**. _____

2. War dein Bruder **stark**? _____

3. Die **jungen** Sportler haben keine Preise (*prizes*) gewonnen. _____

4. Warum kauft ihr einen **langen** Tisch? _____

5. Im Norden (*north*) ist das Wetter oft **kalt**. _____

6. Warum habe ich diesen **langweiligen** Artikel gelesen? _____

7. Sein Puls (*pulse*) ist **schwach** geworden. _____

8. Sie hat den **starken** Gewichtheber (*weight lifter*) fotografiert. _____

9. Meine Tante hatte ein **altes** Auto. _____

10. Meine kleine Tochter schreibt **langsam**. _____

Irregular comparatives

There are a few irregular formations of adjectives and adverbs in the comparative. They are relatively easy to use, because some of them are similar to the irregularities that occur in the English comparative. For example:

POSITIVE	COMPARATIVE	ENGLISH
bald	eher	*sooner*
groß	größer	*bigger*
gut	besser	*better*
hoch	höher	*higher, taller*
nah	näher	*nearer*
viel	mehr	*more*

A small group of adjectives and adverbs end in **-el**, **-en**, or **-er**. Although such words are not necessarily irregular, they have an idiosyncrasy that must be noted: the final **-e** is dropped before the comparative **-er** is added. For example:

POSITIVE	COMPARATIVE	ENGLISH
dunkel	dunkler	*darker*
teuer	teurer	*more expensive*
trocken	trockner	*drier*

No matter what kind of irregularity occurs in the comparative, the regular rules of declensions still apply.

Predicate adjective	Dieses Hotel ist näher.	*This hotel is nearer.*
Declined adjective	Wirst du die größere Stadt besuchen?	*Will you visit the bigger city?*
Adverb	Tina schreibt besser als Lars.	*Tina writes better than Lars.*

Rewrite the adjectives and adverbs in bold in the comparative. For example:

Er hilft dem **kleinen** Kind. *kleineren*

1. Werden Sie der **armen** Familie helfen? _____

2. Dieser Wolkenkratzer (*skyscraper*) ist **hoch**. _____

3. Der Zug nach Bremen wird **bald** kommen. _____

4. Klaus hat ein **gutes** Gedicht geschrieben. _____

5. Ist dein Sohn **krank** geworden? _____

6. Der Professer spricht **viel** aber sagt **wenig**. _____

7. Ich benutze (*use*) einen **kurzen** Bleistift. _____

8. Jetzt wird es **dunkel** im Theater. _____

9. Es ist **nah** bis zum Bahnhof. _____

10. Es ist **gut**, dass du zu Hause bleibst. _____

11. Der Richter (*judge*) war wirklich **nett**. _____

12. Die Tage im Juli sind meistens (*mostly*) **warm**. _____

13. Meine Probleme waren **groß**. _____

14. Wir brauchen ein **neues** Sofa. _____

15. Habt ihr den **hohen** Glockenturm (*bell tower*) gesehen? _____

The comparative is used in two special ways:

1. To suggest that something is *rather* big or tall or nice. Any variety of adjectives can be used with this expression: **ein netterer Mann** (*a rather nice man*), **ein billigeres Haus** (*a rather cheap house*).

2. To emphasize the comparative adjective or adverb by preceding it with **immer**. English just repeats the word for this emphasis: **immer größer** (*bigger and bigger*), **immer schneller** (*faster and faster*).

Je... desto

English uses the definite article *the* with a comparative to say that *the more* one thing occurs, *the more* another thing occurs. German forms a similar expression but with the words **je... desto**. For example:

Je schneller der Zug fährt, **desto** nervöser wird meine Frau.	*The faster the train travels, **the more** nervous my wife becomes.*
Je kälter es wird, **desto** mehr wollen wir nach Mexiko verreisen.	*The colder it gets, **the more** we want to travel to Mexico.*

The word **umso** can replace **desto** in sentences like these, but the original meaning of the sentence is retained.

Je kälter es wird, **umso** mehr wollen wir nach Mexiko verreisen.	*The colder it gets, **the more** we want to travel to Mexico.*

Superlatives

In the superlative of adjectives and adverbs, English and German once again follow a similar pattern. The English superlative ending is **-est**, and the German superlative ending is **-st**. The main difference between the two is that German adds declensional endings in the superlative and English does not. When a German superlative is an adverb or a predicate adjective, it is preceded by **am** (**an dem**) and the dative case. The English translation usually adds the word *the*.

POSITIVE	SUPERLATIVE	ENGLISH
hell	am hellsten	*(the) brightest*
klein	am kleinsten	*(the) smallest*
reich	am reichsten	*(the) richest*
schnell	am schnellsten	*(the) fastest*
schön	am schönsten	*(the) nicest, prettiest*

When an adjective or adverb has several syllables or is a word of foreign origin, the English translation requires the use of the superlative word *most*. For example:

POSITIVE	SUPERLATIVE	ENGLISH
langweilig	am langweiligsten	*(the) most boring*
lächerlich	am lächerlichsten	*(the) most ridiculous*

ÜBUNG
8·5

In the blanks provided, write the superlative of the adjective provided and the translation into English of that superlative. For example:

klein *am kleinsten   the smallest*

1. hässlich   _____   _____

2. kühl   _____   _____

3. weich   _____   _____

4. scharf   _____   _____

5. wenig   _____   _____

6. angenehm   _____   _____

7. tief   _____   _____

8. wichtig   _____   _____

9. gewöhnlich   _____   _____

10. schwierig   _____   _____

If an adjective or adverb ends in **-d, -t, -s, -ß,** or **-z,** an **-e** is added to the superlative suffix. For example:

POSITIVE	SUPERLATIVE	ENGLISH
breit	am breitesten	*the broadest*
heiß	am heißesten	*the hottest*
wild	am wildesten	*the wildest*

And adjectives and adverbs of one syllable with an umlaut vowel often add the umlaut in the superlative. Look at the following examples:

POSITIVE	SUPERLATIVE	ENGLISH
alt	am ältesten	*the oldest*
arm	am ärmsten	*the poorest*
dumm	am dümmsten	*the dumbest, most stupid*
hart	am härtesten	*the hardest*
jung	am jüngsten	*the youngest*
kalt	am kältesten	*the coldest*
klug	am klügsten	*the smartest, most clever*
krank	am kränksten	*the sickest*
kurz	am kürzesten	*the shortest*
lang	am längsten	*the longest*
schwach	am schwächsten	*the weakest*
stark	am stärksten	*the strongest*
warm	am wärmsten	*the warmest*

When a superlative adjective modifies a noun directly, **am (an dem)** is not used. Instead, the superlative adjective is declined normally. For example:

Sie sieht den **nettesten** Jungen.   *She sees the **nicest** boy.*

Das ist mein **wärmster** Mantel.   *That is my **warmest** coat.*

Fill in the blank with the correct German translation of the phrase in parentheses in the case indicated. For example:

nominative

(the hottest coffee) *der heißeste Kaffee*

nominative

1. (the longest poem) _____

2. (your youngest brother) _____

3. (our oldest cat) _____

4. (the shortest days) _____

accusative

5. (the smartest students) _____

6. (his poorest neighbors) _____

7. (my richest relatives) _____

8. (the weakest lightbulbs) _____

dative

9. (the worst idea) _____

10. (the loudest voice) _____

11. (her newest picture) _____

12. (our most pleasant surprise) _____

genitive

13. (the warmest water) _____

14. (the most interesting story) _____

15. (the most stupid joke) _____

Irregular superlatives

The same adjectives and adverbs that have an irregular comparative form also have an irregular superlative form.

POSITIVE	SUPERLATIVE	ENGLISH
bald	am ehesten	*the soonest*
groß	am größten	*the biggest*
gut	am besten	*the best*
		(continued)

POSITIVE	SUPERLATIVE	ENGLISH
hoch	am höchsten	*the highest, tallest*
nah	am nächsten	*the nearest*
viel	am meisten	*the most*

There is no irregularity in the superlative for words ending in **-el**, **-en**, and **-er**: **am dunkelsten** (*the darkest*), **am teuersten** (*the most expensive*), **am trockensten** (*the driest*).

ÜBUNG
8·7

Complete each sentence twice with the adjectives and adverbs shown in bold: once with the adjective or adverb changed to the comparative and once with the adjective or adverb changed to the superlative. For example:

Das Haus ist **klein**.

Das Haus ist kleiner.

Das Haus ist am kleinsten.

1. Kennen Sie den **jungen** Mann?

   _____

   _____

2. Erik arbeitet mit meinem **alten** Bruder.

   _____

   _____

3. Sonja hat mein **großes** Zelt geborgt (*borrowed tent*).

   _____

   _____

4. Der Vogel sitzt auf dem **hohen** Zaun (*fence*).

   _____

   _____

5. Hast du die **langen** Bretter (*boards*)?

   _____

   _____

6. Ist unsere Bushaltestelle (*bus stop*) **nah**?

   _____

   _____

7. Mein Vater hat immer **viel** gearbeitet.

_____

_____

8. Im Sommer ist es **heiß**.

_____

_____

9. Meine Freundin kann **weit** laufen.

_____

_____

10. Der Brandwein (*brandy*) schmeckt **mild** (*tastes smooth*).

_____

_____

Four superlative forms have some special usages. They are **meist, mindest-, längst,** and **bestens.**

Meist is an adverb and means *mostly, most of the time,* or *usually.* It can also be written as **meistens.** For example:

Er hat **meist** wenig Zeit.	*He usually has little time.*
Wir sind **meistens** unterwegs.	*Most of the time we're on the road.*
Der arme Mann ist **meist** betrunken.	*The poor man is drunk most of the time.*

Mindest- is an adjective and follows the regular declensional patterns. It means *the slightest* or *the least.* For example:

Die Frau hat nicht die **mindeste** Ahnung.	*The woman doesn't have the slightest idea.*
Das ist das **Mindeste**, was er tun kann.	*That's the least he can do.*
Ich verstehe nicht das **Mindeste** vom Ski laufen.	*I don't know the first thing about skiing.*

When this word is written as **mindestens**, it is an adverb.

Mindestens kannst du mir damit helfen.	*At least you can help me with that.*

Längst is also an adverb and means *for a long time* or *a long time ago,* although its translation into English sometimes requires some rewording. It is also written as **längstens.** For example:

Ich wusste **längst**, dass sie mich nicht liebte.	*I knew **long ago** that she didn't love me.*
Erik war **längst** noch nicht fertig.	*Erik wasn't **anywhere near** finished.*
Ich bleibe **längstens** ein paar Tage.	***At the most** I'll stay a couple days.*

Bestens is an adverb and means *very well*, *splendidly*, or *excellently*, but sometimes it requires some rewording in its English translation. Let's look at a few examples:

Die beiden Jungen verstehen sich **bestens**.	*The two boys get along together **very well**.*
Ich möchte Frau Bauer **bestens** grüßen.	*I'd like to give my **best** wishes to Mrs. Bauer.*
Sie haben ihm **bestens** gedankt.	*They thanked him **very much**.*

ÜBUNG
8·8

Circle the letter of the word or phrase that best completes each sentence.

1. Ist dieses Museum _____?
   a. neuere   b. am ältesten   c. großes   d. bestens

2. Je größer die Hitze wird, _____ weniger kann ich arbeiten.
   a. umso   b. mindestens   c. mehr   d. viele

3. Mein Sohn spricht viel _____ als meine Tochter.
   a. am schnellsten   b. gut   c. wichtigere   d. lauter

4. Ich finde Heidelberg eine sehr _____ Stadt.
   a. schöne   b. bessere   c. näher   d. am weitesten

5. Seine Fragen werden _____ schwieriger.
   a. desto   b. immer   c. eher   d. als

6. Frau Benz möchte eine _____ Bluse anprobieren.
   a. buntere   b. rot   c. längsten   d. am kürzesten

7. Dieses Auto ist _____ teuersten.
   a. je   b. die   c. mehr   d. am

8. Meine Familie braucht _____ Wohnung.
   a. ein viel besseres   b. eine neuere   c. am billigsten   d. einen reichen

9. _____ Schüler kommen um acht Uhr zur Schule.
   a. Nur am besten   b. Die schlechteste   c. Die meisten   d. Viel jünger

10. Ich habe sie _____ vergessen.
    a. am größten   b. längst   c. breiter   d. langweiligere

Modal auxiliaries and double infinitives

The modal auxiliaries play an important role in the German language. They are the verbs that *nuance* the meaning of the verbs they accompany in a sentence. Let's look at how the meaning of a verb is altered by the use of modals in some English examples:

I go home at six P.M.	*a statement without a modal auxiliary*
I have to go home at six P.M.	*a strict obligation*
I should go home at six P.M.	*a weaker obligation*
I want to go home at six P.M.	*a desire*

In German it works the same way. For example:

Um sechs Uhr gehe ich nach Hause.

Um sechs Uhr muss ich nach Hause gehen.

Um sechs Uhr soll ich nach Hause gehen.

Um sechs Uhr will ich nach Hause gehen.

The present tense conjugation of the modal auxiliaries has some irregularities that need to be addressed. With all of the modals, there is a distinction between the conjugations with singular subjects and conjugations with plural subjects.

dürfen *may,* *to be allowed to*		**können** *can,* *to be able to*	
ich darf	wir dürfen	ich kann	wir können
du darfst	ihr dürft	du kannst	ihr könnt
er, sie, es darf	sie, Sie dürfen	er, sie, es kann	sie, Sie können

mögen *to want, like*		**müssen** *must,* *to have to*	
ich mag	wir mögen	ich muss	wir müssen
du magst	ihr mögt	du musst	ihr müsst
er, sie, es mag	sie, Sie mögen	er, sie, es muss	sie, Sie müssen

sollen *should, to be supposed to*		wollen *to want to*	
ich soll	wir sollen	ich will	wir wollen
du sollst	ihr sollt	du willst	ihr wollt
er, sie, es soll	sie, Sie sollen	er, sie, es will	sie, Sie wollen

This group of verbs most frequently acts as the auxiliary verb of another verb, in this case, a verb in infinitive form. For example:

Das **darfst** du nicht **tun**.	*You're not allowed to do that.*
Können Sie mir damit **helfen**?	*Can you help me with that?*
Ich **muss** ihn vom Bahnhof **abholen**.	*I have to pick him up at the train station.*
Sie **will** diesen Rock **kaufen**.	*She wants to buy this skirt.*

ÜBUNG
9·1

Rewrite each sentence in the present tense with the modal auxiliaries provided in parentheses. For example:

Er kauft einen VW.

(wollen) *Er will einen VW kaufen.*

1. Mein Vater arbeitet zehn Stunden pro Tag (*per day*).

   (müssen) _____

   (wollen) _____

2. Ich schreibe keine Briefe.

   (können) _____

   (müssen) _____

3. Die Gäste tanzen und singen.

   (sollen) _____

   (dürfen) _____

4. Sie beantworten diese Fragen nicht.

   (wollen) _____

   (mögen) _____

5. Erwartest du deine Freundin an der Ecke?

   (sollen) _____

   (müssen) _____

Past tense

In the past tense, the modals *look like* regular verbs. However, the modal auxiliaries that have an umlaut in the infinitive drop the umlaut in the past tense. For example:

dürfen *may, to be allowed to*		**können** *can, to be able to*	
ich durfte	wir durften	ich konnte	wir konnten
du durftest	ihr durftet	du konntest	ihr konntet
er, sie, es durfte	sie, Sie durften	er, sie, es konnte	sie, Sie konnten

mögen *to want, like*		**müssen** *must, to have to*	
ich mochte	wir mochten	ich musste	wir mussten
du mochtest	ihr mochtet	du musstest	ihr musstet
er, sie, es mochte	sie, Sie mochten	er, sie, es musste	sie, Sie mussten

sollen *should, to be supposed to*		**wollen** *to want to*	
ich sollte	wir sollten	ich wollte	wir wollten
du solltest	ihr solltet	du wolltest	ihr wolltet
er, sie, es sollte	sie, Sie sollten	er, sie, es wollte	sie, Sie wollten

In the present and past perfect tenses, the modals always use **haben** as their auxiliary. It is the modal that determines whether to use **haben** or **sein** and not the accompanying verb. Consider these examples:

Er **ist** in die Stadt gefahren. (**Fahren** uses **sein** as its auxiliary.)	*He drove to the city.*
Er **hat** in die Stadt fahren wollen. (Modals use **haben** as their auxiliary.)	*He wanted to drive to the city.*

In the perfect tenses and the future tense, the auxiliary is conjugated (**haben** or **werden**), and the verb and the auxiliary appear at the end of the sentence as a *double infinitive*. For example:

Wir **hatten** unsere Freunde **besuchen wollen**.	*We had wanted to visit our friends.*
Habt ihr diese Bücher **lesen müssen**?	*Did you have to read these books?*
Ich **werde** euch **helfen können**.	*I will be able to help you.*
Lars **wird** sich besser **benehmen müssen**.	*Lars will have to behave better.*

With the subject provided in parentheses, rewrite each phrase in the specified tenses.

1. (der Arzt) können diese Krankheit (*disease*) nicht verstehen.

    PRESENT _____

    PAST _____

    PRESENT PERFECT _____

    FUTURE _____

2. (die Schüler) dürfen hereinkommen (*come in*).

    PRESENT _____

    PAST _____

    PRESENT PERFECT _____

    FUTURE _____

3. (ich) müssen ein paar Tage in Bonn bleiben.

    PRESENT _____

    PAST _____

    PRESENT PERFECT _____

    FUTURE _____

4. (der Wanderer [*hiker*]) wollen in die Berge fahren.

    PRESENT _____

    PAST _____

    PRESENT PERFECT _____

    FUTURE _____

5. (der kranke Herr) dürfen das Krankenhaus nicht verlassen (*leave*).

    PRESENT _____

    PAST _____

    PRESENT PERFECT _____

    FUTURE _____

Mögen

Mögen requires a little extra explanation. This verb is often used without an accompanying infinitive when it means *like*. For example:

Sie **mag** den neuen Reiseführer sehr gern.	*She really likes the new tour guide.*
Meine Tochter **mag** keinen Kaffee.	*My daughter doesn't like coffee.*
Wir **mochten** die Oper einfach nicht.	*We just didn't like the opera.*

This verb is used in certain pat phrases to mean *may* when suggesting that something is possible. For example:

Das **mag** wohl sein, aber ich verstehe es nicht.	*That may well be, but I don't understand it.*
Herr Bauer **mag** dreißig Jahre alt sein.	*Mr. Bauer may be about thirty years old.*
Es **mag** kommen, was will.	*Come what may.*

Perhaps the most high-frequency use of **mögen** is when it is conjugated in subjunctive II: **ich möchte, du möchtest, er möchte, wir möchten, ihr möchtet, sie/Sie möchten**. It is often used as a polite replacement for **wollen**. For example:

Ich will kein Bier.	*I don't want any beer.*
Ich **möchte** kein Bier.	*I wouldn't care for any beer.*
Willst du eine Tasse Tee?	*Do you want a cup of tea?*
Möchtest du eine Tasse Tee?	*Would you like a cup of tea?*

In its subjunctive II conjugation, it can also act as the auxiliary of an accompanying infinitive. For example:

Ich will ein paar Wochen in den Alpen verbringen.	*I want to spend a couple weeks in the Alps.*
Ich **möchte** ein paar Wochen in den Alpen verbringen.	*I would like to spend a couple weeks in the Alps.*
Wir wollen zu Hause bleiben.	*We want to stay home.*
Wir **möchten** zu Hause bleiben.	*We would like to stay home.*

ÜBUNG 9·3

Rewrite each sentence with any appropriate phrase, based upon the suggestion given in parentheses. For example:

Die Kinder mögen _____. (*a beverage*)

Die Kinder mögen kalte Limonade.

1. Magst du _____ gern? (*three people*)

_____

_____

_____

2. Ich möchte _____. (*three infinitive phrases*)

_____

_____

_____

3. Das mag wohl sein, aber _____. (*three clauses*)

_____

_____

_____

4. Meine Frau mochte _____ nicht. (*three people*)

_____

_____

_____

5. Sie möchte _____ bestellen. (*three foods*)

_____

_____

_____

Können

The verb **können** is often used in a special way to state that someone knows a language well or is competent in a subject area. The verb is not accompanied by an infinitive. For example:

Mein Onkel **kann** Englisch und Russisch.	*My uncle knows English and Russian.*
Können Sie Deutsch?	*Do you speak German?*
Meine Schwester **kann** Mathe.	*My sister knows math.*
Kannst du das Gedicht noch?	*Do you still know the poem?*

In instances when an accompanying infinitive could be in the sentence, it is omitted and merely implied or understood. For example:

Können Sie noch?	*Can you still go on?*
Die Kinder laufen, was sie **können**.	*The children run as fast as they can.*
Was **kann** ich dafür?	*What can I do about it?*

Rewrite each sentence with any appropriate phrase, based on the suggestion given in parentheses. For example:

Die Kinder können nur _____. (*a language*)

Die Kinder können nur Deutsch.

1. Kann dein Bruder _____? (*three languages*)

_____

_____

_____

2. _____ liefen, was sie konnten. (*three subjects of the sentence*)

_____

_____

_____

3. Können wir _____? (*three infinitive phrases*)

_____

_____

_____

4. Was können _____ dafür? (*three subjects of the sentence*)

_____

_____

_____

5. Erik kann _____ ziemlich gut. (*three school subjects*)

_____

_____

_____

When a double infinitive structure is in a perfect tense or the future tense in a *subordinate clause*, the auxiliary is not placed at the end of the sentence as occurs with other verbs. The auxiliary **haben** or **werden** precedes the double infinitive.

Ich wusste nicht, dass er ihm **hat** helfen wollen.

Sie bleibt zu Hause, weil sie ein paar Briefe **wird** schreiben müssen.

Hätte tun sollen

When a modal auxiliary is in the present perfect tense and the auxiliary (**haben**) is conjugated in subjunctive II, the phrase takes on a new and useful meaning. Let's look at some examples with **sollen**:

Das **hättest** du nicht tun **sollen**.	*You shouldn't have done that.*
Ich **hätte** ihnen helfen **sollen**.	*I should have helped them.*
Was **hätten** wir sagen **sollen**?	*What should we have said?*

This same kind of structure is used with other modal auxiliaries. Take **können**, for example:

Sie **hätte** es machen **können**.	*She could have done it.*
Du **hättest** viel weiter schwimmen **können**.	*You could have swum a lot farther.*
Hätte ich es gewinnen **können**?	*Could I have won it?*

And the same structure is used with **dürfen**:

Das **hätte** Erik nicht fragen **dürfen**.	*Erik shouldn't have been allowed to ask that.*

It can also be used with **müssen**:

Ich **hätte** nicht alleine reisen **müssen**.	*I shouldn't have had to travel alone.*

ÜBUNG
9·5

*Rewrite each sentence in the present perfect tense with the auxiliary in subjunctive II (**hätten**). For example:*

Ich soll es nicht tun.

Ich hätte es nicht tun sollen.

1. Du sollst ihn gar nicht fragen.

   _____

2. Sollen wir sie am Montag anrufen?

   _____

3. Ich soll meinen Bruder in Oldenburg besuchen.

   _____

4. Ihr sollt ihn nicht um Geld bitten.

   _____

5. Sie sollen es mir früher sagen.

   _____

6. Der alte Mann kann lauter sprechen.

   _____

7. Martin kann ihr damit helfen.

_____

8. Das darfst du nicht kaufen.

_____

9. Wir dürfen nicht in den Wald gehen.

_____

10. Frau Schneider muss sich besser ausdrücken (*express*).

_____

Participles

When modal auxiliaries are used in a sentence without any accompanying infinitive, the present perfect and past perfect tenses do not require a double infinitive structure. Instead, a normal participle is used. For example:

ich habe gekonnt	*I have been able to*
du hast gedurft	*you have been allowed to*
er hat gemocht	*he has liked*
wir hatten gemusst	*we had had to*
ihr hattet gewollt	*you had wanted to*
sie/Sie hatten gesollt	*they/you had been supposed to*

ÜBUNG
9·6

Circle the letter of the word or phrase that best completes each sentence.

1. Die Milch _____ in der Wärme verderben (*spoil*).
   a. wollen   b. kann   c. dürfen   d. musstet

2. So ein Hemd habe ich nicht _____.
   a. gewollt   b. kaufen   c. sollen   d. mochte

3. Jeder _____ die neue Volksbücherei benutzen (*use*).
   a. darf   b. gemusst   c. können   d. wollt

4. Meine Schwester _____ gern Schokolade.
   a. konnte   b. mochte   c. möchten   d. können

5. Möchten Sie uns morgen _____?
   a. gekonnt   b. dürfen   c. fahren wollen   d. besuchen

6. Das Mädchen _____ das Geld verlieren können.
   a. hätte   b. wollt   c. könnt   d. möchtet

7. Ich _____ gestern abend ein paar Briefe schreiben.
   a. will   b. musste   c. gesollt   d. soll

8. Man _____ seine Pflicht (*duty*) tun.
   a. mögen   b. gemusst   c. müssen   d. soll

9. Tina _____ nicht in die Abteilung für Schwimmer (*swimmers' area*) gehen.
   a. konntet   b. wollt   c. darf   d. gemusst

10. Das _____ wohl sein.
    a. dürfen   b. durftet   c. mag   d. möchten

11. Ich kann diese Prüfung jetzt noch nicht _____.
    a. bestehen   b. gemacht   c. machen müssen   d. gesollt

12. Meine Geschwister _____ auch Italienisch.
    a. will lernen b. können   c. sprechen müssen d. gewollt

13. Ich habe es einfach nicht _____.
    a. gekonnt   b. müssen   c. möchten   d. verkauft haben

14. Du magst _____, wohin du willst.
    a. wollen   b. gelaufen   c. gehen   d. geworden

15. _____ wir Ihnen unsere Plätze anbieten (*offer*)?
    a. Möchte   b. Dürfen   c. Sitzen müssen   d. Haben gewollt

Sehen, hören, lassen, helfen, and double infinitives

10

There are four special verbs in German that function in two different ways. First, they are conjugated as transitive verbs and can function in all the tenses. For example:

	SEHEN *TO SEE*	HÖREN *TO HEAR*	LASSEN *TO LET, ALLOW*	HELFEN *TO HELP*
pres.	er sieht	er hört	er lässt	er hilft
past	er sah	er hörte	er ließ	er half
pres. perf.	er hat gesehen	er hat gehört	er hat gelassen	er hat geholfen
fut.	er wird sehen	er wird hören	er wird lassen	er wird helfen

An important reminder: The verbs **sehen**, **hören**, and **lassen** can be followed by an object in the accusative case.

Ich sehe **den Mann** an der Ecke.	*I see **the man** on the corner.*
Er hörte **ihre Stimme**.	*He heard **her voice**.*
Lass **ihn** in Frieden!	*Leave **him** in peace (alone)!*

But **helfen** is followed by an object in the dative case:

Helfen Sir **mir** damit!	*Help me with that!*
Sie hat **ihrer Großmutter** geholfen.	*She helped her grandmother.*

ÜBUNG
10·1

Rewrite each sentence in the missing tenses.

1. PRESENT Tina sieht meine neue Brille (*glasses*).

PAST _____

PRESENT PERFECT _____

PAST PERFECT _____

FUTURE _____

2. PRESENT _____

   PAST Wir hörten oft Radio.

   PRESENT PERFECT _____

   PAST PERFECT _____

   FUTURE _____

3. PRESENT _____

   PAST _____

   PAST PERFECT Erik hat den armen Mann nicht allein gelassen.

   PRESENT PERFECT _____

   FUTURE _____

4. PRESENT _____

   PAST _____

   PRESENT PERFECT _____

   PAST PERFECT Ich hatte ihr über die Straße geholfen.

   FUTURE _____

5. PRESENT _____

   PAST _____

   PRESENT PERFECT _____

   PAST PERFECT _____

   FUTURE Er wird schon bessere Zeiten (*better times*) sehen.

Double infinitives

In Chapter 9 you encountered the use of *double infinitives* with the modal auxiliaries. In a double infinitive structure, a verb in infinitive form is followed by a modal auxiliary in infinitive form. This occurs in the perfect tenses and the future. For example:

Ich kann ihn verstehen.	*I can understand him.*
Ich konnte ihn verstehen.	*I could understand him.*
Ich habe ihn **verstehen können**.	*I was able to understand him.*
Ich hatte ihn **verstehen können**.	*I had been able to understand him.*
Ich werde ihn **verstehen können**.	*I will be able to understand him.*

Musst du wieder arbeiten?	*Do you have to work again?*
Musstest du wieder arbeiten?	*Did you have to work again?*
Hast du wieder **arbeiten müssen**?	*Did you have to work again?*
Hattest du wieder **arbeiten müssen**?	*Had you had to work again?*
Wirst du wieder **arbeiten müssen**?	*Will you have to work again?*

With **sehen**, **hören**, **lassen**, and **helfen**, the double infinitive structures function in the same way and in the same tenses as with the modal auxiliaries. Except for **lassen**, the meaning of each of the verbs remains unchanged. For example:

Er sieht den Mann arbeiten.	*He sees the man working.*
Er sah den Mann arbeiten.	*He saw the man working.*
Er hat den Mann **arbeiten sehen**.	*He saw the man working.*
Er hatte den Mann **arbeiten sehen**.	*He had seen the man working.*
Er wird den Mann **arbeiten sehen**.	*He will see the man working.*
Hörst du die Kinder singen?	*Do you hear the children singing?*
Hörtest du die Kinder singen?	*Did you hear the children singing?*
Hast du die Kinder **singen hören**?	*Did you hear the children singing?*
Hattest du die Kinder **singen hören**?	*Had you heard the children singing?*
Wirst du die Kinder **singen hören**?	*Will you hear the children singing?*
Ich helfe ihm das Auto reparieren.	*I help him repair the car.*
Ich half ihm das Auto reparieren.	*I helped him repair the car.*
Ich habe ihm das Auto **reparieren helfen**.	*I helped him repair the car.*
Ich hatte ihm das Auto **reparieren helfen**.	*I had helped him repair the car.*
Ich werde ihm das Auto **reparieren helfen**.	*I will help him repair the car.*

When **lassen** is used with another verb, it can still mean *let* or *allow*: **Sie lassen mich ins Haus kommen.** *They let me come into the house.* But there is an important variance of usage of **lassen** when accompanied by an infinitive that requires a new meaning: *get* or *have something done*. For example:

Er lässt das Auto reparieren.	*He gets the car repaired.*
Sie lässt ein neues Kleid machen.	*She has a new dress made.*

Although the meaning of **lassen** has changed, it still functions in the tenses as the other three verbs and has a double infinitive structure in the perfect tenses and the future tense. For example:

Wir lassen eine neue Garage bauen.	*We have a new garage built.*
Wir ließen eine neue Garage bauen.	*We had a new garage built.*
Wir haben eine neue Garage **bauen lassen**.	*We had a new garage built.*
Wir hatten eine neue Garage **bauen lassen**.	*We had had a new garage built.*
Wir werden eine neue Garage **bauen lassen**.	*We will have a new garage built.*

Rewrite each sentence in the missing tenses.

1. PRESENT Sie lässt die Türglocke ertönen (*ring the doorbell*).

   PAST _____

   PRESENT PERFECT _____

   PAST PERFECT _____

   FUTURE _____

2. PRESENT _____

   PAST Er hörte seine Mutter sprechen.

   PRESENT PERFECT _____

   PAST PERFECT _____

   FUTURE _____

3. PRESENT _____

   PAST _____

   PRESENT PERFECT Herr Bauer hat die Jungen spielen sehen.

   PAST PERFECT _____

   FUTURE _____

4. PRESENT _____

   PAST _____

   PRESENT PERFECT _____

   PAST PERFECT Wie lange hatten sie arbeiten müssen?

   FUTURE _____

5. PRESENT _____

   PAST _____

   PRESENT PERFECT _____

   PAST PERFECT _____

   FUTURE Wir werden ihm das Gepäck (*luggage*) tragen helfen.

6. PRESENT Ich sehe den Zug in den Bahnhof (*railroad station*) kommen.

   PAST _____

   PRESENT PERFECT _____

   PAST PERFECT _____

   FUTURE _____

7. PRESENT _____

   PAST Wo ließ der Kanzler seine Anzüge (*suits*) machen?

   PRESENT PERFECT _____

   PAST PERFECT _____

   FUTURE _____

8. PRESENT _____

   PAST _____

   PRESENT PERFECT Ich habe sie flüstern (*whispering*) hören.

   PAST PERFECT _____

   FUTURE _____

9. PRESENT _____

   PAST _____

   PRESENT PERFECT _____

   PAST PERFECT Sabine hatte mir den Brief schreiben helfen.

   FUTURE _____

10. PRESENT _____

   PAST _____

   PRESENT PERFECT _____

   PAST PERFECT _____

   FUTURE Sie wird nach Italien reisen wollen.

Es lässt sich

There is another important function of the verb **lassen** when it is used as a reflexive verb. It tends to be conjugated in the third person and has a new idiomatic meaning that sounds like the passive voice in English. For example:

Es **lässt sich** nicht tun.	*It cannot be done.*
Das **ließ sich** leicht beweisen.	*That could be easily proved.*
Seine Fragen **lassen sich** nicht beantworten.	*His questions cannot be answered.*
Das Problem hat **sich** nicht lösen **lassen**.	*The problem could not be solved.*

This use of **lassen** with a reflexive calls for a double infinitive structure in the perfect tenses and the future tense just as it does when it means *get* or *have something done*: **Das Problem hat sich nicht *lösen lassen*.**

*Rewrite each sentence by replacing the subject of the sentence with the direct object and forming it with the correct form of **lässt sich**. Change the verb in the sentence to an infinitive, and retain the same tense as the original sentence. For example:*

Er verstand das Problem nicht. *He did not understand the problem.*

<u>Das Problem ließ sich nicht verstehen.</u> *The problem could not be understood.*

1. Er ändert (*changes*) unsere Pläne schnell.

   _____

2. Er macht es nicht.

   _____

3. Er reparierte die alte Uhr leicht.

   _____

4. Er hat die Fenster nicht leicht geöffnet.

   _____

5. Er wird diese Theorie (*theory*) nicht beweisen.

   _____

Fahren and gehen

Two verbs of motion, **fahren** and **gehen**, are used with an accompanying infinitive in the present, past, and future tenses in the same way as **sehen**, **hören**, **helfen**, and **lassen**. But in the perfect tenses, a double infinitive structure is not used. For example:

Sie fährt jeden Montag einkaufen.	*She goes (drives) shopping every Monday.*
Sie fuhr jeden Montag einkaufen.	*She went shopping every Monday.*
Sie ist jeden Montag einkaufen **gefahren**.	*She went shopping every Monday.*
Sie wird jeden Montag **einkaufen fahren**.	*She will go shopping every Monday.*
Ich gehe um acht Uhr schwimmen.	*I go swimming at eight o'clock.*
Ich ging um acht Uhr schwimmen.	*I went swimming at eight o'clock.*
Ich bin um acht Uhr schwimmen **gegangen**.	*I went swimming at eight o'clock.*
Ich werde um acht Uhr **schwimmen gehen**.	*I will go swimming at eight o'clock.*

Rewrite each sentence twice: once with **fahren** and once with **gehen**. Retain the same tense of the original sentence. For example:

Sie kauft heute ein.

Sie fährt heute einkaufen.

Sie geht heute einkaufen.

1. Er läuft heute morgen Ski.

_____

_____

2. Wir wanderten oft.

_____

_____

3. Ich jogge morgen.

_____

_____

4. Erik und Sonja werden oft schwimmen.

_____

_____

5. Er tanzte heute abend mit Tina.

_____

_____

Lehren, lernen, and schicken

Three more verbs, **lehren**, **lernen**, and **schicken**, follow a pattern similar to the one used with **fahren** and **gehen**: in the perfect tenses a double infinitive structure is not formed. For example:

Sie lehrt die Kinder schreiben.	*She teaches the children to write.*
Sie lehrte die Kinder schreiben.	*She taught the children to write.*
Sie hat die Kinder schreiben **gelehrt**.	*She taught the children to write.*
Sie wird die Kinder **schreiben lehren**.	*She will teach the children to write.*
Wir lernen schwimmen.	*We learn to swim.*
Wir lernten schwimmen.	*We learned to swim.*
Wir haben schwimmen **gelernt**.	*We learned to swim.*
Wir werden **schwimmen lernen**.	*We will learn to swim.*

Tina schickt uns einkaufen.	*Tina sends us shopping.*
Tina schickte uns einkaufen.	*Tina sent us shopping.*
Tina hat uns einkaufen **geschickt**.	*Tina sent us shopping.*
Tina wird uns **einkaufen schicken**.	*Tina will send us shopping.*

**ÜBUNG
10·5**

Rewrite each sentence in the missing tenses.

1. PRESENT Herr Benz lehrt uns rechnen.

    PAST _____

    PRESENT PERFECT _____

    PAST PERFECT _____

    FUTURE _____

2. PRESENT _____

    PAST Mein Freund lernte schnell Spanisch sprechen.

    PRESENT PERFECT _____

    PAST PERFECT _____

    FUTURE _____

3. PRESENT _____

    PAST _____

    PRESENT PERFECT Sie hat ihn sich die Hände waschen (*wash his hands*) geschickt.

    PAST PERFECT _____

    FUTURE _____

4. PRESENT _____

    PAST _____

    PRESENT PERFECT _____

    PAST PERFECT Lars war mit Sonja mexikanisch essen gegangen.

    FUTURE _____

5. PRESENT _____

    PAST _____

    PRESENT PERFECT _____

    PAST PERFECT _____

    FUTURE Die Lehrerin wird die Schüler zeichnen (*draw*) lehren.

6. PRESENT Es lässt sich kaum glauben (*hardly believe*).

   PAST _____

   PRESENT PERFECT _____

   PAST PERFECT _____

   FUTURE _____

7. PRESENT _____

   PAST _____

   PRESENT PERFECT Der Student hat programmieren (*programming*) gelernt.

   PAST PERFECT _____

   FUTURE _____

8. PRESENT _____

   PAST _____

   PRESENT PERFECT _____

   PAST PERFECT Die Nachricht hatte uns erschrecken (*frightened*) lassen.

   FUTURE _____

9. PRESENT _____

   PAST _____

   PRESENT PERFECT _____

   PAST PERFECT _____

   FUTURE Sie wird die Jungen in den Garten spielen schicken.

10. PRESENT Der Dieb (*thief*) hört die Polizei kommen.

   PAST _____

   PRESENT PERFECT _____

   PAST PERFECT _____

   FUTURE _____

Circle the word or phrase that best completes each sentence.

1. Erik _____ ihr den Koffer tragen.
   a. lasst   b. schickt   c. half   d. lernte

2. Der Lehrer hat mir die Wörter übersetzen _____.
   a. helfen   b. gelernt   c. gehen   d. fahren

3. Das Kind _____ auch selbst sich beschäftigen.
   a. lernt   b. fahrt   c. hörte   d. sah

4. Ich habe meinen Freund vor der Tür _____ hören.
   a. sein   b. werden   c. pfeifen   d. lassen

5. Thomas hat einen Sportwagen fahren _____.
   a. machen   b. tun   c. gelernt   d. gesehen

6. Niemand _____ das Flugzeug landen.
   a. sah   b. hörten   c. schickt   d. lassen

7. Morgen _____ in den Alpen klettern.
   a. lehren   b. gehen wir   c. lässt sich   d. fahren

8. Ich werde im Sommerlager _____.
   a. sich   b. schwimmen lernen c. tanzen gelernt d. drachenfliegen gelehrt
      beschäftigen

9. Ich habe den Dieb aus dem Haus _____.
   a. kommen sehen   b. laufen   c. gestohlen   d. finden lassen

10. Wir werden dem Gärtner _____.
    a. laufen gehen   b. aufstehen   c. schreiben lehren   d. arbeiten helfen

11. Wer _____ die neuen Busse bauen?
    a. hat   b. ließ   c. hilft   d. sieht

12. Es ließ _____ nicht ändern.
    a. kaum   b. davon   c. sich   d. selbst

13. Habt ihr die Vögel _____?
    a. machen müssen b. singen hören   c. fliegen   d. lassen

14. Der Herr hat den Hund nicht hereinkommen _____.
    a. lassen   b. sehen   c. hören   d. geholfen

15. Mein Großvater hat sich die Haare schneiden _____.
    a. fahren   b. waschen sehen   c. lassen   d. helfen

Prefixes

11

Many European languages change the meaning of a word by the addition of a prefix. English is no exception. For example:

have	come	port
behave	income	airport

Prefixes in English tend to be of three distinct types: (1) words or particles derived from older forms of English (*aweigh*), (2) prefixes that have a Latin origin (*extend*), and (3) a contemporary word added to another contemporary word to make a new meaning (*housemother*).

German is similar but not identical. German has (1) a large category of separable and inseparable prefixes (**bekommen, ankommen**), (2) prefixes that have a Latin origin (**Deklaration**), and (3) a contemporary word added to another contemporary word to make a new meaning (**Wunderkind**). This chapter will emphasize the first and third of these categories of prefixes.

Separable prefixes

German has a large number of separable prefixes. They tend to be prepositions and adverbs and are attached to a verb only when the verb is in its infinitive or participial form. If the separable prefix is attached to a word other than a verb, the prefix becomes *inseparable*.

Some commonly used separable prefixes are:

ab	mit
an	nach
auf	vor
bei	um
durch	weg
fern	zurück

Take note of the position of a separable prefix when it is attached to a form of a verb.

INFINITIVE		PARTICIPLE	CONJUGATED IN PRESENT OR PAST
abfahren	*depart*	**ab**gefahren	ich fahre **ab**, wir fuhren **ab**
ausgeben	*spend*	**aus**gegeben	er gibt **aus**, sie gab **aus**
fernsehen	*watch TV*	**fern**gesehen	wir sehen **fern**, du sahst **fern**

(continued)

INFINITIVE		PARTICIPLE	CONJUGATED IN PRESENT OR PAST
mitkommen	*come along*	**mit**gekommen	ich komme **mit**, ihr kamt **mit**
umbringen	*kill*	**um**gebracht	sie bringen **um**, sie brachte **um**

ÜBUNG
11·1

Rewrite each phrase in the tenses specified with the subject in parentheses. For example:

(er) nicht mitkommen.

PRESENT *Er kommt nicht mit.*

PAST *Er kam nicht mit.*

PRESENT PERFECT *Er ist nicht mitgekommen.*

FUTURE *Er wird nicht mitkommen.*

1. (ich) mich umziehen (*change my clothes*).

    PRESENT _____

    PAST _____

    PRESENT PERFECT _____

    FUTURE _____

2. (Frau Bauer) die Türen zumachen (*close*).

    PRESENT _____

    PAST _____

    PRESENT PERFECT _____

    FUTURE _____

3. (Herr Benz) uns Mathe beibringen (*teach*).

    PRESENT _____

    PAST _____

    PRESENT PERFECT _____

    FUTURE _____

4. (das Mädchen) sehr gut aussehen (*look*).

    PRESENT _____

    PAST _____

    PRESENT PERFECT _____

    FUTURE _____

5. (mein Vater) das Frühstück vorbereiten (*prepare breakfast*).

PRESENT _____

PAST _____

PRESENT PERFECT _____

FUTURE _____

6. (wir) am Montag zurückgehen (*go back*).

PRESENT _____

PAST _____

PRESENT PERFECT _____

FUTURE _____

7. (die Vorlesung [*lecture*]) um elf Uhr anfangen (*begin*).

PRESENT _____

PAST _____

PRESENT PERFECT _____

FUTURE _____

8. (Sie) Ihren Mann vorstellen (*introduce*)?

PRESENT _____

PAST _____

PRESENT PERFECT _____

FUTURE _____

9. (du) warum weglaufen (*run away*)?

PRESENT _____

PAST _____

PRESENT PERFECT _____

FUTURE _____

10. (unsere Verwandten) nach dem Konzert vorbeikommen (*come by*).

PRESENT _____

PAST _____

PRESENT PERFECT _____

FUTURE _____

The verb **vorbereiten** was used in item 5 of Übung 11-1. In the present perfect tense, there was no -**ge**- prefix added to the past participle, because the verb already had the inseparable prefix **be**- attached to the stem. Therefore, the past participle became **vorbereitet**.

When verbs are formed in the imperative, the separable prefix must be separated from the verb. This is true whether the imperative is stated for **du**, **ihr**, or **Sie**. For example:

INFINITIVE		du	ihr	Sie
anbieten	*offer*	Biete an!	Bietet an!	Bieten Sie an!
mitnehmen	*take along*	Nimm mit!	Nehmt mit!	Nehmen Sie mit!
ausziehen	*undress*	Ziehe aus!	Zieht aus!	Ziehen Sie aus!

ÜBUNG
11·2

*Rewrite each phrase as **du**-, **ihr**-, and **Sie**- imperatives.*

1. damit aufhören (*stop that*)

_____

_____

_____

2. fortbleiben (*stay away*)

_____

_____

_____

3. alle Fenster aufmachen (*open*)

_____

_____

_____

4. um acht Uhr abfahren (*depart*)

_____

_____

_____

5. das neue Klavier ansehen (*look at the new piano*)

_____

_____

_____

6. die Reise fortsetzen (*continue the trip*)

_____

_____

_____

7. wegfahren (*drive away*)

_____

_____

_____

8. ihn nicht ausschließen (*exclude*)

_____

_____

_____

9. mit viel Wasser nachspülen (*rewash*)

_____

_____

_____

10. die Fahne niederholen (*haul down the flag*)

_____

_____

_____

As stated earlier, a separable prefix separates from a verb only when the verb is conjugated in the present or past tenses or in the imperative. In a participle, it is still part of the verb although separated by -ge- (**fortgesetzt, zugemacht, weggeschickt**, and so on). In an infinitive phrase that requires the use of **zu**, the word **zu** separates the prefix from the infinitive, but it is written as one word. For example:

Sie schlägt vor ein bisschen weniger auszugeben. *She suggests spending a little less.*

When prefixes in this category are attached to other parts of speech such as nouns and adjectives, they remain in the prefix position and cannot be separated. For example:

Infinitive phrase:	abzufallen	*to fall off*
Conjugated verb:	Dabei fällt nicht viel ab.	*Not much will come of it.*
Noun:	der Abfall	*rubbish, garbage*
Adjective:	abfällig	*derogatory*

Infinitive phrase:	zurückzuhalten	*to hold back*
Conjugated verb:	Wir hielten den Dieb zurück.	*We stopped the thief.*
Noun:	die Zurückhaltung	*reserve, restraint*
Adjective:	zurückhaltend	*reserved, restrained*
Infinitive phrase:	abzuhängen	*to depend*
Conjugated verb:	Davon hängt es ab.	*It depends (on that).*
Noun:	der Abhang	*slope*
Adjective:	abhängig	*dependent*

*Keeping in mind the rules of gender described in Chapter 1, in the blank provided write the appropriate definite article (**der**, **die**, or **das**) for each noun.*

1. _____ Ausgang (*exit*)

2. _____ Abstieg (*descent*)

3. _____ Einreise (*entry*)

4. _____ Gegenmeinung (*opposing view*)

5. _____ Wiederherstellung (*restoration*)

6. _____ Zunahme (*increase*)

7. _____ Wegzug (*move*)

8. _____ Einbruch (*burglary*)

9. _____ Durchschnitt (*average*)

10. _____ Rathaus (*city hall*)

Inseparable prefixes

The inseparable prefixes are so named because they are always in the prefix position, no matter what kind of word they are attached to. They are prefixes for verbs, nouns, adjectives, and adverbs. The list of inseparable prefixes is quite small. They are **be-**, **emp-**, **ent-**, **er-**, **ge-**, **ver-**, and **zer-**.

The prefix **emp-** is a variant of **ent-** and is primarily used with three verbs: **empfangen** (*receive*), **empfehlen** (*recommend*), and **empfinden** (*feel*).

The prefix **be-** makes verbs *transitive*; that is, they are verbs that can have a direct object. Compare the base verb with the transitive verb formed with **be-**:

BASE VERB		TRANSITIVE VERB	
antworten	*answer*	beantworten	*answer (a question)*
finden	*find*	sich befinden	*be located*
grüßen	*greet, salute*	begrüßen	*greet, welcome*
kommen	*come*	bekommen	*receive*
nehmen	*take*	sich benehmen	*behave oneself*
sitzen	*sit*	besitzen	*own, possess*
stellen	*put, place*	bestellen	*order*

One verb that has the prefix **be-** that does not act as a transitive verb is **begegnen**. The object of this verb is in the dative case, and the verb uses **sein** as its auxiliary.

Wir sind alten Freunden im Park begegnet.   *We met old friends in the park.*

The prefix **ent-** (**emp-**) usually implies a motion *away* or *removal* from someone or something, or literally *escaping* or *fleeing* from someone or something. If the meaning is *escaping,* the verb will often be accompanied by a dative object. For example:

Der Dieb entläuft dem Polizisten.	*The thief escapes from the policeman.*
Unser Vogel ist uns entflogen.	*Our bird flew away from our house.*
Wie kann ich diesem Problem entkommen?	*How can I get away from this problem?*

If the verbs are verbs of motion, their auxiliary will be **sein**. For example: **Er ist dem Polizisten entlaufen.** (*He has escaped from the policeman.*) Other verbs with the prefix **ent-** do not always require a dative object and use the auxiliary **haben**.

Der Chef hat ihn aus seinem Amt entfernt.	*The boss dismissed him from his office.*
Ich habe das Gewehr entladen.	*I unloaded the rifle.*
Er hat mich dem Tod entrissen.	*He saved me from a certain death.*

The prefix **er-** is frequently employed to suggest a *change of condition or state.* For example:

Erik errötet vor Freude.	*Erik blushes with joy.*
Er ist endlich erwacht.	*He finally woke up.*
Die Frau erblindet.	*The woman goes blind.*

The same prefix suggests a *worsening condition, violence,* and even *death.*

ermüden	*get tired*
erschlagen	*strike dead*
ersticken	*choke*
ertrinken	*drown*
erwürgen	*strangle*
sich erkälten	*catch a cold*

But these meanings for **er-** are only some of the commonly used ones. In many cases, the meaning of the prefix cannot be predicted. For example:

erfahren	*experience*
erfüllen	*fulfill*
erkennen	*recognize*
erlauben	*allow*

The prefix **ge-** is used with many verbs, but a precise meaning for its usage is not possible.

gehören	*belong to*
genießen	*enjoy*
geschehen	*happen*

The meaning of the prefix **ver-** cannot be clearly described. It is often used to suggest a *change in condition or state* or the *exaggeration of a condition or state*. For example: **verstärken** (*strengthen*), **verhungern** (*starve*), **verschlimmern** (*make worse*).

Like the prefix **ge-**, **ver-** is used in a variety of ways that cannot always be predicted.

vereinigen	*unite*
vergessen	*forget*
verkaufen	*sell*
verschwinden	*disappear*
verstehen	*understand*

The prefix **zer-** is more predictable. It suggests the meaning of something *disintegrating* or *going to pieces*. For example:

Warum hast du das Fenster zerbrochen?	*Why did you break the window?*
Hat Lars die Zeitung zerrissen?	*Did Lars tear up the newspaper?*

ÜBUNG
11·4

Using the words in parentheses as your cue, write an appropriate sentence. For example:

(zerreißen, Buch) *Warum hast du das alte Buch zerrissen?*

1. (bekommen, zehn Euro) _____

2. (empfehlen, das Restaurant) _____

3. (entfliehen, der Feind [*enemy*]) _____

4. (erwarten, ein paar Freunde) _____

5. (gefallen [*like*], diese Schuhe) _____

6. (vergessen, meine Bücher) _____

7. (zerstören [*destroy*], die Stadt) _____

8. (besuchen [*visit*]), unsere Tante) _____

9. (geschehen, an der Ecke) _____

10. (erreichen [*catch*], der Zug) _____

No matter what the prefix is, verbs tend to be conjugated as they are without a prefix. Consider the following pairs of regular and irregular verbs:

	REGULAR VERB **STELLEN/BESTELLEN**	IRREGULAR VERB **GEBEN/AUSGEBEN**
Pres.	ich stelle/bestelle	er gibt/gibt aus
Past	ich stellte/bestellte	er gab/gab aus
Pres. perf.	ich habe gestellt/habe bestellt	er hat gegeben/hat ausgegeben
Fut.	sich werde stellen/werde bestellen	er wird geben/wird ausgeben

ÜBUNG
11·5

Rewrite each verb phrase in the tenses specified with the subject in parentheses. For example:

(ich) einen Euro bekommen.

PRESENT *Ich bekomme einen Euro.*

PAST *Ich bekam einen Euro.*

PRESENT PERFECT *Ich habe einen Euro bekommen.*

FUTURE *Ich werde einen Euro bekommen.*

1. (die Musik) mir nicht gefallen.

   PRESENT _____

   PAST _____

   PRESENT PERFECT _____

   FUTURE _____

2. (sie *s.*) nicht erröten (*blush*).

   PRESENT _____

   PAST _____

   PRESENT PERFECT _____

   FUTURE _____

3. (die alte Frau) nach einer Krankheit umkommen (*die after an illness*).

   PRESENT _____

   PAST _____

PRESENT PERFECT _____

FUTURE _____

4. (er) nicht mit dem Unsinn (*nonsense*) aufhören.

PRESENT _____

PAST _____

PRESENT PERFECT _____

FUTURE _____

5. (der Direktor) ihn aus der Schule entfernen (*remove*).

PRESENT _____

PAST _____

PRESENT PERFECT _____

FUTURE _____

Like separable prefixes, inseparable prefixes can be used with other parts of speech. Let's look at a few examples of nouns:

das Besteck	*cutlery*
die Empfehlung	*recommendation*
die Enttäuschung	*disappointment*
der Ersatz	*replacement*
das Geschenk	*gift*
der Verkäufer	*salesman*
die Zerstörung	*destruction*

Here are some examples of adjectives (which can also be used as adverbs):

beschwipst	*tipsy*
entfernt	*remote*
gesetzlich	*legal*
verräterisch	*treacherous*
zerbrechlich	*fragile*

Separable-inseparable prefixes

A few prefixes can act either as separable prefixes or inseparable prefixes. These prefixes are **durch-**, **hinter-**, **über-**, **um-**, **unter-**, **voll-**, **wider-**, and **wieder-**. It is easy to determine whether the prefix is being used as a separable one or an inseparable one. If the accented syllable is the prefix, the prefix is inseparable. If the accented syllable is the verb stem, the prefix is separable. Let's look at some examples:

SEPARABLE PREFIX		INSEPARABLE PREFIX	
dúrchfallen	*fail*	durchréisen	*travel through*
N/A		hinterlássen	*leave, make a bequest*
überwerfen	*throw over*	übersétzen	*translate*
úmkommen	*die*	umármen	*embrace*
únterlegen	*put beneath*	untersúchen	*examine*
vólltanken	*fill up with gas*	vollbríngen	*achieve*
wíderrufen	*retract*	widerspréchen	*contradict*
wíederkehren	*return*	wiederhólen	*repeat*

Although the prefixes are identical in both lists of verbs, the position of the accent determines how the verb is conjugated. For example:

	SEPARABLE PREFIX **WÍEDERKEHREN**	INSEPARABLE PREFIX **WIEDERHÓLEN**
Pres.	ich kehre wieder	ich wiederhole
Past	ich kehrte wieder	ich wiederholte
Pres. perf.	ich bin wiedergekehrt	ich habe wiederholt
Fut.	ich werde wiederkehren	ich werde wiederholen

ÜBUNG
11·6

Rewrite each verb phrase in the tenses specified with the subject in parentheses.

1. (die Tänzerin) sich umziehen.

   PRESENT _____

   PAST _____

   PRESENT PERFECT _____

   FUTURE _____

2. (wir) das Gedicht übersetzen.

   PRESENT _____

   PAST _____

   PRESENT PERFECT _____

   FUTURE _____

3. (sie *s.*) ihn ärztlich (*medically*) untersuchen.

   PRESENT _____

   PAST _____

   PRESENT PERFECT _____

   FUTURE _____

4. (ich) in Heidelberg volltanken.

PRESENT _____

PAST _____

PRESENT PERFECT _____

FUTURE _____

5. (der Diplomat) sich selbst widersprechen.

PRESENT _____

PAST _____

PRESENT PERFECT _____

FUTURE _____

Latin prefixes

Many words in German are derived from a Latin (sometimes a Greek) source just like in English. Unless someone is familiar with Latin or Greek, he or she has to accept the dictionary meaning of the foreign word without analysis of the prefix and stem. This is true of German speakers and English speakers. Some examples of vocabulary derived from a classical source include:

die Absolution	*absolution*
demonstrativ	*demonstrative*
der Exponent	*exponent*
transzentdent	*transcendent*

Other words used in the prefix position

Where English *tends* to use a noun as an adjective, German combines that noun with a second noun to form a new noun. The first noun now sits in the prefix position. (In some cases, English also combines the two nouns.) Let's look at a few examples with the word **Haus** placed in the prefix position:

der Hausangestellte	*household servant*
das Hausboot	*houseboat*
der Hauseingang	*entrance to the house*
der Hausfreund	*family friend*
der Hausschlüssel	*house key*

A large abundance of similar combinations of nouns with other nouns or other parts of speech occurs in German. For example:

das Autoradio	*car radio*
der Bücherfreund	*book lover*

buchstäblich	*literal*
kaufmännisch	*commercial, business*
die Türangel	*door hinge*
der Turmbau	*building of a tower*

Other parts of speech can combine with a variety of other words to form new words.

bisherig	*previous*
eindeutig	*clear*
kurzsichtig	*shortsighted*
langbeinig	*long-legged*
saubermachen	*clean*

ÜBUNG

11·7

Place the first word given in the pair of words in the prefix position, and combine it appropriately with the second word to conform to the English translation provided. For example:

Haus / halten *der Haushalt* (*household*)

1. Bücher/Regal _____ (*bookcase*)

2. blitzen/Krieg _____ (*lightning war*)

3. Not/Fall _____ (*emergency*)

4. sparen/Kasse _____ (*savings bank*)

5. Theater/Stück _____ (*theatrical play*)

6. ab/hängen _____ (*dependent*)

7. Liebling/Film _____ (*favorite movie*)

8. Frieden/Hof _____ (*churchyard, cemetery*)

9. wild/Pferd _____ (*wild horse*)

10. schnell/Imbiss _____ (*snack bar*)

Imperatives

The imperative form of a verb is a *command* to the second-person singular or plural pronoun (*you*). In German, that means there are three forms of imperative, because German has three pronouns that mean *you*: **du**, **ihr**, and **Sie**.

The imperative of regular verbs is quite simple. The meaning of all three forms is the same for each pronoun. Let's look at some examples:

INFINITIVE	DU-FORM		IHR-FORM	SIE-FORM
singen	Sing(e)!	*sing*	Singt!	Singen Sie!
lachen	Lach(e)!	*laugh*	Lacht!	Lachen Sie!
trinken	Trink(e)!	*drink*	Trinkt!	Trinken Sie!

The **du**-form in the imperative can have an -**e** ending, which is optional: **Singe! Lache! Trinke!**

Infinitives ending in -**eln**, -**ern**, -**igen**, or -**men** must retain the -**e** ending in the **du**-form imperative. It is not optional. For example:

lächeln	Lächele!	*smile*
wandern	Wandere!	*hike*
öffnen	Öffne!	*open*
besichtigen	Besichtige!	*go sightseeing*
atmen	Atme!	*breathe*

If a verb has an irregular conjugation in the present tense, that irregularity occurs in the **du**-form of the imperative if the irregularity is the change of the vowel **e** in the stem of the verb to the vowel **i** or **ie**. For example:

INFINITIVE	IRREGULAR PRESENT	DU-FORM	
geben	du gibst, er gibt	Gib!	*give*
nehmen	du nimmst, er nimmt	Nimm!	*take*
sehen	du siehst, er sieht	Sieh!	*see*

The optional -**e** ending that is used with regular verbs is not an option in this form of imperative.

If the irregular present tense is formed by the addition of an umlaut, that irregularity does not occur in the **du**-form imperative.

INFINITIVE	IRREGULAR PRESENT	**DU**-FORM	
fahren	du fährst, er fährt	Fahr(e)!	*drive*
laufen	du läufst, er läuft	Lauf(e)!	*run*

Irregular verbs that add an umlaut in the present tense can have the optional **-e** ending in the **du**-form of the imperative. For example: **Fahre! Laufe!**

A German command is always punctuated with an exclamation point: **Sing(e)! Fahre!**

ÜBUNG

12·1

*Rewrite each infinitive in the **du**-form, **ihr**-form, and **Sie**-form of the imperative.*

1. kommen _____ _____ _____

2. gehen _____ _____ _____

3. schlafen _____ _____ _____

4. bringen _____ _____ _____

5. fangen _____ _____ _____

6. tragen _____ _____ _____

7. helfen _____ _____ _____

8. schreiben _____ _____ _____

9. essen _____ _____ _____

10. brechen _____ _____ _____

11. halten _____ _____ _____

12. sprechen _____ _____ _____

13. rennen _____ _____ _____

14. sagen _____ _____ _____

15. reinigen _____ _____ _____

Prefixes

If a verb has an inseparable prefix, the three imperative forms are formed like verbs without prefixes. For example:

INFINITIVE	DU-FORM		IHR-FORM	SIE-FORM
verkaufen	Verkauf(e)!	*sell*	Verkauft!	Verkaufen Sie!
besuchen	Besuch(e)!	*visit*	Besucht!	Besuchen Sie!
zerstören	Zerstör(e)!	*destroy*	Zerstört!	Zerstören Sie!

But separable prefixes detach from the infinitive and stand at the end of the imperative phrase.

INFINITIVE	DU-FORM		IHR-FORM	SIE-FORM
anfangen	Fang(e) an!	*begin*	Fangt an!	Fangen Sie an!
aufhören	Hör(e) auf!	*stop*	Hört auf!	Hören Sie auf!
ansehen	Sieh an!	*look at*	Seht an!	Sehen Sie an!

ÜBUNG

12·2

*Rewrite each infinitive in the **du**-form, **ihr**-form, and **Sie**-form of the imperative.*

1. ausgeben _____ _____ _____

2. beschreiben _____ _____ _____

3. mitkommen _____ _____ _____

4. entfliehen _____ _____ _____

5. abfahren _____ _____ _____

6. aufstehen _____ _____ _____

7. erschlagen _____ _____ _____

8. anrufen _____ _____ _____

9. befehlen _____ _____ _____

10. aussprechen _____ _____ _____

11. bearbeiten _____ _____ _____

12. annehmen _____ _____ _____

13. ausziehen _____ _____ _____

14. umsteigen _____ _____ _____

15. werfen _____ _____ _____

Haben, sein, and werden

The verbs **haben**, **sein**, and **werden** play an important role in the formation of tenses and other verb structures. Their imperative forms are equally important. Let's look at them:

INFINITIVE	DU-FORM		IHR-FORM	SIE-FORM
haben	Hab!	*have*	Habt!	Haben Sie!
sein	Sei!	*be*	Seid!	Seien Sie!
werden	Werde!	*become*	Werdet!	Werden Sie!

ÜBUNG
12·3

*Rewrite each sentence in the **du**-form, **ihr**-form, and **Sie**-form imperative. For example:*

Er singt es besser.

Sing(e) es besser!

Singt es besser!

Singen Sie es besser!

1. Sie spielt nicht im Garten.

   _____

   _____

   _____

2. Wir helfen dem alten Mann.

   _____

   _____

   _____

3. Die Frauen fangen mit der Arbeit an.

   _____

   _____

   _____

4. Ich probiere den Kuchen (*cake*).

   _____

   _____

   _____

5. Sie empfehlen kein Restaurant.

_____

_____

_____

6. Er ist mein Freund.

_____

_____

_____

7. Die Kinder essen Pommes frites (*French fries*).

_____

_____

_____

8. Die Frau macht alle Fenster auf.

_____

_____

_____

9. Ich belege (*enroll in*) einen Kurs in Deutsch.

_____

_____

_____

10. Er zieht sich um (*changes clothes*).

_____

_____

_____

Let's and Let

When English uses *let's* to begin an utterance, the inference is that the speaker or writer is *included in this form of command*. For example:

> Let's go to the movies.

The speaker is suggesting that you go to the movies, and the speaker is going to join you. The speaker is included in the command.

German does something similar. The speaker or writer is included in the command when the structure begins with a present tense verb conjugated with **wir**, but the pronoun **wir** follows the verb. Let's look at some examples:

Gehen **wir** heute in die Stadt!	*Let's go into the city today.*
Bleiben **wir** morgen zu Hause!	*Let's stay home tomorrow.*
Essen **wir** am Freitag chinesisch!	*Let's go out for Chinese on Friday.*

ÜBUNG
12·4

Rewrite each sentence as a wir-command. Be careful: the sentences are provided in a variety of tenses. For example:

Sie machte die Fenster zu.

Machen wir die Fenster zu!

1. Erik hat das Gedicht auswendig gelernt.

   _____

2. Die Jungen gehen heute nachmittag schwimmen.

   _____

3. Ich spreche nur Russisch.

   _____

4. Sie stand auf.

   _____

5. Er wird ein paar Ansichtskarten (*picture postcards*) schreiben.

   _____

6. Sie besuchten das Kunstmuseum.

   _____

7. Ihr seid zum Stadtpark gelaufen.

   _____

8. Tina zieht sich schnell an.

   _____

9. Ich habe den neuen Roman gelesen.

   _____

10. Ich nahm einen Regenschirm (*umbrella*) mit.

    _____

Lassen

The verb **lassen** is also used to give a command, in which the speaker or writer is also included, but this imperative does not mean *let's*. Its translation is *let*. **Lassen** is conjugated as an imperative in the three forms and is often accompanied by another verb in infinitive form. Let's look at an example with **ihn singen lassen** (*let him sing*):

DU-FORM	**IHR**-FORM	**SIE**-FORM
Lass ihn singen!	Lasst ihn singen!	Lassen Sie ihn singen.

This pattern is used with any variety of verbs. For example:

Lass Erik den Kuchen backen!   *Let Erik bake the cake!*
Lasst die Mädchen Schach spielen!   *Let the girls play chess!*
Lassen Sie mich mitkommen!   *Let me come along!*

If the object of the verb **lassen** is a form of **wir**, that phrase can be translated as *let's*. For example:

Lass uns jetzt gehen!   *Let's go now!*

ÜBUNG
12·5

*Rewrite each phrase as a **lassen**-command in the three forms of imperative. For example:*

sie eine Bank (*bench*) bauen lassen
Lass sie eine Bank bauen!
Lasst sie eine Bank bauen!
Lassen Sie sie eine Bank bauen!

1. mich ihnen helfen lassen

   _____

   _____

   _____

2. ihn die Vögel fotografieren lassen

   _____

   _____

   _____

3. die Schüler über die Straße gehen lassen

_____

_____

_____

4. das Konzert beginnen lassen

_____

_____

_____

5. sie das Gemälde (*painting*) zeigen lassen

_____

_____

_____

Circle the letter of the word or phrase that best completes each sentence.

1. Schicken _____ den Brief heute!
   a. lass   b. sie   c. wir   d. uns

2. _____ ein bisschen freundlicher!
   a. Sei   b. Werden   c. Habt   d. Lassen Sie

3. Kinder, _____ langsamer!
   a. iss   b. trinken   c. trinke   d. esst

4. _____ mir bitte die Zeitung!
   a. Kaufen   b. Wir verkaufen   c. Gib   d. Gebt ihr

5. Gehen _____ jetzt einkaufen!
   a. wir   b. sie   c. uns   d. ihn

6. _____ den armen Mann in Ruhe!
   a. Lasst   b. Wir sind   c. Seien Sie   d. Werdet

7. _____ Sie Erik auch spielen!
   a. Haben   b. Werden   c. Machen wir   d. Lassen

8. Lass mich die Briefe _____ !
   a. bekommt   b. versuche   c. lesen   d. gehabt

9. _____ in die Schweiz!
   a. Wohnen wir   b. Bleibt   c. Reisen wir   d. Lass

10. Lass _____ helfen!
    a. den Sohn dem   b. uns sie   c. meinem Onkel   d. mich dich
        Vater   meine Tante

11. Sonja, _____ fleißiger!
    a. Arbeit   b. üben   c. übt   d. arbeite

12. Herr Bauer, _____ vor einer Erkältung!
    a. schützen   b. schützt euch   c. schütze   d. sie schützt sich
        Sie sich

13. _____, ruft mich um elf Uhr an!
    a. Martin   b. Professor Benz   c. Lars und Erik   d. Frau Schneider

14. _____ damit zufrieden!
    a. Lernen wir   b. Sei   c. Haben Sie   d. Warte

15. Lass mich mit den Kindern _____!
    a. nach   b. spielen   c. gelaufen   d. seien

Verbs with specific prepositions

·13·

People who speak a language fluently probably never consider the fact that they use only certain prepositions with certain verbs. But those new to a language must make this kind of analysis in order to speak accurately, because the meaning of a sentence can be altered or even lost if the preposition accompanying a verb is the wrong one. In English, for example, the preposition *for* is used with the verb *wait*:

> I'll **wait** in the car **for** you.
>
> We have to **wait for** the next train.

This combination of *wait* and *for* is merely the result of a long-developing tradition of using these two words together. And although the usage of *wait* with *for* could be considered accidental and other prepositions could have been paired with the verb, this combination is the current one in usage and the one that speakers and writers who want to use English correctly should learn.

Other prepositions could have been combined with *wait*:

> I'll wait in the car **to** you.
>
> We have to wait **of** the next train.

But English speakers have chosen *for*.

Sentences like those just illustrated make some sense even with the wrong preposition and suggest the meaning desired by the speaker or writer, but they are not accurate. The prepositions *to* and *of* are not paired with *wait* in English.

This pairing of a verb and a specific preposition occurs with numerous verbs. For example:

> to be interested in
>
> to care for
>
> to talk about
>
> to drive to, from
>
> to ask about

The purpose of these few lines of explanation about English verbs and prepositions is meant to convey to German learners that the same traditional use of a verb and a preposition also occurs in German. It cannot always be explained why a certain verb is combined with a specific preposition. It's what has become the habit of the users of the language; it's their tradition. And so we shall look at German verbs and their traditional prepositional partners.

An and auf

The prepositions **an** and **auf** are so-called *accusative-dative* prepositions, because they are followed by either of those two cases. Usually, the accusative case is used when there is motion to a place, and the dative case is used when location is indicated. For example:

Er geht an die Tür. (*motion*)	*He goes to the door.*
Er steht an der Tür. (*location*)	*He stands by the door.*

But when paired with certain verbs those rules about the choice of case do not always apply. Therefore, it is wise to learn what preposition is paired with a certain verb and simultaneously what case is used with that preposition and verb. Let's look at a few verbs that use the preposition **an** (the required case will be indicated by *A* [accusative] and *D* [dative]):

Ich denke oft an meine Eltern. A	*I often think about my parents.*
Hast du dich daran erinnert? A	*Did you remember it?*
Sie glaubt an mich. A	*She believes in me.*
Erik schreibt an seinen Bruder. A	*Erik writes to his brother.*
Ich erkannte ihn an seiner Stimme. D	*I recognized him by his voice.*
Sie leidet an einer Lungenentzündung. D	*She suffers from pneumonia.*
Ich habe an diesem Stück teilgenommen. D	*I took part in this play.*
Das Bild hängt an der Wand. D	*The picture hangs on the wall.*

Let's look at some examples with the preposition **auf**:

Sie freute sich auf die Party. A	*She looked forward to the party.*
Wie lange hast du auf mich gewartet? A	*How long have you waited for me?*
Ich antworte ihr auf die Frage. A	*I respond to her question.*
Wir blicken auf das schöne Tal. A	*We gaze upon the beautiful valley.*
Müssen wir auf den Turm steigen? A	*Do we have to climb up the tower?*
Du kannst dich auf mich verlassen. A	*You can rely on me.*

With most all prepositions, a prepositional phrase is not formed when a pronoun replaces an inanimate noun. Instead, a *prepositional adverb* is used. Compare the following pairs of phrases:

PREPOSITIONAL PHRASE	PRONOUN REPLACEMENT	
mit dem Mann (*animate*)	mit ihm	*with him*
mit dem Bus (*inanimate*)	damit	*with it*
an meine Eltern (*animate*)	an sie	*about them*
an der Tür (*inanimate*)	daran	*by it*

In questions, the prefix **wo(r)-** is used: **Womit? Woran?**

*In the blanks provided, write the missing preposition (**an** or **auf**) and add the appropriate declension of the modifiers. For example:*

Ich warte *auf* mein*en* Freund.

1. Mein Vater stieg _____ d_____ alt_____ Leiter (*ladder*).

2. Sie erinnerte sich _____ sein_____ Geburtstag (*birthday*).

3. _____ d_____ Wand hing ein großer Spiegel (*mirror*).

4. Ich konnte mich _____ mein_____ Schwester verlassen.

5. Wir freuen uns schon _____ d_____ Wochenende (*weekend*).

6. Glaubst du _____ Gott?

7. Er schreibt einen langen Brief _____ sein_____ neu_____ Freundin.

8. Er hat ihn _____ sein_____ lang_____ Bart (*beard*) erkannt.

9. Sie möchte _____ unser_____ Schachspiel teilnehmen.

10. Lars dachte manchmal (*sometimes*) _____ sein_____ Großmutter.

11. Wir blickten _____ d_____ Fluss (*river*).

12. Antworte mir sofort _____ dies_____ Frage!

13. Sie leidet wieder _____ ein_____ Fieber (*fever*).

14. Ich habe zehn Minuten _____ d_____ Zug gewartet.

15. Erinnerst du dich noch _____ unser_____ Hochzeit (*wedding*)?

Rewrite the underlined prepositional phrases with the correct pronoun replacement. Use prepositional adverbs where necessary. For example:

Ich sprach *mit meiner Schwester*.

mit ihr

1. Der Lehrer wartet <u>auf seine Schüler</u>.

_____

2. Ich glaube <u>an meinen Onkel</u>.

_____

3. Wir freuten uns sehr <u>auf das nächste Fußballspiel</u>.

_____

4. Schreiben Sie oft an Ihre Kinder?

_____

5. Sein Porträt hängt an der Wand.

_____

Follow the same instructions, but form the prepositional phrase as a question. For example:

Ich sprach *mit meiner Schwester*.

Mit wem?

6. An der Ecke warten wir auf den Bus.

_____

7. Ich habe mich immer auf Tante Luise verlassen.

_____

8. Denkst du wieder an deine Probleme?

_____

9. Wir erkennen sie an ihren blonden Haaren.

_____

10. Er kann sich an seine Geschwister nicht erinnern.

_____

In, um, über, and vor

Four more prepositions fall into the category of accusative-dative prepositions: **in**, **um**, **über**, and **vor**. Let's look at some sentences that show some example verbs that are used with these prepositions:

Martin verliebt sich in Sabine. A	*Martin falls in love with Sabine.*
Er bewirbt sich um den letzten Job. A	*He applies for the last job.*
Ich bitte sie um den nächsten Tanz. A	*I ask her for the next dance.*
Warum musst du dich darüber beklagen? A	*Why do you have to complain about it?*
Sie hat sich über das Geschenk gefreut. A	*She was happy about the gift.*
Er redet/spricht über den Artikel. A	*He talks about the article.*
Wir werden über den Unfall schreiben. A	*We will write about the accident.*
Die Mauer schützt uns vor dem Wind. D	*The wall protects us from the wind.*
Ich habe dich vor diesem Mann gewarnt. D	*I warned you about this man.*

*In the blanks provided, write the missing preposition (**in, um, über,** or **vor**) and add the appropriate declension of the modifiers. For example:*

Ich verliebte mich *in* dein*e* Schwester.

1. Ich möchte mich _____ dies_____ Stellung bewerben.

2. Warne ihn _____ jen_____ Frau!

3. Wer hat _____ d_____ Zweit_____ Weltkrieg (*world war*) geschrieben?

4. Wir haben uns _____ Ihr_____ Besuch gefreut.

5. Sie beklagt sich _____ jed_____ klein_____ Problem.

6. Das Zelt (*tent*) wird uns _____ d_____ Regen schützen.

7. Die Jungen sprechen _____ d_____ Schülerinnen.

8. Ich muss Sie _____ Ihr_____ Hilfe bitten.

9. Warum hast du dich _____ dies_____ Mädchen verliebt?

10. Reden Sie bitte _____ Ihr_____ Afrikareise!

Rewrite the underlined prepositional phrases with the correct pronoun replacement. Use prepositional adverbs where necessary. For example:

Ich sprach *über meine Schwester*.

Über sie

1. Sie hat uns <u>vor dem Gewitter</u> (*storm*) gewarnt.

   _____

2. Haben Sie sich wirklich <u>in Sonja</u> verliebt?

   _____

3. Wir freuten uns sehr <u>über die schönen Geschenke</u>.

   _____

4. Schreiben Sie oft <u>über Ihre Reisen</u>?

   _____

5. Er bat <u>um etwas zu essen</u>.

   _____

Follow the same instructions, but form the prepositional phrase as a question. For example:

Ich sprach <u>*über seine Schwester.*</u>
<u>*Über wen?*</u>

6. Niemand hat <u>über die Kanzlerin</u> geredet.

_____

7. Sie hat sich <u>um meinen Job</u> beworben.

_____

8. Ich freue mich sehr <u>über deinen Erfolg</u> (*success*).

_____

9. Ich warne die Kinder <u>vor dem Dieb</u>.

_____

10. Mein Bruder hat sich <u>in die Frau des Bürgermeisters</u> verliebt.

_____

Für and gegen

Für and **gegen** are accusative prepositions. And they, too, are often paired with specific verbs. Let's look at some example sentences:

Herr Schneider bezahlt für das Abendessen.	*Mr. Schneider pays for the dinner.*
Ich interessiere mich für Physik.	*I'm interested in physics.*
Alle kämpfen gegen den Feind.	*Everyone fights against the enemy.*
Sie ist allergisch gegen Milch.	*She is allergic to milk.*

Dative prepositions

Several dative prepositions accompany specific verbs. They are **aus**, **bei**, **mit**, **nach**, **von**, and **zu**. Let's look at a few sentences with some verbs that combine with these prepositions:

Ich komme aus Deutschland.	*I come from Germany.*
Ich möchte mich bei Ihnen bedanken.	*I'd like to say thanks to you.*
Tina wohnt noch bei ihren Eltern.	*Tina still lives with her parents.*
Er arbeitet bei einer Firma in Berlin.	*He works for a company in Berlin.*
Wir beschäftigen uns viel mit den Kindern.	*We are very busy with the children.*
Man muss mit der Straßenbahn fahren.	*You have to go by streetcar.*
Sie ist mit Erik Benz verlobt.	*She is engaged to Erik Benz.*

Sie fährt/fliegt/reist nach Bremen.	*She's driving/flying/traveling to Bremen.*
Sie fragten nach seiner kranken Frau.	*They asked about his sick wife.*
Habt ihr lange nach ihm gesucht?	*Did you search for him for a long time?*
Sie bekam die Rosen von Stefan.	*She received the roses from Stefan.*
Frau Bauer erzählte von ihrer Party.	*Ms. Bauer told about her party.*
Die Studenten sprechen von der Vorlesung.	*The students talk about the lecture.*
Warum laufen sie zum Stadtpark?	*Why are they running to the city park?*
Gehen die Kinder zur Schule?	*Are the children going to school?*
Es gehört dazu.	*That's part of it. It's natural.*

In many cases, a verb phrase is paired with a specific preposition. This occurs most often with the verbs **haben** and **sein**. For example:

Angst vor jemandem/etwas haben	*to be afraid of someone/something*
Die Kinder hatten Angst vor dem alten Mann.	*The children were afraid of the old man.*
mit jemanden böse sein	*to be mad at someone*
Warum bist du wieder böse mit mir?	*Why are you mad at me again?*

Note: **böse sein** is often used with **auf** (A) rather than **mit**.

ÜBUNG 13·5

*In the blanks provided, write the missing preposition (**für, gegen, aus, bei, mit, nach, von,** or **zu**) and add the appropriate declension of the modifiers. For example:*

Er bekommt einen Brief *von* sein*em* Freund.

1. Interessierst du dich noch _____ Musik?

2. Sie hat _____ ein_____ neu_____ Film gesprochen.

3. Er kämpft _____ dies_____ gefährlich_____ (*dangerous*) Ideologie.

4. Gehört es wirklich da_____?

5. Meine Großeltern kamen _____ Frankreich.

6. Arbeiten Sie noch _____ d_____ Bank?

7. Ich werde mich _____ dies_____ Problemen beschäftigen.

8. Wann seid ihr _____ Amerika gereist?

9. Erzähle bitte _____ dein_____ Leben in China!

10. Ich muss _____ d_____ Briefmarken bezahlen.

11. Wir haben _____ d_____ verloren_____ (*lost*) Kind gesucht.

12. Onkel Peter fragte _____ mein_____ Studium in Hamburg.

13. Sie war allergisch _____ Muschel (*clams*).

14. Erik will _____ sein_____ Verwandten in der Stadt wohnen.

15. Morgen fahren wir _____ Dänemark.

16. Bist du _____ ein_____ Ausländer verlobt?

17. Am Freitag gehen wir _____ d_____ Rathaus.

18. Er hat sich _____ d_____ Hauswirtin (*landlady*) bedankt.

19. Sonja hat sich nie _____ Wildwestfilme (*cowboy movies*) interessiert.

20. Oma (*granny*) hat wieder _____ d_____ letzt_____ Krieg erzählt.

Identifying verb-preposition combinations

It is important to read dictionary entries with an eye for correct prepositional usage. If you were to look for the German translation of *to be interested in*, you would find an entry similar to the following:

> **interessieren** *reflexive verb* **sich für jemanden** or **etwas interessieren**: *to be interested in someone or something.*

This entry tells you that **sich interessieren** is paired with **für** and requires the use of the accusative case with that preposition (**für jemanden**). Always check for prepositions when looking up a verb.

ÜBUNG
13·6

Finish each sentence with any two completions of your choosing. For example:

Ich komme aus _____.

Deutschland

Amerika

1. Die Jungen haben nach _____ gesucht.

_____

_____

2. Ich möchte mich bei _____ bedanken.

_____

_____

3. Bitte erzählen Sie von _____!

_____

_____

4. Sie denkt so oft an _____.

_____

_____

5. Warum wartet ihr noch auf _____?

_____

_____

6. Der Mann bittet uns um _____.

_____

_____

7. Warum hast du mich nicht vor _____ gewarnt?

_____

_____

8. Er hat früher (*previously*) bei _____ gearbeitet.

_____

_____

9. Er fährt jeden Tag mit _____.

_____

_____

10. Ich freue mich schon auf _____.

_____

_____

Categories of
irregular verbs

Most German verbs have a regular conjugation. Once the endings and the auxiliaries for the tenses of the regular verbs have been learned, they can be applied to any number of verbs. For example:

	PRESENT	PAST	PRESENT PERFECT	FUTURE
ich	brauche	brauchte	habe gebraucht	werde brauchen
du	brauchst	brauchtest	hast gebraucht	wirst brauchen
er/sie/es	braucht	brauchte	hat gebraucht	wird brauchen
wir	brauchen	brauchten	haben gebraucht	werden brauchen
ihr	braucht	brauchtet	habt gebraucht	werdet brauchen
Sie/sie	brauchen	brauchten	haben gebraucht	werden brauchen

The translation of the tenses in the third-person singular with the verb **brauchen** is *he needs, he needed, he has needed/he needed*, and *he will need*.

Sometimes English speakers believe that a verb is an irregular verb if its auxiliary in the perfect tenses is **sein** rather than **haben**. This is not true. Many regular verbs use **sein** in the perfect tenses. For example:

	PRESENT	PAST	PRESENT PERFECT	FUTURE
ich	reise	reiste	bin gereist	werde reisen
du	reist	reistest	bist gereist	wirst reisen
er/sie/es	reist	reiste	ist gereist	wird reisen
wir	reisen	reisten	sind gereist	werden reisen
ihr	reist	reistet	seid gereist	werdet reisen
Sie/sie	reisen	reisten	sind gereist	werden reisen

The translation of the tenses in the third-person singular with the verb **reisen** is *he travels, he traveled, he has traveled/he traveled*, and *he will travel*.

English once used both *have* and *be* as its auxiliaries in the perfect tenses, but that practice began to fade a couple centuries ago. It still can be found in older literature or older versions of the Bible. For example: *The Lord **is** come.* = *The Lord has come.*

Irregular patterns

Irregular verbs follow some patterns that are helpful in determining their conjugation in the various tenses. Not all irregular verbs are irregular in the present tense, but most are in the past tense, and most have an irregular participle that ends in -**en**. Irregularities do not occur in the future tense. The future tense auxiliary **werden** has an irregular present tense conjugation, which is used as the future tense auxiliary and then means *shall* or *will*. But the irregular verb that accompanies **werden** in the future tense is always in infinitive form.

Let's look at a verb that has no present tense irregularity: **verstehen** (*to understand*).

	PRESENT	PAST	PRESENT PERFECT	FUTURE
ich	verstehe	verstand	habe verstanden	werde verstehen
du	verstehst	verstandest	hast verstanden	wirst verstehen
er/sie/es	versteht	verstand	hat verstanden	wird verstehen
wir	verstehen	verstanden	haben verstanden	werden verstehen
ihr	versteht	verstandet	habt verstanden	werdet verstehen
Sie/sie	verstehen	verstanden	haben verstanden	werden verstehen

Verbs of motion (**gehen** *to go*, **fahren** *to drive*) and verbs that show a change of condition (**sterben** *to die*, **werden** *to become*) use **sein** as the perfect tense auxiliary: **ich bin gegangen, er ist gefahren, sie sind gestorben, du bist geworden**.

Note: Refer to the appendix at the back of this book for a complete list of irregular verbs.

ÜBUNG
14·1

Rewrite each sentence in the missing tenses. Be aware that some of the verbs in these sentences are regular, and others are irregular.

1. PRESENT Wir hören Radio.

   PAST _____

   PRESENT PERFECT _____

   FUTURE _____

2. PRESENT _____

   PAST Stefan ging nach Hause.

   PRESENT PERFECT _____

   FUTURE _____

3. PRESENT _____

   PAST _____

   PRESENT PERFECT Wir haben kein Bier getrunken.

   FUTURE _____

4. PRESENT _____

   PAST _____

   PRESENT PERFECT _____

   FUTURE Ich werde in Italien bleiben.

5. PRESENT Schreibst du an deinen Vater?

   PAST _____

   PRESENT PERFECT _____

   FUTURE _____

6. PRESENT _____

   PAST Die alte Dame weinte vor Freude (*cried with joy*).

   PRESENT PERFECT _____

   FUTURE _____

7. PRESENT _____

   PAST _____

   PRESENT PERFECT Die Mädchen haben sehr gut gesungen.

   FUTURE _____

8. PRESENT _____

   PAST _____

   PRESENT PERFECT _____

   FUTURE Lars wird auf dem Boden (*floor*) sitzen.

9. PRESENT Er schwimmt einen neuen Record (*swims a new record time*).

   PAST _____

   PRESENT PERFECT _____

   FUTURE _____

10. PRESENT _____

    PAST Was kauften Sie?

    PRESENT PERFECT _____

    FUTURE _____

Present tense irregularities: e to i or ie

Some irregular verbs that have a verb stem **e** change that **e** to an **i** or an **ie** in the present tense. They also have an irregular past tense and an irregular participle. Take note that the present tense irregularity occurs only in the second-person and third-person singular. For example:

geben *to give*

	PRESENT	PAST	PRESENT PERFECT	FUTURE
ich	gebe	gab	habe gegeben	werde geben
du	gibst	gabst	hast gegeben	wirst geben
er/sie/es	gibt	gab	hat gegeben	wird geben
wir	geben	gaben	haben gegeben	werden geben
ihr	gebt	gabt	habt gegeben	werdet geben
Sie/sie	geben	gaben	haben gegeben	werden geben

sehen *to see*

	PRESENT	PAST	PRESENT PERFECT	FUTURE
ich	sehe	sah	habe gesehen	werde sehen
du	siehst	sahst	hast gesehen	wirst sehen
er/sie/es	sieht	sah	hat gesehen	wird sehen
wir	sehen	sahen	haben gesehen	werden sehen
ihr	seht	saht	habt gesehen	werdet sehen
Sie/sie	sehen	sahen	haben gesehen	werden sehen

Other verbs that have this kind of present tense irregularity are **brechen, bricht** (*break*); **empfehlen, empfiehlt** (*recommend*); **essen, isst** (*eat*); **fressen, frisst** (*eat like an animal*); **geschehen, geschieht** (*happen*); **helfen, hilft** (*help*); **lesen, liest** (*read*); **nehmen, nimmt** (*take*); **sprechen, spricht** (*speak*); **stehlen, stiehlt** (*steal*); **sterben, stirbt** (*die*); **treffen, trifft** (*meet*); **vergessen, vergisst** (*forget*); **werfen, wirft** (*throw*).

ÜBUNG
14·2

Conjugate each verb in the present, past, and present perfect.

1. brechen

   ich _____ _____ _____

   du _____ _____ _____

   er _____ _____ _____

   wir _____ _____ _____

   ihr _____ _____ _____

   Sie _____ _____ _____

2. nehmen

ich   _____   _____   _____

du   _____   _____   _____

er   _____   _____   _____

wir   _____   _____   _____

ihr   _____   _____   _____

Sie   _____   _____   _____

3. helfen

ich   _____   _____   _____

du   _____   _____   _____

er   _____   _____   _____

wir   _____   _____   _____

ihr   _____   _____   _____

Sie   _____   _____   _____

4. geschehen

es   _____   _____   _____

sie *pl.*   _____   _____   _____

5. sprechen

ich   _____   _____   _____

du   _____   _____   _____

er   _____   _____   _____

wir   _____   _____   _____

ihr   _____   _____   _____

Sie   _____   _____   _____

*Rewrite each sentence in the present tense with the third-person pronoun **er**. For example:*

Wir haben kein Wasser getrunken.

Er trinkt kein Wasser.

1. Sehen Sie die Elefanten?

_____

2. Ich werde ihren neuen Roman lesen.

_____

3. Sie hat oft mexikanisch gegessen.

_____

4. Warum wird er sterben?

_____

5. Was stahl der Dieb?

_____

Present tense irregularities: umlaut

Several irregular verbs with the vowel **a** in the stem add an umlaut in the present tense in the second- and third-person singular. They also have an irregular past tense and an irregular past participle. For example:

fahren *to drive*

	PRESENT	PAST	PRESENT PERFECT	FUTURE
ich	fahre	fuhr	bin gefahren	werde fahren
du	fährst	fuhrst	bist gefahren	wirst fahren
er/sie/es	fährt	fuhr	ist gefahren	wird fahren
wir	fahren	fuhren	sind gefahren	werden fahren
ihr	fahrt	fuhrt	seid gefahren	werdet fahren
Sie/sie	fahren	fuhren	sind gefahren	werden fahren

Other verbs that have this kind of present tense irregularity are **backen**, **bäckt** (*bake*); **braten**, **brät** (*roast*); **fallen**, **fällt** (*fall*); **fangen**, **fängt** (*catch*); **halten**, **hält** (*hold*); **lassen**, **lässt** (*let*); **laufen**, **läuft** (*run*); **raten**, **rät** (*advise*); **schlafen**, **schläft** (*sleep*); **schlagen**, **schlägt** (*hit*); **tragen**, **trägt** (*carry*); **wachsen**, **wächst** (*grow*); **waschen**, **wäscht** (*wash*).

One verb adds the umlaut to the vowel **o** in the present tense: **stoßen**, **stößt** (*punch*, *kick*).

ÜBUNG

14·4

Conjugate each verb in the present, past, and present perfect.

1. braten

   ich _____ _____ _____

   du _____ _____ _____

   er _____ _____ _____

   wir _____ _____ _____

   ihr _____ _____ _____

   Sie _____ _____ _____

2. lassen

   ich _____ _____ _____

   du _____ _____ _____

   er _____ _____ _____

   wir _____ _____ _____

   ihr _____ _____ _____

   Sie _____ _____ _____

3. wachsen

   ich _____ _____ _____

   du _____ _____ _____

   er _____ _____ _____

   wir _____ _____ _____

   ihr _____ _____ _____

   Sie _____ _____ _____

*Rewrite each sentence in the present tense with the second-person pronoun **du**.
For example:*

Wir haben kein Wasser getrunken.

Du trinkst kein Wasser.

1. Haben Sie sich gewaschen?

_____

2. Er schlug den armen Hund.

_____

3. Ich stoße mich am Tisch.

_____

4. Bist du auf der Treppe gefallen?

_____

5. Sie wird in die Apotheke (*drugstore*) laufen.

_____

Mixed verbs

There is a small category of verbs called *mixed verbs*. They are so named, because they combine some patterns of regular verbs and some patterns of irregular verbs. These verbs are:

INFINITIVE		PAST	PRESENT PERFECT
brennen	*burn*	er brannte	er hat gebrannt
bringen	*bring*	er brachte	er hat gebracht
denken	*think*	er dachte	er hat gedacht
kennen	*know*	er kannte	er hat gekannt
nennen	*name*	er nannte	er hat genannt
rennen	*run*	er rannte	er ist gerannt
senden	*send*	er sandte	er hat gesandt
wissen	*know*	er wusste	er hat gewusst

The verb **wissen** follows the pattern of a modal auxiliary (Chapter 9) in the present tense: with singular subjects it has a verb stem different from the verb stem with plural subjects.

ich weiß	wir wissen
du weißt	ihr wisst
er/sie/es weiß	sie wissen
	Sie wissen

Rewrite each sentence in the missing tenses.

1. PRESENT Die Lampe brennt dunkel (*dark*).

   PAST _____

   PRESENT PERFECT _____

   FUTURE _____

2. PRESENT _____

   PAST Der Polizist brachte eine gute Nachricht (*news*).

   PRESENT PERFECT _____

   FUTURE _____

3. PRESENT _____

   PAST _____

   PRESENT PERFECT Ich habe wieder an meine Familie gedacht.

   FUTURE _____

4. PRESENT _____

   PAST _____

   PRESENT PERFECT _____

   FUTURE Er wird den Chef persönlich kennen.

5. PRESENT Wir nennen unsere Tochter Angela.

   PAST _____

   PRESENT PERFECT _____

   FUTURE _____

6. PRESENT _____

   PAST Die Jungen rannten zum Sportplatz.

   PRESENT PERFECT _____

   FUTURE _____

7. PRESENT _____

   PAST _____

   PRESENT PERFECT Wer hat den Katalog zur Ansicht gesandt?

   FUTURE _____

8. PRESENT _____

PAST _____

PRESENT PERFECT _____

FUTURE Du wirst nichts wissen.

Verbs that end in -ieren

Verbs that end in **-ieren** tend to come from a foreign source and have their own unique past participle formation, which does not require the suffix **ge-**. This lack of a participial prefix is essentially the only irregularity with this category of verbs. Depending upon the meaning of the verb, these verbs can use either **haben** or **sein** as the auxiliary in the perfect tenses. Let's look at some examples:

INFINITIVE		PAST	PRESENT PERFECT
diskutieren	*discuss*	er diskutierte	er hat diskutiert
komponieren	*compose*	er komponierte	er hat komponiert
kontrollieren	*control*	er kontrollierte	er hat kontrolliert
marschieren	*march*	er marschierte	er ist marschiert
reparieren	*repair*	er reparierte	er hat repariert
riskieren	*risk*	er riskierte	er hat riskiert
studieren	*study*	er studierte	er hat studiert
tolerieren	*tolerate*	er tolerierte	er hat toleriert

There are two notable exceptions to the **-ieren** conjugational patterns: **frieren** (*freeze*) and **verlieren** (*lose*).

	PRESENT	PAST	PRESENT PERFECT
er	friert	er fror	er ist gefroren
er	verliert	er verlor	er hat verloren

ÜBUNG
14·7

Rewrite each sentence in the missing tenses.

1. PRESENT Sie diskutieren stundenlang.

PAST _____

PRESENT PERFECT _____

FUTURE _____

2. PRESENT _____

   PAST **Er disziplinierte sich nicht** (*did not discipline himself*).

   PRESENT PERFECT _____

   FUTURE _____

3. PRESENT _____

   PAST _____

   PRESENT PERFECT **Die Soldaten sind nach Hause marschiert.**

   FUTURE _____

4. PRESENT _____

   PAST _____

   PRESENT PERFECT _____

   FUTURE **Ich werde dir ein Glas Bier spendieren** (*get a glass of beer*).

Dative verbs

Some dative verbs have a regular conjugation, and others have an irregular conjugation. They are included in this chapter not for any particular irregularity but because English speakers often have difficulty assigning the dative case to the object of such a verb. This is because in English those objects tend to be direct objects, which normally means the accusative case in German. Let's look at some examples:

Transitive verb

Er sieht **den alten Herrn**.   *He sees the old gentleman.*

In this sentence the accusative case is used because **den alten Herrn** is the direct object of the verb **sieht**. In the English translation, *the old gentleman* is also a direct object.

Dative verb

Er hilft **dem alten Herrn**.   *He helps the old gentleman.*

In this sentence the dative case is used because the object **dem alten Herrn** is the object of the dative verb **hilft**. However, in the English translation, *the old gentleman* is still a *direct object*. English speakers need to differentiate between the English meaning of a sentence and the case required when an object follows a dative verb in the German sentence.

Let's look at how the tenses of some commonly used dative verbs are formed:

INFINITIVE		PAST	PRESENT PERFECT
begegnen	*meet*	er begegnete	er ist begegnet
dienen	*serve*	er diente	er hat gedient
drohen	*threaten*	er drohte	er hat gedroht
folgen	*follow*	er folgte	er ist gefolgt

INFINITIVE		PAST	PRESENT PERFECT
gefallen	*please, like*	es gefiel	es hat gefallen
gehören	*belong*	es gehörte	es hat gehört
gelingen	*succeed*	es gelang	es ist gelungen
glauben	*believe*	er glaubte	er hat geglaubt
schaden	*harm*	er schadete	er hat geschadet
vertrauen	*trust*	er vertraute	er hat vertraut
zuhören	*listen to*	er hörte zu	er hat zugehört

ÜBUNG
14·8

Rewrite each sentence with the objects provided in parentheses. For example:

Sie hilft _____.

(der Mann) *Sie hilft dem Mann.*

(die Frau) *Sie hilft der Frau.*

Wo seid ihr _____ begegnet?

1. (euer Professor) _____

2. (meine Verwandten) _____

3. (der junge Künstler [*artist*]) _____

Hör _____ zu!

4. (ich) _____

5. (sie *pl.*) _____

6. (die Ärztin) _____

Können Sie _____ folgen?

7. (seine Rede) _____

8. (diese langweilige Vorlesung [*boring lecture*]) _____

Warum hast du _____ nicht geglaubt?

9. (er) _____

10. (meine Brüder) _____

Passive voice versus participles as adjectives

German and English both form the passive voice in the same way: an auxiliary verb is conjugated and accompanied by a past participle. In English, the auxiliary is the verb *be,* and the past participle that is used comes from a transitive verb. This formation looks like this: *to be broken, to be found, to be repaired.*

There can be some confusion with the English passive voice, because in certain tenses it is not always clear whether the past participle is used in a passive structure or as an adjective. For example: *The chair is broken.* If the meaning intended is that the *condition of the chair* is *broken*, then the past participle is being used as an adjective. However, if the meaning intended is that *someone is breaking the chair*, then the past participle is part of a passive voice structure. This confusion can be avoided by changing the auxiliary to mean that the action is *in process* and not complete.

> *The chair **is being** broken.*

Or the person carrying out the action of the verb can be included in the sentence.

> *The chair is broken **by the clumsy delivery man**.*

Consider the same sentence in various tenses, and note where the intended meaning is not always clear and the participle can be either part of the passive voice or used as an adjective:

> *The chair is broken.* (passive voice or adjective)
>
> *The chair is being broken.* (passive voice)
>
> *The chair was broken.* (passive voice or adjective)
>
> *The chair was being broken.* (passive voice)
>
> *The chair has been broken.* (passive voice or adjective)
>
> *The chair had been broken.* (passive voice or adjective)
>
> *The chair will be broken.* (passive voice or adjective)

It is important to be aware of this confusion in the English passive voice in order to come up with the appropriate German sentence that has the same meaning intended by the English sentence. This chapter on the German passive voice deals with this very issue.

The auxiliary for the German passive voice is **werden**. But the typical meaning of **werden** (*become, get*) is not used in the passive voice. It must be translated as *be*. For example:

gebrochen werden	*to be broken*
gefunden werden	*to be found*
gelernt werden	*to be learned*

In the German passive voice, **werden** is combined with past participles formed from transitive verbs. Transitive verbs are those that can be followed by a direct object in an active voice sentence. For example:

Er liest **den Brief**. (den Brief = *direct object*)	*He reads the letter.*
Sie fand **das Buch**. (das Buch = *direct object*)	*She found the book.*

The active voice sentence, **Er liest den Brief.**, can be changed to the passive voice by doing the following:

1. Make the direct object the subject of the passive voice sentence: **der Brief**.

2. Conjugate **werden** for the new subject in the tense of the verb in the active voice sentence: **wird**.

3. Make the subject of the active voice sentence the object of the dative preposition **von**: **von ihm**.

4. Form the verb in the active voice sentence as a past participle: **gelesen**.

Der Brief wird von ihm gelesen.	*The letter is read by him.*

The same procedure is used for changing other active voice sentences to the passive voice: **Sie fand das Buch.**

1. Make the direct object the subject of the passive voice sentence: **das Buch**.

2. Conjugate **werden** for the new subject in the tense of the verb in the active voice sentence: **wurde**.

3. Make the subject of the active voice sentence the object of the dative preposition **von**: **von ihr**.

4. Form the verb in the active voice sentence as a past participle: **gefunden**.

Das Buch wurde von ihr gefunden.	*The book was found by her.*

These example sentences look like the following in the other tenses:

Present	Der Brief wird von ihm gelesen.	*The letter is read by him.*
Past	Der Brief wurde von ihm gelesen.	*The letter was read by him.*
Present perfect	Der Brief ist von ihm gelesen worden.	*The letter has been read by him.*
Past perfect	Der Brief war von ihm gelesen worden.	*The letter had been read by him.*
Future	Der Brief wird von ihm gelesen werden.	*The letter will be read by him.*
Present	Das Buch wird von ihr gefunden.	*The book is found by her.*
Past	Das Buch wurde von ihr gefunden.	*The book was found by her.*
Present perfect	Das Buch ist von ihr gefunden worden.	*The book has been found by her.*
Past perfect	Das Buch war von ihr gefunden worden.	*The book had been found by her.*
Future	Das Buch wird von ihr gefunden werden.	*The book will be found by her.*

In the perfect tenses of the verb **werden** (*become, get*), the past participle is **geworden**. However, when **werden** is part of a passive voice structure, the past participle is **worden**.

Es ist gefunden **worden**.	*It has been found.*
Der Brief ist von ihm gelesen **worden**.	*The letter has been read by him.*

ÜBUNG
15·1

Rewrite each active voice sentence in the passive voice. Retain the tense of the original sentence.

1. Der Junge zerbricht das Fenster.

   _____

2. Wirst du einen Artikel schreiben?

   _____

3. Der Lehrer fragte mich.

   _____

4. Der Maler malt (*painter paints*) das Bild.

   _____

5. Wir haben ein Geschenk geschickt (*sent*).

   _____

6. Die Soldaten schützten (*protected*) die Stadt.

   _____

7. Die Kinder werden den Ball suchen.

   _____

8. Ich kaufe ein paar Ansichtskarten (*picture postcards*).

   _____

9. Der Tourist hat die Schiffe fotografiert.

   _____

10. Gutenberg hat die Bibel gedruckt (*Bible printed*).

    _____

11. Die Schüler werden die Aufgabe lernen.

    _____

12. Ihr seht die alten Flugzeuge.

    _____

13. Er hat die Schlüssel (*keys*) vergessen.

    _____

14. Erik aß zwei Äpfel (*apples*).

    _____

15. Meine Mutter heizt den Ofen (*heats the oven*).

    _____

ÜBUNG
15·2

Rewrite each passive sentence in the missing tenses.

1. PRESENT Die Bücher werden in den Schrank (*bookcase*) gestellt.

   PAST _____

   PRESENT PERFECT _____

   FUTURE _____

2. PRESENT _____

   PAST Von wem wurde der Brief in den Briefkasten gesteckt?

   PRESENT PERFECT _____

   FUTURE _____

3. PRESENT _____

   PAST _____

   PRESENT PERFECT Die schönen Waren sind auf den Tisch gelegt worden.

   FUTURE _____

4. PRESENT _____

   PAST _____

   PRESENT PERFECT _____

   FUTURE Hier wird Weihnachten auch gefeiert (*Christmas celebrated*) werden.

5. PRESENT Das Wort wird von dem Schüler buchstabiert.

   PAST _____

   PRESENT PERFECT _____

   FUTURE _____

Past participles as adjectives

If a German speaker or writer intends to use a past participle as an adjective in a sentence that resembles the passive voice, the verb **sein** replaces **werden**. There is no confusion about the intended meaning, because the passive voice auxiliary **werden** has been replaced. Compare the following pairs of sentences:

Passive	Der alte Stuhl **wird** repariert.	*The old chair is being repaired.*
Adjective	Der alte Stuhl **ist** repariert.	*The old chair is repaired. (It is in repaired condition.)*
Passive	Der Ofen **wurde** geheizt.	*The oven was being heated.*
Adjective	Der Ofen **war** geheizt.	*The oven was heated. (It was hot.)*

When a past participle is used as an adjective, the verb **sein** can be conjugated in any tense. For example:

Present	Der alte Stuhl **ist** repariert.	*The old chair is repaired.*
Past	Der alte Stuhl **war** repariert.	*The old chair was repaired.*
Present perfect	Der alte Stuhl **ist** repariert **gewesen**.	*The old chair has been repaired.*
Future	Der alte Stuhl **wird** repariert **sein**.	*The old chair will be repaired.*

ÜBUNG
15·3

Using the string of words provided, write a present tense passive voice sentence. Then rewrite the sentence with the past participle used as an adjective. For example:

die Suppe/kochen

Die Suppe wird gekocht.

Die Suppe ist gekocht.

1. die Wunde/heilen

_____

_____

2. das Fahrrad/verkaufen

_____

_____

3. der Laden/eröffnen

_____

_____

4. eine neue Kirche/bauen

_____

_____

5. das kleine Dorf/zerstören

_____

_____

Dative case

It is common to use the accusative case for direct objects in German. But some verbs require the use of the dative case with objects. These verbs are called **dative verbs**. Some of the most common dative verbs are:

danken	_thank_
dienen	_serve_
drohen	_threaten_
glauben	_believe_
helfen	_help_
imponieren	_impress_
raten	_advise_
schenken	_give, make a gift_
vertrauen	_trust_

Nouns and pronouns that follow dative verbs will be in the dative case, even though the English translation of the nouns and pronouns indicates that they are direct objects. For example:

Ich danke meinem Freund.	_I thank my friend._
Wir halfen dem alten Herrn.	_We helped the old gentleman._

Even though the objects of the verbs are not direct objects, a passive voice sentence can be formed. The only difference between the passive voice formation from an accusative case object and the passive voice formation from a dative case object is that _the object of a dative verb remains in the dative case._ For example:

Meinem Freund wird von mir gedankt.	_My friend is thanked by me._
Dem alten Herrn wurde von uns geholfen.	_The old gentleman was helped by us._

If a German active voice sentence has both a direct object and an indirect object, it can be made a passive voice sentence. The direct object becomes the subject of the passive voice sentence, and the indirect object remains in the dative case in the passive voice sentence. Either the new subject or the dative case object can begin the passive voice sentence. For example:

Active	Sie gibt **dem Lehrer einen Bleistift**.	*She gives the teacher a pencil.*
Passive	Ein Bleistift wird **dem Lehrer** von ihr gegeben.	*A pencil is given to the teacher by her.*
	Dem Lehrer wird ein Bleistift von ihr gegeben.	*The teacher is given a pencil by her.*

ÜBUNG
15·4

Rewrite each active voice sentence in the passive voice. Retain the tense of the original sentence.

1. Er hat dem Matrosen für seine Hilfe gedankt.

   _____

2. Lars glaubte mir nicht.

   _____

3. Der junge Pianist imponiert der Managerin sehr.

   _____

4. Der Richter wird ihnen mit dem Todesurteil (*death penalty*) drohen.

   _____

5. Wer hat Ihnen gedient?

   _____

6. Ich schenkte ihr ein paar CDs zum Geburtstag.

   _____

7. Der Bräutigam (*groom*) wird seiner Braut (*bride*) Ohrringe geben.

   _____

8. Wir vertrauen dir nicht.

   _____

9. Sabine hat uns etwas Schönes (*something nice*) geschickt.

   _____

10. Was werdet ihr eurer Schwester raten?

   _____

Modal auxiliaries

It is possible to use modal auxiliaries with passive voice structures. Remember that modals are accompanied by infinitives: **ich muss gehen** (*I have to go*), **wir können verstehen** (*we can understand*), and so on. When using a passive voice structure with a modal, the modal is conjugated normally, but the passive voice structure is formed as a passive voice infinitive. Note that the modal auxiliary can be conjugated in any tense. For example:

Es soll schnell **gebaut werden**.	*It should be built quickly.*
Konnte die ganze Stadt **geschützt werden**?	*Could the whole city be protected?*
Sie hat **fotografiert werden** wollen.	*She wanted to be photographed.*
Tina wird auch **eingeladen werden** müssen.	*Tina will also need to be invited.*

ÜBUNG
15·5

Rewrite each passive voice sentence with the modal auxiliary in parentheses. Retain the tense of the original sentence. For example:

Sie wird nicht geküsst.

(wollen) *Sie will nicht geküsst werden.*

1. Diese Probleme werden von uns gelöst (*solved*).

   (müssen) _____

2. Das Geld wurde nicht gefunden.

   (können) _____

3. Der Hund ist von Thomas gewaschen worden.

   (sollen) _____

4. Der Dieb wird nicht verhaftet (*arrested*) werden.

   (wollen) _____

5. Den Mädchen wurde mit ihrer Schularbeit geholfen.

   (müssen) _____

6. Solche Wörter werden nicht geschrieben.

   (dürfen) _____

7. Der Fernsehapparat (*TV set*) ist von ihr repariert worden.

   (können) _____

8. Er wurde nicht von mir geraten.

   (wollen) _____

9. Ihm wird für seine Großzügigkeit (*generosity*) gedankt.

   (sollen) _____

10. Das kranke Pferd ist durch einen Schuss getötet worden.

    (müssen) _____

The prepositional phrase that tells *by whom* or *what* something was done does not always begin with **von** in German.

> Ihm ist damit **von Erik** geholfen worden.　　*He was helped with that by Erik.*

In many cases, the preposition to use is **durch**. Use **durch** when the object of that preposition is the *cause* of the action or is the *means* by which the action was carried out. For example:

> Das Haus wurde **durch** ein Feuer bedroht.　　*The house was threatened by a fire.*
> Die Krankheit wurde **durch** Bakterien verursacht.　　*The disease was caused by bacteria.*

In Chapter 10, you encountered the use of the verb **lassen** to form a passive meaning. This occurs when the verb is accompanied by its reflexive pronoun and, most commonly, is conjugated in the third person.

> Das lässt sich leicht beweisen.　　*That can be easily proved.*
> Diese Probleme ließen sich nicht lösen.　　*These problems could not be solved.*

This structure is a replacement for the modal **können** followed by a passive voice infinitive.

ÜBUNG
15·6

Circle the letter of the word or phrase that best completes each sentence.

1. Das Rathaus ist _____ den Angriff zerstört worden.
   a. wird　　　　　　b. durch　　　　　　c. von　　　　　　d. konnte

2. Das Brot _____ von Frau Bauer gekauft.
   a. werden　　　　　b. lässt sich　　　　c. wurde　　　　　d. ließen sich

3. Diese Klasse wird von Herrn Brecht _____.
   a. unterrichtet werden　　b. geholfen werden　　c. lernen lassen　　d. studieren können

4. _____ wurde für seine interessante Rede gedankt.
   a. Dem Bürgermeister　b. Mein Chef　　　c. Unseren Freund　d. Diese Professorin

5. Ein Kaufhaus _____ nicht im Stadtzentrum gebaut werden.
   a. durch　　　　　　b. sollen　　　　　　c. wurde　　　　　d. kann

6. Die Maus wurde von dem Adler _____.
   a. gefangen   b. fressen wollen   c. essen   d. genommen werden

7. _____ ist das Glas Bier bestellt worden?
   a. Durch ihn   b. Dadurch   c. Wer   d. Von wem

8. Es hat _____ nicht tun lassen.
   a. sie   b. ihren   c. sich   d. mich

9. Der Polizist ist von meiner Tante gefragt _____.
   a. worden   b. geworden   c. werden   d. wurden

10. Manche Krankheiten _____ vielleicht niemals geheilt werden.
    a. wird   b. kann   c. müsst   d. werden

Subjunctive mood

Sometimes English speakers consider the German subjunctive mood simply a nuisance. It's hardly that, but it's understandable that English speakers occasionally feel this way. The English subjunctive still exists, but it has been in decline for a long time, and people just don't believe there's much of a need for it. Remnants of the subjunctive appear here and there in people's usage, but often those same people don't even know that the verb in a sentence they just uttered was in the subjunctive mood. For example:

> Be that as it **may**, I won't participate in this plan.
> Long **live** the king!
> I suggest you **be** on time from now on.

About the only time English speakers use the subjunctive mood consistently is with the auxiliary *would*.

> *I would really like to meet your sister.*
> *She would help me if she had more time.*

Because the English subjunctive mood is losing its popularity, the German subjunctive mood sometimes suffers and is not looked at carefully enough by those learning the language. This chapter will attempt to alter that point of view and show the significant areas where the subjunctive mood is used and how to apply its conjugations.

Subjunctive I

Let's look first at how the subjunctive I is formed. It is sometimes called the *present subjunctive* because it is derived from the infinitive stem of a verb and resembles the present tense. The subjunctive I verb endings are quite consistent: **-e**, **-est**, **-e**, **-en**, **-et**, **-en**. The conjugation of a verb with these endings is rather simple, because nearly all verbs are conjugated exactly the same way. There are only a few irregularities.

The process is simple: Identify the stem of the verb (e.g., **lachen = lach**). Apply the subjunctive I endings:

ich lache	wir lachen
du lachest	ihr lachet
er lache	sie/Sie lachen

For the most part, verbs conjugated in subjunctive I do not change their meaning in any way: **ich lache** (*I laugh*), **du lachest** (*you laugh*), **er lache** (*he laughs*), and so on. Let's look at a variety of other verbs, some of which have an irregular present tense conjugation. Any such irregularity is not used in subjunctive I.

suchen	kommen	sehen	fahren	wissen
to look for	to come	to see	to drive	to know
ich suche	komme	sehe	fahre	wisse
du suchest	kommest	sehest	fahrest	wissest
er suche	komme	sehe	fahre	wisse
wir suchen	kommen	sehen	fahren	wissen
ihr suchet	kommt	sehet	fahret	wisset
sie/Sie suchen	kommen	sehen	fahren	wissen

The verbs **haben**, **sein**, and **werden** always deserve a special look, because they are the building blocks of other tenses:

haben	sein	werden
ich habe	sei	werde
du habest	seiest	werdest
er habe	sei	werde
wir haben	seien	werden
ihr habt	seiet	werdet
sie/Sie haben	seien	werden

ÜBUNG
16·1

Conjugate each infinitive in the present tense and in subjunctive I.

1. warten

ich _____ _____

du _____ _____

er _____ _____

wir _____ _____

ihr _____ _____

sie/Sie _____ _____

2. vergessen

ich _____ _____

du _____ _____

er _____ _____

wir _____ _____

ihr _____ _____

sie/Sie _____ _____

3. schlagen

ich _____ _____

du _____ _____

er _____ _____

wir _____ _____

ihr _____ _____

sie/Sie _____ _____

4. ausgeben

ich _____ _____

du _____ _____

er _____ _____

wir _____ _____

ihr _____ _____

sie/Sie _____ _____

5. empfehlen

ich   _____ _____

du   _____ _____

er   _____ _____

wir   _____ _____

ihr   _____ _____

sie/Sie   _____ _____

The modal auxiliaries are not exceptional in subjunctive I. The stem of the verb is identified, and the subjunctive I endings are applied. This means that modals with an umlaut in the infinitive retain that umlaut, unlike the present tense conjugation. Compare the two conjugations of **müssen** and **wollen**:

	PRESENT TENSE	SUBJUNCTIVE I	PRESENT TENSE	SUBJUNCTIVE I
ich	muss	müsse	will	wolle
du	musst	müssest	willst	wollest
er	muss	müsse	will	wolle
wir	müssen	müssen	wollen	wollen
ihr	müsst	müsset	wollt	wollet
sie/Sie	müssen	müssen	wollen	wollen

ÜBUNG
16·2

Conjugate each verb in the present tense and in subjunctive I.

1. können

ich _____ _____

du _____ _____

er _____ _____

wir _____ _____

ihr _____ _____

sie/Sie _____ _____

2. mögen

ich _____ _____

du _____ _____

er _____ _____

wir _____ _____

ihr _____ _____

sie/Sie _____ _____

3. sollen

ich _____ _____

du _____ _____

er _____ _____

wir _____ _____

ihr _____ _____

sie/Sie _____ _____

4. dürfen

ich _____ _____

du _____ _____

er _____ _____

wir _____ _____

ihr _____ _____

sie/Sie _____ _____

5. sein

ich	_____	_____
du	_____	_____
er	_____	_____
wir	_____	_____
ihr	_____	_____
sie/Sie	_____	_____

The subjunctive I conjugation is used primarily in *indirect discourse*. When someone's statement is reported by someone else, that is *indirect discourse*. For example:

Direct discourse
Mary: "John is acting like a fool."

Indirect discourse
Mary said that John is acting like a fool.

In English indirect discourse, there usually is no change in the verb in the statement that was direct discourse. German is different. The verb in indirect discourse is usually conjugated in subjunctive I. This occurs in sentences that report the discourse in the past tense and that are more formal in nature. Compare the following pairs of sentences:

DIRECT DISCOURSE		FORMAL INDIRECT DISCOURSE
Er wohnt in Bonn.	*He lives in Bonn.*	Sie sagte, dass er in Bonn **wohne**.
Sie ist Deutsche.	*She is German.*	Er berichtete, dass sie Deutsche **sei**.
Wird es regnen?	*Will it rain?*	Lars fragte, ob es regnen **werde**.

ÜBUNG
16·3

Using the phrase provided, rewrite each direct discourse sentence as indirect discourse.

Meine Mutter sagte, dass _____

1. Mein Bruder ist wieder krank geworden.

_____

2. Unser Lehrer hat heute nachmittag (*afternoon*) angerufen.

_____

3. Herr Bauer will seinen Wagen verkaufen.

_____

4. Ihre Nachbarin wird Schauspielerin (*actress*).

_____

5. Niemand kann das Problem lösen.

_____

Thomas fragte, ob _____

6. Ist der Vogel von Erik gefangen worden?

_____

7. Muss eure Schwester hier in der Küche spielen?

_____

8. Singt sie gut?

_____

9. Hat er jetzt genug Geld?

_____

10. Verstehst du es?

_____

Subjunctive II

Subjunctive II is sometimes called the *past subjunctive* because it is formed from the past tense stem of a verb. The subjunctive II endings are identical to the endings in subjunctive I: **-e, -est, -e, -en, -et, -en**. The past tense conjugations of regular verbs use the suffix **-te**. Most verbs that form their past tense in this way are identical to that tense when in subjunctive II.

PAST TENSE	SUBJUNCTIVE I
ich lachte	lachte
du lachtest	lachtest
er lachte	lachte
wir lachten	lachten
ihr lachtet	lachtet
sie/Sie lachten	lachten

Irregular verbs use their irregular past tense stem followed by the endings **-e, -est, -e, -en, -et, -en** in subjunctive II. If the verb has an umlaut vowel (**a, o, u**), an umlaut is added in subjunctive II. For example:

	schlafen, schlief	fahren, fuhr	essen, aß	trinken, trank
ich	schliefe	führe	äße	tränke
du	schliefest	führest	äßest	tränkest
er	schliefe	führe	äße	tränke
wir	schliefen	führen	äßen	tränken
ihr	schliefet	führet	äßet	tränket
sie/Sie	schliefen	führen	äßen	tränken

Let's take a look at what happens to **haben**, **sein**, and **werden** as well as the modal auxiliaries:

	haben	**sein**	**werden**	**können**	**wollen**
ich	hätte	wäre	würde	könnte	wollte
du	hättest	wärest	würdest	könntest	wolltest
er	hätte	wäre	würde	könnte	wollte
wir	hätten	wären	würden	könnten	wollten
ihr	hättet	wäret	würdet	könntet	wolltet
sie/Sie	hätten	wären	würden	könnten	wollten

Verbs that have a mixed conjugation (see Chapter 14) have a unique formation for subjunctive II. Compare the two forms of subjunctive:

INFINITIVE		SUBJUNCTIVE I	SUBJUNCTIVE II
brennen	*burn*	er brenne	er brennte
bringen	*bring*	er bringe	er brächte
denken	*think*	er denke	er dächte
kennen	*know*	er kenne	er kennte
nennen	*name*	er nenne	er nennte
rennen	*run*	er renne	er rennte
senden	*send*	er sende	er sendete
wissen	*know*	er wisse	er wüsste

The subjunctive II conjugations are used in indirect discourse when a statement is reported *casually*.

DIRECT DISCOURSE		CASUAL INDIRECT DISCOURSE
Er wohnt in Bonn.	*He lives in Bonn.*	Sie sagte, dass er in Bonn **wohnte**.
Sie ist Deutsche.	*She is German.*	Er berichtete, dass sie Deutsche **wäre**.
Wird es regnen?	*Will it rain?*	Lars fragte, ob es regnen **würde**.

In formal indirect discourse, the subjunctive II conjugation is used where the present tense conjugation and the subjunctive I conjugation are identical. This occurs with the first- and third-person plural. For example:

DIRECT DISCOURSE	FORMAL INDIRECT DISCOURSE
Sie wohnen in Bonn.	Sie sagte, dass sie in Bonn **wohnten**.
Die Jungen haben keine Zeit.	Sie sagte, dass die Jungen keine Zeit **hätten**.
Können Sie uns verstehen?	Er fragte, ob Sie uns verstehen **könnten**.

If a direct discourse statement is in the past tense or a perfect tense, it is structured as a perfect tense in subjunctive I or II. For example:

Er war krank.	Sie sagte, dass er krank gewesen sei/wäre.
Er ist krank gewesen.	Sie sagte, dass er krank gewesen sei/wäre.
Er war krank gewesen.	Sie sagte, dass er krank gewesen sei/wäre.

Using the phrase provided, rewrite each direct discourse sentence as casual indirect discourse.

Der Reporter berichtete, dass _____

1. Der Wissenschaftler (*scientist*) ist heute gestorben.

   _____

2. Er kann sich nicht daran gewöhnen (*get used to it*).

   _____

3. Der Dieb wurde von den Polizisten gesehen.

   _____

4. Man soll den Arzt täglich benachrichtigen (*keep informed daily*).

   _____

5. Viele waren beim Unglück (*accident*) umgekommen.

   _____

Die Schauspielerin fragte, (ob) _____

6. Warum fährt die Eisenbahn (*railroad*) nicht mehr?

   _____

7. Hat der Fluss die Brücke fortgerissen (*ripped away*)?

   _____

8. Befinden sie sich auf einer Insel (*located on an island*)?

   _____

9. Wie lange können die Männer wandern?

   _____

10. Will Ihre Tante nach Paris reisen?

    _____

Wenn

The interrogative **wenn** means *when* or *whenever*. However, it is also used to introduce a subjunctive II clause, and in such a case it means *if*. For example:

Wenn er nur hier wäre!	*If only he were here!*
Wenn das Dorf nicht so weit gewesen wäre!	*If only the village were not so far away!*

A **wenn**-clause can be accompanied by a second clause. That second clause usually contains the auxiliary **würde** (*would*) followed by an infinitive. Let's look at some examples:

Wenn Martin mehr Geld hätte, würde er einen Sportwagen kaufen.	*If Martin had more money, he would buy a sports car.*
Wenn das Wetter besser wäre, würden wir zum Stadtpark gehen.	*If the weather were better, we would go to the city park.*

In the second clause of such sentences, **würde** is usually avoided if there is more than one verb in the clause. For example:

Wenn er Deutsch verstehen könnte, könnte er mit meinem Großvater sprechen.	*If he could understand German, he could speak with my grandfather.*
Wenn ich in Amerika gewesen wäre, hätte ich meinen Onkel besucht.	*If I had been in America, I would have visited my uncle.*

Just like in English, in German the **wenn**-clause can be in either the first or second position of the sentence.

Wenn Martin mehr Geld hätte, würde er einen Sportwagen kaufen.

Martin würde einen Sportwagen kaufen, wenn er mehr Geld hätte.

ÜBUNG
16·5

Complete each sentence with any appropriate clause.

1. Wenn _____, würde ich ihr ein Geschenk geben.

2. Wenn _____, hätte Stefan seine Schwester mitgebracht.

3. Wenn er vierzig Euro hätte, _____.

4. Wenn Sabine besser gelernt hätte, _____.

5. Der Lehrer würde ihm helfen, wenn _____.

6. Niemand wäre in dieses Restaurant gegangen, wenn _____.

7. Der Chef hätte Sonja gelobt (*praised*), wenn _____.

8. _____, wenn der Schauspieler mit mir tanzte.

9. _____, wenn er zu Hause gewesen wäre.

10. Wenn _____, könnten wir das verlorene Geld finden.

Als ob

Als ob is a conjunction that introduces a clause that requires a subjunctive II conjugation. It is sometimes said and written as **als wenn** and means *as if*. For example:

Martin tut so, als ob er das Problem lösen könnte.	*Martin acts as if he could solve the problem.*
Sie redet immer, als ob sie reich wäre.	*She always talks as if she were rich.*

A few verbs form the subjunctive II conjugation with a stem different from the past tense stem. The most common of these verbs are:

INFINTIVE		SUBJUNCTIVE II
empfehlen	*recommend*	empföhle
helfen	*help*	hülfe
schwimmen	*swim*	schwömme
stehen	*stand*	stünde, stände
sterben	*die*	stürbe
verderben	*spoil*	verdürbe
verstehen	*understand*	verstünde, verstände
werfen	*throw*	würfe

ÜBUNG
16·6

Using the phrase provided, write a complete sentence with each sentence.

Sie tat so, als ob _____

1. Sie ist in Thomas verliebt.

   _____

2. Sie hat mich gar nicht gesehen.

   _____

3. Wir sind nicht ihre Freunde gewesen.

   _____

4. Der Film ist langweilig.

   _____

5. Ich bin heute abend müde (*tired*).

   _____

Der Mann singt, als ob _____

6. Er hat eine wunderbare Stimme (*voice*).

   _____

7. Alle klatschen Beifall (*applaud*).

   _____

8. Er ist allein im Wartesaal (*waiting room*).

   _____

9. Er steht vor einem Mikrofon.

   _____

10. Er erwartet Geld von uns.

   _____

Ihre Augen sahen aus (*looked like*), als wenn _____

11. Sie ist krank geworden.

   _____

12. Sie wollte weinen.

   _____

13. Sie hat ein Ungeheuer (*monster*) gesehen.

   _____

14. Sie kann nicht klar sehen.

   _____

15. Die Lampe ist zu hell gewesen.

   _____

 # Numbers and numerals

You are already familiar with numbers and counting in German: **eins**, **zwei**, **drei**, **vier**, **fünf**, and so on. The number **eins** is used when counting numbers in a row. When **eins** refers to the *amount* of persons or things, **eins** is not the only form used, because gender and case play a role. For example:

Wie viele Bleistifte sind das?	*How many pencils are there?*
Einer. (**Bleistift** *is masculine.*)	*One.*
Wie viele Bleistifte hast du?	*How many pencils do you have?*
Einen. (*masculine, direct object*)	*One.*
Wie viele Blumen sind das?	*How many flowers are there?*
Wie viele Blumen hast du?	*How many flowers do you have?*
Eine. (**Blume** *is feminine.*)	*One.*
Wie viele Bücher sind das?	*How many books are there?*
Wie viele Bücher hast du?	*How many books do you have?*
Eins. (**Buch** *is neuter.*)	*One.*

This usage of **einer**, **eine**, **eins** is pronominal. Let's look at a few more examples:

Siehst du die beiden Jungen dort drüben?	*Do you see the two boys over there?*
Ja, aber ich kenne sie nicht.	*Yes, but I don't know them.*
Einer ist mein Cousin. Der Andere ist sein Freund.	*One is my cousin. The other is his friend.*
Diese Frauen sind Touristinnen.	*These women are tourists.*
Ja, **eine** kommt aus Deutschland.	*Yes, one is from Germany.*
Wessen Geschenke sind das?	*Whose gifts are those?*
Eins ist für meinen Bruder, und **eins** ist für mich.	*One is for my brother, and one is for me.*

*Answer each question with words of your choice. Use a form of **einer** as a replacement for the word in bold. For example:*

Hast du einen **Bleistift**?

Ja, ich habe einen in meiner Tasche.

1. Wie viele **Männer** wohnen in diesem Haus?

   _____

2. Für wen sind die beiden **Zeitungen**?

   _____

3. Kennst du die **Kinder** an der Ecke?

   _____

4. Wie viele **Wagen** hat euer Vater?

   _____

5. Wie viele **Universitäten** gibt es in unserer stadt?

   _____

6. Siehst du die neuen **Lehrerinnen**?

   _____

7. Wie viele **Schiffe** waren im Hafen (*harbor*)?

   _____

8. Warum hast du drei **Pullover**?

   _____

9. Hast du viele neue **Blusen** gekauft?

   _____

10. Hat Erik mit allen neuen **Studentinnen** gesprochen?

    _____

Mathematik

Numbers are used in mathematics in German in the same way as in English. Only some of the terminology is different. In addition and subtraction, there are two ways to form statements. For example:

Drei und vier ist sieben.	*Three plus/and four is seven.*
Drei plus vier gleich sieben.	
Acht weniger zwei ist sechs.	*Eight minus two is six.*
Acht minus zwei ist sechs.	

In multiplication there is one general way of expressing statements, although the product follows either **ist** or **gleich** as in addition and subtraction. For example:

Drei mal sechs ist achtzehn.   *Three times six is eighteen.*
Drei mal sechs gleich achtzehn.

The option of **ist** or **gleich** occurs in division as well. There is also the option of using **geteilt** (*divided*) in the statement. For example:

Zwölf (geteilt) durch vier ist drei.   *Twelve divided by four is three.*
Zwölf (geteilt) durch vier gleich drei.

ÜBUNG
17·2

Rewrite the formulas as German sentences.

1. 8 + 7 = 15

_____

2. 7 × 3 = 21

_____

3. 14 ÷ 7 = 2

_____

4. 99 − 59 = 40

_____

5. 48 ÷ 8 = 6

_____

Ordinal numbers

Ordinal numbers are used to describe *what order* persons or things are in: *first*, *second*, *third*, and so on. In German, there are only a few irregular ordinal numbers. Most ordinal numbers from *first* to *nineteenth* merely add the suffix **-te** with any needed adjective ending. For example:

zweite	*second*
vierte	*fourth*
fünfte	*fifth*
sechste	*sixth*
elfte	*eleventh*
siebzehnte	*seventeenth*
neunzehnte	*nineteenth*

The few irregularities are:

erste	*first*
dritte	*third*
siebte	*seventh*

All numbers greater than nineteen form the ordinal with the suffix **-ste** and any needed adjective ending. For example:

zwanzigste	*twentieth*
vierzigste	*fortieth*
achtundneunzigste	*ninety-eighth*
hundertste	*hundredth*
tausendste	*thousandth*

ÜBUNG
17·3

Write the ordinal form of each of the numbers provided.

1. zehn _____

2. fünfzehn _____

3. dreißig _____

4. zweiundachtzig _____

5. eins _____

6. dreizehn _____

7. sieben _____

8. zweihundert _____

9. siebzig _____

10. drei _____

Since ordinals are adjectives, they conform to the rules of adjective usage like any other adjective. For example:

Kennst du den Mann in der **ersten** Reihe?	*Do you know the man in the first row?*
Sie ist am **zwanzigsten** März geboren.	*She was born on the twentieth of March.*
Sein **drittes** Buch war nicht interessant.	*His third book was not interesting.*

When using ordinals with dates, use the nominative case to tell *what date* it is. Use the dative case following **am** (contraction of **an dem**) to say *on what date* something occurs. For example:

Heute ist **der vierte** Oktober.	*Today is the fourth of October.*
Tina kommt **am vierten** Oktober nach Hause.	*Tina is coming home on the fourth of October.*

To ask what the date is, use one of two expressions:

Welches Datum haben wir heute?   *What is today's date?*

Der Wievielte ist heute?   *What is today's date?*

ÜBUNG

17·4

Use the dates provided to write three sentences. The first sentence will be the question What is today's date? *Use either of the two forms to ask the question. In the second sentence, say that* today is *the date provided. In the third sentence, write an original sentence that tells when something occurred. For example:*

sechs September

Der Wievielte ist heute?

Heute ist der sechste September.

Erik fährt am sechsten September nach Italien.

1. zehn Dezember

_____

_____

_____

2. eins Januar

_____

_____

_____

3. einunddreißig Juli

_____

_____

_____

4. drei April

_____

_____

_____

5. sieben Mai

_____

_____

_____

When large numbers are used as years, they are said in two parts just like in English: *1912 = nineteen twelve, 2011 = twenty eleven.* (In the years after 1999, many people made the first part of the year *two thousand* rather than *twenty*. Therefore, 2011 becomes *two thousand eleven*. German tends to use that format as well.) Let's look at a few examples of how years are said:

neunzehnhundertzweiundzwanzig = 1922

neunzehnhunderteinundachtzig = 1981

zweitausendfünf = 2005

zweitausendzwölf = 2012

When saying *in what year* something occurs, there are two formats to use: (1) simply add the year to the sentence without any preposition; (2) make the year the object of the preposition **im** (contraction of **in dem**) and the word **Jahre**. For example:

Meine Tante ist 1998 gestorben.   *My aunt died in 1998.*

Meine Tante ist **im Jahre** 1998 gestorben.

ÜBUNG
17·5

*Using the string of words provided, write two sentences. In one sentence just use the year, and in the other use the year together with the phrase **im Jahre**. For example:*

Martin / fahren / 2005 / nach Italien

Martin ist 2005 nach Italien gefahren.

Martin ist im Jahre 2005 nach Italien gefahren.

1. wir / kaufen / unser Haus / 1985

   _____

   _____

2. ich / reisen / 2011 / in die Schweiz

   _____

   _____

3. Zwillinge / 1998 / geboren

   _____

   _____

4. er / anfangen / 2001 / in Amerika / zu arbeiten

   _____

   _____

5. mein Bruder / dienen / 2009 / in Afghanistan

   _____

   _____

Indefinite numerals

Indefinite numerals are so named because they do not denote a specific amount. One such word is **viel** (*much, many*). **Viel** could refer to five people or things or a hundred people or things. The amount is *indefinite*. The most commonly used of the indefinite numerals that *cannot be declined* are:

alles	*everything*
etwas	*some*
mehr	*more*
nichts	*nothing*
viel	*much*
wenig	*little*

Endings do not attach themselves to these indefinite numerals no matter what case or gender is involved. For example:

nom.	Mehr Geld wird euch nicht helfen.	*More money will not help you.*
acc.	Ich brauche mehr Geld.	*I need more money.*
dat.	Wie kannst du von mehr Geld sprechen?	*How can you talk about more money?*
gen.	Trotz mehr Geldes sind sie noch arm.	*Despite more money, they are still poor.*

Alles and **nichts** are unique in that they do not modify an accompanying noun. For example:

nom.	Nichts kann das Problem lösen.	*Nothing can solve the problem.*
acc.	Sie verlangt nichts.	*She demands nothing.*
dat.	Die Frauen reden von nichts.	*The women talk about nothing.*
gen.	Anstatt nichts bekam sie drei Geschenke.	*Instead of nothing, she got three gifts.*

ÜBUNG
17·6

Rewrite each sentence with the indefinite numerals provided.

Die Kinder trinken _____ Milch.

1. mehr _____

2. etwas _____

3. wenig _____

4. viel _____

Sie braucht wieder _____ Zeit.

5. mehr _____

6. etwas _____

7. wenig _____

8. viel _____

Other indefinite numerals tend to be used with plural nouns, some of which require a declension. They are:

alle	*all*
die meisten	*the most*
ein paar	*a couple*
einige	*some*
manche	*many a*
viele	*many*
wenige	*few*

Alle, **die meisten**, and **manche** are declined like **der**-words.

nom.	alle netten Leute	die meisten Kinder	manche alten Frauen
acc.	alle netten Leute	die meisten Kinder	manche alten Frauen
dat.	allen netten Leuten	den meisten Kindern	manchen alten Frauen
gen.	aller netten Leute	der meisten Kinder	mancher alten Frauen

Viele and **wenige** require a special declension.

nom.	viele alte Bücher	wenige schwere Probleme
acc.	viele alte Bücher	wenige schwere Probleme
dat.	vielen alten Büchern	wenigen schweren Problemen
gen.	vieler alter Bücher	weniger schwerer Probleme

Ein paar is unique in that it is not declined when used with cases and gender.

Er spricht mit ein paar englischen Touristen.	*He speaks with a couple English tourists.*

Refer to Chapter 7 for a thorough look at these numerals.

ÜBUNG
17·7

Circle the letter of the word or phrase that best completes each sentence.

1. _____ Ausländer studieren in Deutschland.
   a. Viele   b. Nichts   c. Den Meisten   d. Alles

2. _____ Studenten haben Deutsch schon gelernt.
   a. Einige   b. Allen   c. Eins   d. Etwas

3. Ich kenne _____ Gäste nicht.
   a. wenig   b. die meisten   c. etwas   d. alles

4. Weihnachten ist _____ Dezember.
   a. fünfundzwanzig   b. fünfundzwanzigste   c. fünfundzwanzigsten   d. am fünfundzwanzigsten

5. Mein Onkel hat _____ Bier getrunken.
   a. viel   b. viele   c. vieles   d. vielen

6. Meine Schwester will _____ neue Kleider kaufen.
   a. wenig   b. eins   c. ein paar   d. manches

7. Einige _____ machen täglich einen Fehler.
   a. Schülern   b. Menschen   c. die Mädchen   d. Ärztin

8. _____ alte Männer dienen in der Armee.
   a. Manche   b. Alle   c. Nichts   d. Wenige

9. Vierundzwanzig _____ zehn ist vierzehn.
   a. plus   b. weniger   c. gleich   d. viel

10. Mozart wurde _____ 1756 in Salzburg geboren.
    a. in   b. im Jahre   c. am   d. an

Infinitive clauses

German infinitives have a variety of endings. The most common ending is -**en** (**gehen, fahren, sehen, haben, werden**). Other infinitive ends are -**eln** (**entwickeln, handeln, schütteln**) and -**ern** (**dauern, hämmern**). And one verb has its own special formation as an infinitive: **sein**.

Infinitives can be accompanied by the modal auxiliaries (see Chapter 9) as well as **sehen, hören, lassen**, and **helfen** (see Chapter 10). For example:

Modals

Ich kann es nicht **verstehen**.

Er sollte im Garten **arbeiten**.

Wir haben in die Stadt **fahren** wollen.

Wirst du zu Hause **bleiben** müssen?

Sehen, hören, lassen, helfen

Ich sehe die Kinder **spielen**.

Wer hörte meine Tochter **singen**?

Lars hat den Wagen **waschen** lassen.

Ich werde euch **aufräumen** helfen.

Es

When other verbs are used that are accompanied by an infinitive, the infinitive is often preceded by the word **zu**. This usually occurs following a statement that begins with **es** and that *anticipates* the action of the infinitive. Let's look at some example sentences:

Es ist wichtig diese Probleme **zu** lösen.	*It is important to solve these problems.*
Es wird nicht möglich sein früher ab**zu**fahren.	*It will not be possible to depart earlier.*
Es wurde leicht ihn **zu** betrügen.	*It became easy to deceive him.*
Es kann schwer sein im Ausland **zu** leben.	*It can be hard to live abroad.*

With separable prefixes, the word **zu** is placed between the prefix and the infinitive, and the verb is written as one word. With inseparable prefixes, **zu** stands separately before the infinitive.

wegzulaufen	*to run away*
mitzubringen	*to bring along*
zu versprechen	*to promise*
zu erwarten	*to await, expect*

ÜBUNG
18·1

Using the infinitive provided in parentheses, complete each sentence with an original infinitive clause. For example:

Es ist wichtig _____.

(helfen) *diesen alten Leuten zu helfen*

Es war sehr unangenehm (*unpleasant*) _____.

1. (besuchen) _____

2. (sprechen) _____

3. (arbeiten) _____

4. (anrufen) _____

5. (essen) _____

Es fiel mir nicht ein (*didn't occur to me*) _____.

6. (begrüßen) _____

7. (schenken) _____

8. (danken) _____

9. (mitbringen) _____

10. (erklären [*explain*]) _____

Es ist unmöglich _____.

11. (retten [*save*]) _____

12. (reisen) _____

13. (verkaufen) _____

14. (kennen lernen) _____

15. (verstehen) _____

Infinitive clauses can be formed from verb phrases that have any variety of auxiliaries. However, it is the auxiliary that becomes the infinitive and is preceded by **zu**. For example:

Modal auxiliary

Ich **kann** mit den Kindern spielen.	*I can play with the children.*
... mit den Kindern spielen **zu können**.	*. . . to be able to play with the children.*

Haben

Wir **haben** mit Herrn Bauer gesprochen.	*We (have) spoke(n) with Mr. Bauer.*
... mit Herrn Bauer gesprochen **zu haben**.	*. . . to have spoken with Mr. Bauer.*

Sein

Sie **ist** nach Belgien gefahren.	*She (has) traveled to Belgium.*
... nach Belgien gefahren **zu sein**.	*. . . to have traveled to Belgium.*

Lassen

Martin **ließ** einen neuen Anzug machen.	*Martin had a new suit made.*
... einen neuen Anzug machen **zu lassen**.	*. . . to have a new suit made.*

Passive voice

Sie wurde von Erik geküsst.	*She was kissed by Erik.*
... von Erik geküsst **zu werden**.	*. . . to be kissed by Erik.*

To reflect the perfect tenses in an infinitive clause, the auxiliary is accompanied by a past participle.

Er hat es gesehen.	*He saw it.*
... es gesehen **zu haben**.	*. . . to have seen it.*
Wir sind nach Hause gegangen.	*We went home.*
... nach Hause gegangen **zu sein**.	*. . . to have gone home.*
Sie ist von Erik geküsst worden.	*She was kissed by Erik.*
... von Erik geküsst worden **zu sein**.	*. . . to have been kissed by Erik.*

ÜBUNG 18·2

Rewrite each sentence as an infinitive clause. If the sentence is in a perfect tense, retain that tense in the infinitive clause.

1. Wir kaufen ein paar Blumen.

_____

2. Sie wollen mit der Ausländerin tanzen.

_____

3. Die alte Kirche ist von ihnen zerstört worden.

_____

4. Ich habe kein Eis gemocht.

_____

5. Der Witz (*joke*) wird von Tina erzählt.

_____

6. Die Touristen hören das Orchester spielen.

_____

7. Der Fahrer wird von dem Polizisten bestraft.

_____

8. Ich sehe euch bald wieder.

_____

9. Wir waren mit derselben Straßenbahn gefahren.

_____

10. Niemand hat dem weinenden Kind geholfen.

_____

ÜBUNG
18·3

Using the infinitive provided in parentheses, complete each sentence with an original infinitive clause. For example:

Es fiel mir nicht ein _____.

(helfen) *diesen alten Leuten zu helfen*

Ich musste ihm raten (*advise*) _____.

1. (gehen) _____

2. (schlafen) _____

3. (sparen [*save*]) _____

Der Taschendieb behauptete (*pickpocket maintained*) _____.

4. (gesagt haben) _____

5. (gestohlen haben) _____

6. (verstehen können) _____

Es hat mir überhaupt nicht gefallen _____.

7. (betrügen) _____

8. (singen müssen) _____

9. (gearbeitet haben) _____

Sie hat ihm versprochen _____.

10. (bleiben) _____

11. (werden) _____

12. (sprechen lernen) _____

Plötzlich (*suddenly*) fing es an _____.

13. (regnen) _____

14. (werden) _____

15. (schneien) _____

Prepositions and infinitives

Infinitive clauses are often introduced by four prepositions: **anstatt**, **außer**, **ohne**, and **um**. When combined with **zu**, three of these prepositions alter their meaning only slightly. However, **um zu** takes on a new meaning. For example:

anstatt zu gehen	*instead of going*
außer zu schreien	*except to scream*
ohne zu wissen	*without knowing*
um zu verstehen	*in order to understand*

Let's look at these prepositions in some example sentences:

Anstatt in Bonn zu bleiben, fuhr er nach Köln.	*Instead of remaining in Bonn, he went to Cologne.*
Was konnte ich tun, außer mit ihr zu streiten?	*What could I do except argue with her?*
Er ging nach Hause, ohne seiner Mutter zu danken.	*He went home without thanking his mother.*
Erik ist nicht stark genug, um mir damit zu helfen.	*Erik is not strong enough (in order) to help me with that.*

ÜBUNG
18·4

Complete each sentence with an original infinitive clause introduced by the prepositions ***anstatt, außer, ohne****, and* ***um****. For example:*

Es fiel mir nicht ein, ohne _____.

meine Frau zu kommen

Thomas saß im Garten, ohne _____.

1. _____

2. _____

3. _____

4. _____

5. _____

Was muss ich tun, außer _____?

6. _____

7. _____

8. _____

9. _____

10. _____

Sie sind um acht Uhr abgefahren, ohne _____.

11. _____

12. _____

13. _____

14. _____

15. _____

Er arbeitete viel, um _____.

16. _____

17. _____

18. _____

19. _____

20. _____

Circle the letter of the word or phrase that best completes each sentence.

1. Sie verurteilte mich, _____ mich zu hören.
   a. ohne   b. dass   c. um zu   d. es

2. Es ist wirklich _____ diesen Text zu übersetzen.
   a. unmöglich   b. anstatt   c. geraten   d. außer

3. Er hat versucht sein Fahrrad reparieren _____.
   a. zu lassen   b. haben   c. gewesen   d. zu sein

4. Es kann lange dauern, _____ ein fremdes Volk zu verstehen.
   a. kann   b. ist   c. es   d. um

5. Was haben sie getan, _____?

   a. um die Ecke zu   b. außer zu   c. von ihm geküsst   d. gestorben zu sein
      kommen   protestieren   zu werden

6. Herr Benz braucht neues Werkzeug, um eine Mauer _____ bauen.
   a. ohne   b. haben   c. zu   d. werden

7. Man muss lernen, um eine neue Sprache _____.

   a. studiert haben   b. zu erlernen   c. gelernt worden   d. lernen
                                                 zu sein

8. _____ mir zu helfen, fordert er hundert Euro von mir.
   a. Außer   b. Es   c. Sein   d. Anstatt

9. Es fällt ihr nicht ein _____.

   a. dem alten Herrn   b. um ihn zu   c. ohne es zu   d. außer zu lachen
      zu helfen   besuchen   erklären

10. _____ meinem Rat zu folgen, geht sie ihre eigenen Wege.
    a. Es   b. Ohne   c. Um zu   d. Es war wichtig

Relative clauses

A relative clause is a clause that gives additional information about an element in another clause or sentence. That element is the *antecedent*. The antecedent is most often a noun or noun phrase but can also be a pronoun or even an entire sentence. Let's look at some English examples.

Two sentences that have the same element in them can be changed to one sentence with a relative clause attached. The relative clause is formed from one of the sentences. For example, in the following two sentences, the word *mayor* is the element that is identical in both sentences:

> The **mayor** will travel to Washington. The **mayor** is a friend of mine.

The English relative pronouns are *who*, *that*, and *which*. Since *mayor* is a person, *who* can replace *mayor* as the relative pronoun that introduces the relative clause:

> The **mayor**, **who** is a friend of mine, will travel to Washington.

All relative clauses provide additional information about an element in the sentence to which they are attached. This is also true about relative clauses in the German language.

In German, the two most frequently used relative pronouns are a form of the definite article (**der, die, das**) or a form of **welcher**. Their declensions are as follows:

	MASCULINE	FEMININE	NEUTER	PLURAL	
nom.	der	die	das	die	*who*
acc.	den	die	das	die	*whom*
dat.	dem	der	dem	denen	*whom*
gen.	dessen	deren	dessen	deren	*whose*

	MASCULINE	FEMININE	NEUTER	PLURAL	
nom.	welcher	welche	welches	welche	*who*
acc.	welchen	welche	welches	welche	*whom*
dat.	welchem	welcher	welchem	welchen	*whom*
gen.	dessen	deren	dessen	deren	*whose*

Note that the genitive case (the possessive pronoun form) is identical with both definite articles and **welcher**: **dessen, deren, dessen, deren**.

German always conforms to case and gender, and relative pronouns are no exception. If the noun that is replaced is masculine nominative, the relative pronoun will be masculine nominative. If the noun is feminine dative, the relative pronoun will be feminine dative. For example:

Der Mann kommt aus Berlin. Der Mann ist ein
Freund von mir. (der Mann = *nominative*)

Der Mann, **der/welcher** ein Freund von mir ist,
kommt aus Berlin.

*The man, who is a friend of mine,
comes from Berlin.*

Das ist die Frau. Ich habe mit der Frau
gesprochen. (mit der Frau = *dative*)

Das ist die Frau, **mit der/welcher** ich
gesprochen habe.

That is the woman with whom I spoke.

In English, a preposition that accompanies a relative pronoun does not always have to precede the relative pronoun. In German, it must precede the pronoun.

*This is the man, **with** whom I spoke./This is the man, whom I spoke **with**.*
Das ist der Mann, **mit** dem ich gesprochen habe.

ÜBUNG
19·1

*Combine each sentence with the list of sentences that follow with a form of **der**. Use the second sentence as the relative clause. For example:*

Der Lehrer spricht Deutsch.

Der Lehrer ist ziemlich jung. *Der Lehrer, der ziemlich jung ist, spricht Deutsch.*

Ich kenne den Lehrer nicht. *Der Lehrer, den ich nicht kenne, spricht Deutsch.*

Die Kinder müssen jetzt nach Hause gehen.

1. Die Kinder besuchen Tina und Erik.

   _____

2. Wir haben die Kinder heute kennen gelernt.

   _____

3. Ich gab den Kindern die Bücher.

   _____

4. Die Mutter der Kinder ist krank geworden.

   _____

Das Haus ist sehr groß.

5. Das Haus ist mehr als fünfzig Jahre alt.

_____

6. Mein Onkel hat das Haus gekauft.

_____

7. Viele Bäume stehen neben dem Haus.

_____

8. Die Farbe des Hauses ist weiß.

_____

Lars tanzte mit der Schauspielerin.

9. Die Schauspielerin ist Französin.

_____

10. Ich will die Schauspielerin interviewen.

_____

11. Monika hat ein Geschenk von der Schauspielerin bekommen.

_____

12. Der Mann der Schauspielerin ist Komponist.

_____

Sie sprechen von dem Arzt.

13. Der Arzt hat 100.000 Euro gewonnen.

_____

14. Meine Tante arbeitet für den Arzt.

_____

15. Der Detektiv fragt nach dem Arzt.

_____

16. Die Praxis des Arztes ist in der Hauptstadt.

_____

*Rewrite each of the answers in Übung 19-1 with the correct form of **welcher**.*

1. _____
2. _____
3. _____
4. _____
5. _____
6. _____
7. _____
8. _____
9. _____
10. _____
11. _____
12. _____
13. _____
14. _____
15. _____
16. _____

There are clauses that *look like relative clauses* but are not. Instead, they are clauses that use a definite article as a substitute for a pronoun. For example:

Es war einmal eine Königin; **die** hatte zwei hübsche Töchter.	*There once was a queen; **she** had two beautiful daughters.*

It is clear that the article **die** in the second clause is not a relative pronoun, because in a relative clause, the conjugated verb is the last element. The preceding example sentence can be written with a relative clause. Notice where the verb is positioned:

Es war einmal eine Königin, **die** zwei hübsche Töchter hatte.	*There once was a queen, **who** had two beautiful daughters.*

Let's look at another example of this concept:

Das ist ein wunderbares Hotel; **das** kann ich euch empfehlen.	*That is a wonderful hotel; I can recommend **it** to you.*
Das ist ein wunderbares Hotel, **das** ich euch empfehlen kann.	*That is a wonderful hotel, **which** I can recommend to you.*

Complete each sentence with original relative clauses. Put the relative pronoun in the case indicated in parentheses. Use a form of the definite article. For example:

Er findet den Stuhl.

(**auf** with the dative case) Er findet den Stuhl, *auf dem eine Katze schläft.*

Kennen Sie die Leute, _____?

1. (nominative) _____

2. (accusative direct object) _____

3. (accusative preposition) _____

Ich habe einen Wagen gekauft, _____.

4. (nominative) _____

5. (**mit** with the dative case) _____

6. (genitive possessive) _____

Wir erwarten die Gäste, _____.

7. (**über** with the accusative case) _____

8. (genitive possessive) _____

Sie kaufte einen Bücherschrank, _____.

9. (**in** with the dative case) _____

10. (**in** with the accusative case) _____

Using the string of words provided, write a sentence with a relative clause. For example:

Witwe / Frau / Mann / gestorben

Eine Witwe ist eine Frau, deren Mann gestorben ist.

1. Schimmel / Pferd / Farbe / weiß

_____

2. Russe / Mann / Heimat / Russland

_____

3. weltbekannte Sängerin / Sängerin / Name / Welt / bekannt

_____

4. Handwerker / Arbeiter / Beruf / schwierg

_____

5. Waisenkind / Kind / Vater und Mutter / tot

_____

Wer

Some relative clauses are introduced by a form of **wer**. In such a sentence, **wer** can be translated as _he who_. Note that this relative pronoun does not refer to a specific person but infers a generality. Some examples in English:

> _He who lives by the sword shall perish by the sword._
> _I am grateful to him who spares the weak._

Often, _whoever_ replaces _he, who_:

> _Whoever lives by the sword shall perish by the sword._

In German, this concept of a relative pronoun is carried out by **wer** and is followed in a second clause by a form of **der**. But as is always the case in German, **wer** and **der** can function in other cases besides the nominative. For example:

nom.	Wer in Not ist, dem gebe ich mein Brot.	_I give my bread to him who is in need._
acc.	Wen seine Freunde lieben, den hassen seine Feinde.	_His enemies hate him whom his friends love._
dat.	Wem nicht zu glauben ist, dem ist nicht zu helfen.	_He cannot be helped who cannot be believed._
gen.	Wessen Wein wir trinken, dem ist immer zu danken.	_He is always to be thanked whose wine we drink._

ÜBUNG
19·5

Complete each sentence with two original clauses that require the use of **wer**, **der**.

1. _____, der ist mein Feind.

_____

_____

2. Wen sie trifft, _____.

_____

_____

3. Wem man nicht trauen kann, _____.

_____

_____

4. _____, dem wird man nie glauben.

_____

_____

5. Wer nicht arbeiten will, _____.

_____

_____

Was

The relative pronoun **was, das** (often translated as *what* or *that, which*) is similar to **wer** in that it does not refer to a specific object and is a generality. Let's look at a couple examples in English:

> *I find **what** you said most interesting.*
> ***What** he found now belongs to him.*

Let's look at the same concept in German:

> **Was** das Kind in einer Stunde fragt, **das** kann man nicht in einer Woche beantworten.
>
> *What a child asks in an hour, one cannot answer in a week.*

> **Was** er gefunden hat, **das** gehört jetzt ihm.
>
> *What he found now belongs to him.*

Was is also used with certain indefinite numerals. For example:

alles, was	*all that*
etwas, was	*some that*
manches, was	*many a thing that*
nichts, was	*nothing that*
vieles, was	*much that*

In sentences, they are used as follows:

> **Alles, was** ich habe, jetzt gehört Ihnen.
>
> *All that I have now belongs to you.*

> Ich verstehe **nichts, was** sie sagt.
>
> *I do not understand anything that she says.*

> Es gibt **vieles, was** uns sehr gefällt.
>
> *There is much that we really like.*

In addition to these phrases, **was** becomes the relative pronoun for numerous superlatives. For example:

das Beste, was	*the best thing that*
das Schönste, was	*the most beautiful thing that*

Complete each sentence with any appropriate phrase that uses the concept of the relative pronoun **was**.

1. Alles, was _____, wird immer bewundert.

2. Nichts, was gut und rein ist, _____.

3. Das ist das Schlimmste, was _____.

4. Ich habe etwas gekauft, was _____.

5. Vieles, was _____, ist total richtig.

6. Ich möchte das Beste, was _____.

7. Das ist das Schrecklichste, was _____.

8. Was _____, das ist leider nicht zu glauben.

9. Rede nichts, was _____!

10. Was das Teuerste ist, das _____.

The relative pronoun **was** can also refer to a complete sentence as its antecedent. It does not refer to a specific element in the sentence but rather to the meaning of the entire sentence. Consider this example in English:

Johnny finally got a passing grade, which pleased his parents immensely.

In that sentence, the relative pronoun *which* does not refer to *Johnny*. It does not refer to *a passing grade*. The antecedent to *which* is the entire sentence *Johnny finally got a passing grade*. This occurs in German, and the relative pronoun for this concept is **was**.

Der Weihnachtsmann hat ihnen viele Geschenke gebracht, **was** den Kindern sehr gefiel.	*Santa Claus brought them many gifts, which pleased the children very much.*
Die Armen bleiben arm, **was** eine Tragödie ist.	*The poor remain poor, which is a tragedy.*

Complete each sentence with any appropriate phrase.

1. Herr Schulze hat 5000 Euro gewonnen, was _____.

2. _____, was seiner Frau nicht gefällt.

3. Er behauptet, dass er unschuldig ist, was _____.

4. _____, was ich nicht glauben konnte.

5. _____, was eine Lüge ist.

6. Erik hat sein Abitur gemacht, was _____.

7. Sie essen und trinken zu viel, was _____.

8. _____, was niemand verstehen kann.

9. _____, was die beste Nachricht ist.

10. Ihr Sohn hat einen neuen BMW gestohlen, was _____.

When **was** is combined with prepositions, it is formed like a prepositional adverb with the prefix **wo(r)-**. For example:

Sie braucht nicht alles, **womit** sie nach Hause gekommen ist.

She does not need everything that she came home with.

Ihr Geburtstag ist am Freitag, **worauf** sie sich sehr freut.

Her birthday is on Friday, which she really is looking forward to.

Circle the letter of the word or phrase that best completes each sentence.

1. Er liest ein bisschen von dem, _____ ich geschrieben habe.
   a. womit   b. was   c. wer   d. von wem

2. Thomas spricht mit einer Freundin, _____ Sonja neulich kennen gelernt hat.
   a. der   b. den   c. die   d. deren

3. Ich besuchte einen Herrn, _____ Schwester Schauspielerin war.
   a. die   b. dessen   c. der   d. deren

4. Warum willst du ein Auto, _____ so teuer ist?
   a. den   b. dem   c. welcher   d. welches

5. Frau Benz hatte einen schlechten Unfall, _____ die Nachbarn sprechen.
   a. der   b. den   c. dessen   d. worüber

6. Einem Mann, _____, ist nicht zu helfen.
   a. den besuche ich   b. dem nicht zu   c. wem ich dafür   d. welches sehr
      jeden Tag   raten ist   danken will   unglücklich ist

7. _____ das Buch nicht gefällt, der soll es nicht lesen.
   a. Wem   b. Dem   c. Deren   d. Wofür

8. _____ Brot wir essen, dessen Lied wir singen.
   a. Wen   b. Deren   c. Was   d. Wessen

9. _____, was der Mann sagt, ist Unsinn.
   a. Welche   b. Alles   c. Jeder   d. An dessen

10. Bremen und Hamburg sind Häfen, die an der Nordsee _____.
    a. gewesen   b. wurden   c. steht   d. liegen

Writing

In this chapter you will have a variety of opportunities to do some creative writing. You will write original sentences in various formats and will complete the missing lines from dialogues. Do not be afraid to experiment and to apply new ideas that you have developed from your experience with the other chapters. Use any resources that will help you write accurately.

ÜBUNG
20·1

Write original sentences with the phrase provided in parentheses. Use the provided phrase as described in each line. For example:

(der alte Mann)

subject of the sentence

Der alte Mann wohnt nicht weit von hier.

object of a dative verb

Ich habe dem alten Mann gedankt.

(unsere ausländischen Gäste)

1. subject of the sentence

   _____

2. direct object

   _____

3. object of the preposition **mit**

   _____

4. indirect object

   _____

5. subject of a passive voice sentence

   _____

6. direct object in a subjunctive sentence

   _____

7. object of the preposition **für**

_____

8. object of the preposition **wegen**

_____

9. subject of a sentence with a double infinitive

_____

10. object of the verb **glauben**

_____

ÜBUNG
20·2

Write original sentences with the phrase provided in parentheses. Use the provided phrase as described in each line.

(das nette Mädchen)

1. subject of the sentence

_____

2. direct object

_____

3. object of the preposition **von**

_____

4. indirect object

_____

5. subject in a relative clause

_____

6. antecedent to a relative clause

_____

7. object of the preposition **ohne**

_____

8. object of the preposition **wegen**

_____

9. subject of a sentence with a modal auxiliary

_____

10. object of the verb **begegnen**

_____

_____

Write original sentences with the phrase provided in parentheses. Use the provided phrase as described in each line.

(meine junge Nichte)

1. subject of the sentence

_____

2. direct object

_____

3. object of the preposition **außer**

_____

4. indirect object

_____

5. subject of a passive voice sentence

_____

6. indirect object in a relative clause

_____

7. object of the preposition **gegen**

_____

8. object of the preposition **an**

_____

9. subject of a present perfect tense sentence

_____

10. object of the verb **helfen**

_____

_____

Write original sentences with the phrase provided in parentheses. Use the provided phrase as described in each line.

(jeder amerikanische Soldat)

1. subject of the sentence

_____

2. direct object

_____

3. object of the preposition **nach**

_____

4. indirect object

_____

5. subject of a future tense sentence

_____

6. antecedent of a possessive in a relative clause

_____

7. object of the preposition **gegen**

_____

8. object of the preposition **neben** in the dative case

_____

9. subject of a past perfect tense sentence

_____

10. object of the preposition **von** in a passive voice sentence

_____

Write original sentences with the phrase provided in parentheses. Use the provided phrase as described in each line.

(diese hohen Berge)

1. subject of a sentence with a comparison made with *als*

_____

2. direct object

_____

3. object of the preposition **zu**

_____

4. subject of a sentence with a superlative adjective

_____

5. subject of a past tense sentence with a modal auxiliary

_____

6. antecedent of a direct object in a relative clause

_____

7. object of the preposition **durch**

_____

8. object of the preposition **auf** in the accusative case

_____

9. subject of a present perfect tense sentence

_____

10. object of the preposition **anstatt**

_____

ÜBUNG
20·6

Complete each sentence with any appropriate phrase that includes the vocabulary in parentheses. For example:

Martin schläft auf dem Sofa, aber _____.

(Boden) Martin schläft auf dem Sofa, aber *die Kinder müssen auf dem Boden schlafen.*

Sabine hat etwas gekauft, was _____.

1. (ihr Mann) _____

2. (teuer) _____

3. (Einkaufszentrum) _____

4. (passen) _____

Der Richter sagte, dass _____.

5. (Gefängnis) _____

6. (unschuldig) _____

7. (Polizei) _____

8. (Verbrecher) _____

Ein Tourist hat uns gefragt, _____.

9. (wo) _____

10. (wann) _____

11. (wie) _____

12. (ob) _____

Die Jungen gehen nicht zur Schule, sondern _____.

13. (Fußball) _____

14. (schwimmen) _____

15. (Kino) _____

16. (Karten spielen) _____

Viele sind im Studentenheim geblieben, weil _____.

17. (kalt und regnerisch) _____

18. (Examen) _____

19. (Faschingfest) _____

20. (eine Rede halten) _____

Ich muss Überstunden machen, um _____.

21. (verdienen) _____

22. (bezahlen) _____

23. (Reise machen) _____

Was konnte ich tun, außer _____?

24. (protestieren) _____

25. (versuchen) _____

In the blank provided, write in a line of dialogue that fits the conversation. For example:

Ich muss in die Stadt fahren.

Fährst du mit dem Bus oder der Straßenbahn?

Ich fahre lieber mit dem Bus.

1. Sabine ist jetzt die Beste in ihrer Klasse.

   _____

   Vielleicht kann Sabine ihr helfen.

2. Willst du heute abend ins Kino gehen?

   _____

   Schade. Du arbeitest aber zu viel.

3. Am Montag hat Lars Geburtstag.

   Was willst du ihm kaufen?

   _____

4. Was für eine Bluse willst du kaufen?

   _____

   Eine weiße Bluse steht dir immer gut.

5. Ich habe leider nur fünfzehn Euro.

   _____

   Nicht weniger als fünfundzwanzig.

6. Meine Söhne fahren nach Italien.

   Können die Jungen Italienisch?

   _____

7. Wie steht mir diese Brille?

   _____

   Schade. Ich mag die Farbe.

8. Ist dieses Hemd die richtige Größe für mich?

   Ja, es passt gut.

   _____

9. Mit wem reist ihr nach Russland?

   _____

   Spricht er ein bisschen Russisch?

10. Wie lange haben die Kinder geschlafen?

_____

Um wie viel Uhr frühstückt ihr?

11. Von wem wurde der Fremde eingeladen?

_____

Nein, ich kenne den Mann überhaupt nicht.

12. Hast du versucht mich anzurufen?

_____

Wie schrecklich. Ich kann ohne Telefon nicht leben.

13. Das Fleisch sieht gut aus. Wo hast du es gekauft?

_____

Ich wusste nicht, das sein Geschäft noch offen ist.

14. In Freiburg sind wir mit der Seilbahn gefahren.

_____

Gar nicht gefährlich. Es war eine angenehme Fahrt.

15. Warum ist deine Mutter froh, dass es regnet?

_____

Ich vergesse, dass sie Nelken und Tulpen liebt.

ÜBUNG
20·8

Complete the lines of dialogue with any appropriate phrases.

SABINE: Guten Tag, Herr Bauer. _____?

HERR BAUER: _____. Ich möchte meiner Frau ein Geschenk kaufen.

SABINE: _____?

HERR BAUER: Nein, ihr Geburtstag ist im April. _____.

SABINE: Ich gehe auch ins Einkaufszentrum. _____.

HERR BAUER: Ich kenne Erik nicht. _____?

SABINE: Nein, ist nur ein Freund von mir. _____.

HERR BAUER: Ist Martin noch Student oder _____?

SABINE: Er ist jetzt Bauingenier. _____.

HERR BAUER: _____. Ich muss mich beeilen. Wiedersehen!

ÜBUNG
20·9

Complete the lines of dialogue with any appropriate phrases.

THOMAS: Ich habe Lars gestern mit einem Mädchen gesehen. _____.

WERNER: Ja, sie ist sehr schön. _____.

THOMAS: Seine Cousine? _____.

WERNER: Sie hat schon einen Freund und ist sogar _____.

THOMAS: Schade. _____?

WERNER: Ich fahre morgen mit meinem Vater in die Stadt. _____.

THOMAS: Was für ein Auto wird es sein? _____.

WERNER: Ein BMW ist zu teuer. _____.

THOMAS: Wenn ich ein Auto hätte, würde _____.

WERNER: Zuerst musst du arbeiten und _____.

ÜBUNG
20·10

Complete the lines of dialogue with any appropriate phrases.

TANTE LUISE: Rolf, warum hast du den Tisch noch nicht gedeckt? _____.

ROLF: Ich bin eben nach Hause gekommen. _____.

TANTE LUISE: Frische Brötchen mit Butter! _____.

ROLF: Ich habe schon Wasser gekocht. _____?

TANTE LUISE: _____. Ich trinke lieber Tee.

ROLF: Onkel Karl hat vor einer halben Stunde angerufen. _____.

TANTE LUISE: Der arme Mann arbeitet so viel. _____.

ROLF: Eine Reise? _____?

TANTE LUISE: Ich möchte gern Paris oder Madrid besuchen, aber _____.

ROLF: Kein Problem. In Europa _____.

TANTE LUISE: Hoffentlich hast du Recht. _____?

ROLF: Nein, nur die Brötchen. _____?

TANTE LUISE: Nein, die Kinder können Apfelsaft trinken. _____?

ROLF: Ich möchte Kaffee. _____.

APPENDIX
The principal parts of irregular verbs

Only the second-person and third-person singular are shown in the present tense. In the past tense, the third-person singular is provided. However, because of the number of irregularities in the conjugations, the full present tense conjugations of **sein** and **tun** are shown.

Indicative				Subjunctive
INFINITIVE	PRESENT	PAST	PAST PARTICIPLE	IMPERFECT
backen	bäckst; bäckt	buk *or* backte	gebacken	büke *or* backte
befehlen	befiehlst; befiehlt	befahl	befohlen	beföhle
befleißen	befleißt; befleißt	befliss	beflissen	beflisse
beginnen	beginnst; beginnt	begann	begonnen	begönne
beißen	beißt; beißt	biss	gebissen	bisse
bergen	birgst; birgt	barg	geborgen	bürge
bersten	birst; birst	barst	geborsten	börste
betrügen	betrügst; betrügt	betrog	betrogen	betröge
bewegen	bewegst; bewegt	bewog	bewogen	bewöge
biegen	biegst; biegt	bog	gebogen	böge
bieten	bietest; bietet	bot	geboten	böte
binden	bindest; bindet	band	gebunden	bände
bitten	bittest; bittet	bat	gebeten	bäte
blasen	bläst; bläst	blies	geblasen	bliese
bleiben	bleibst; bleibt	blieb	geblieben	bliebe
bleichen	bleichst; bleicht	blich	geblichen	bliche
braten	brätst; brät	briet	gebraten	briete
brechen	brichst; bricht	brach	gebrochen	bräche
brennen	brennst; brennt	brannte	gebrannt	brennte
bringen	bringst; bringt	brachte	gebracht	brächte
denken	denkst; denkt	dachte	gedacht	dächte
dingen	dingst; dingt	dingte *or* dang	gedungen *or* gedingt	dingte
dreschen	drischst; drischt	drasch	gedroschen	drösche
dringen	dringst; dringt	drang	gedrungen	dränge

Indicative				Subjunctive
INFINITIVE	PRESENT	PAST	PAST PARTICIPLE	IMPERFECT
dürfen	darfst; darf	durfte	gedurft	dürfte
empfangen	empfängst; empfängt	empfing	empfangen	empfinge
empfehlen	empfiehlst; empfiehlt	empfahl	empfohlen	empföhle
empfinden	empfindest; empfindet	empfand	empfunden	empfände
erbleichen	erbleichst; erbleicht	erbleichte or erblich	erbleicht or erblichen	erbleichte; erbliche
erlöschen	erlischst; erlischt	erlosch	erloschen	erlösche
erschrecken	erschrickst; erschrickt	erschrak	erschrocken	erschäke
erwägen	erwägst; erwägt	erwog	erwogen	erwöge
essen	isst; isst	aß	gegessen	ässe
fahren	fährst; fährt	fuhr	gefahren	führe
fallen	fällst; fällt	fiel	gefallen	fiele
fangen	fängst; fängt	fing	gefangen	finge
fechten	fichtest; ficht	focht	gefochten	föchte
finden	findest; findet	fand	gefunden	fände
flechten	flichtest; flicht	flocht	geflochten	flöchte
fliegen	fliegst; fliegt	flog	geflogen	flöge
fliehen	fliehst; flieht	floh	geflohen	flöhe
fließen	fließt; fließt	floss	geflossen	flösse
fressen	frisst; frisst	fraß	gefressen	frässe
frieren	frierst; friert	fror	gefroren	fröre
gären	gärst; gärt	gor	gegoren	göre
gebären	gebierst; gebiert	gebar	geboren	gebäre
geben	gibst; gibt	gab	gegeben	gäbe
gedeihen	gedeihst; gedeiht	gedieh	gediehen	gediehe
gehen	gehst; geht	ging	gegangen	ginge
gelten	giltst; gilt	galt	gegolten	gälte or gölte
genesen	genest; genest	genas	genesen	genäse
genießen	genießt; genießt	genoss	genossen	genösse
geraten	gerätst; gerät	geriet	geraten	geriete
gewinnen	gewinnst; gewinnt	gewann	gewonnen	gewänne or gewönne
gießen	gießt; gießt	goss	gegossen	gösse
gleichen	gleichst; gleicht	glich	geglichen	gliche
gleiten	gleitest; gleitet	glitt	geglitten	glitte
glimmen	glimmst; glimmt	glomm or glimmte	geglommen or geglimmt	glömme or glimmte
graben	gräbst; gräbt	grub	gegraben	grübe
greifen	greifst; greift	griff	gegriffen	griffe
haben	hast; hat	hatte	gehabt	hätte
halten	hältst; hält	hielt	gehalten	hielte
hangen	hängst; hängt	hing	gehangen	hinge
hauen	haust; haut	hieb	gehauen	hiebe

Indicative				Subjunctive
INFINITIVE	PRESENT	PAST	PAST PARTICIPLE	IMPERFECT
heben	hebst; hebt	hob	gehoben	höbe
heißen	heißt; heißt	hieß	geheißen	hieße
helfen	hilfst; hilft	half	gcholfen	hülfe
kennen	kennst; kennt	kannte	gekannt	kennte
klimmen	klimmst; klimmt	klomm *or* klimmte	geklommen *or* geklimmt	klömme *or* klimmte
klingen	klingst; klingt	klang	geklungen	klänge
kneifen	kneifst; kneift	kniff	gekniffen	kniffe
kommen	kommst; kommt	kam	gekommen	käme
können	kannst; kann	konnte	gekonnt	könnte
kriechen	kriechst; kriecht	kroch	gekrochen	kröche
laden	lädst *or* ladest; lädt *or* ladet	lud *or* ladete	geladen *or* geladet	lüde *or* ladete
lassen	lässt; lässt	ließ	gelassen	ließe
laufen	läufst; läuft	lief	gelaufen	liefe
leiden	leidest; leidet	litt	gelitten	litte
leihen	leihst; leiht	lieh	geliehen	liehe
lesen	liest; liest	las	gelesen	läse
liegen	liegst; liegt	lag	gelegen	läge
lügen	lügst; lügt	log	gelogen	löge
mahlen	mahlst; mahlt	mahlte	gemahlen	mahlte
mciden	meidest; meidet	mied	gemieden	miede
melken	melkst; melkt	melkte	gemelkt *or* gemolken (*adjective*)	mölke
messen	misst; misst	maß	gemessen	mässe
mögen	magst; mag	mochte	gemocht	möchte
müssen	musst; muss	musste	gemusst	müsste
nehmen	nimmst; nimmt	nahm	genommen	nähme
nennen	nennst; nennt	nannte	genannt	nennte
pfeifen	pfeifst; pfeift	pfiff	gepfiffen	pfiffe
pflegen	pflegst; pflegt	pflegte *or* pflog	gepflegt *or* gepflogen	pflegte *or* pflöge
preisen	preist; preist	pries	gepriesen	priese
quellen	quillst; quillt	quoll	gequollen	quölle
raten	rätst; rät	riet	geraten	riete
reiben	reibst; reibt	rieb	gerieben	riebe
reißen	reißt; reißt	riss	gerissen	risse
reiten	reitest; reitet	ritt	geritten	ritte
rennen	rennst; rennt	rannte	gerannt	rennte
riechen	riechst; riecht	roch	gerochen	röche
ringen	ringst; ringt	rang	gerungen	ränge
rinnen	rinnst; rinnt	rann	geronnen	rönne
rufen	rufst; ruft	rief	gerufen	riefe

Indicative				Subjunctive
INFINITIVE	PRESENT	PAST	PAST PARTICIPLE	IMPERFECT
salzen	salzt; salzt	salzte	gesalzt *or* gesalzen (*figurative*)	salzte
saufen	säufst; säuft	soff	gesoffen	söffe
saugen	saugst; saugt	sog	gesogen	söge
schaffen	schaffst; schafft	schuf	geschaffen	schüfe
schallen	schallst; schallt	schallte	geschallt	schallte *or* schölle
scheiden	scheidest; scheidet	schied	geschieden	schiede
scheinen	scheinst; scheint	schien	geschienen	schiene
schelten	schiltst; schilt	schalt	gescholten	schölte
scheren	schierst; schiert	schor *or* scherte	geschoren *or* geschert	schöre *or* scherte
schieben	schiebst; schiebt	schob	geschoben	schöbe
schießen	schießt; schießt	schoss	geschossen	schösse
schinden	schindest; schindet	schund	geschunden	schünde
schlafen	schläfst; schläft	schlief	geschlafen	schliefe
schlagen	schlägst; schlägt	schlug	geschlagen	schlüge
schleichen	schleichst; schleicht	schlich	geschlichen	schliche
schleifen	schleifst; schleift	schliff	geschliffen	schliffe
schleißen	schleißt; schleißt	schliss	geschlissen	schlisse
schliefen	schliefst; schlieft	schloff	geschloffen	schlöffe
schließen	schließt; schließt	schloss	geschlossen	schlösse
schlingen	schlingst; schlingt	schlang	geschlungen	schlänge
schmeißen	schmeißt; schmeißt	schmiss	geschmissen	schmisse
schmelzen	schmilzt; schmilzt	schmolz	geschmolzen	schmölze
schneiden	schneidest; schneidet	schnitt	geschnitten	schnitte
schrecken	schrickst; schrickt	schrak	geschrocken	schräke
schreiben	schreibst; schreibt	schrieb	geschrieben	schriebe
schreien	schreist; schreit	schrie	geschrieen	schriee
schreiten	schreitest; schreitet	schritt	geschritten	schritte
schweigen	schweigst; schweigt	schwieg	geschwiegen	schwiege
schwellen	schwillst; schwillt	schwoll	geschwollen	schwölle
schwimmen	schwimmst; schwimmt	schwamm	geschwommen	schwömme
schwinden	schwindest; schwindet	schwand	geschwunden	schwände
schwingen	schwingst; schwingt	schwang	geschwungen	schwänge
schwören	schwörst; schwört	schwur	geschworen	schwüre
sehen	siehst; sieht	sah	gesehen	sähe
sein	bin bist ist; sind seid sind	war	gewesen	wäre
senden	sendest; sendet	sandte *or* sendete	gesandt *or* gesendet	sendete
sieden	siedest; siedet	sott *or* siedete	gesotten	sötte *or* siedete

Indicative				Subjunctive
INFINITIVE	PRESENT	PAST	PAST PARTICIPLE	IMPERFECT
singen	singst; singt	sang	gesungen	sänge
sinken	sinkst; sinkt	sank	gesunken	sänke
sinnen	sinnst; sinnt	sann	gesonnen	sänne
sitzen	sitzt; sitzt	saß	gesessen	sässe
sollen	sollst; soll	sollte	gesollt	sollte
spalten	spaltest; spaltet	spaltete	gespalten *or* gespaltet	spaltete
speien	speist; speit	spie	gespieen	spiee
spinnen	spinnst; spinnt	spann	gesponnen	spönne
spleißen	spleißt; spleißt	spliss	gesplissen	splisse
sprechen	sprichst; spricht	sprach	gesprochen	spräche
sprießen	sprießt; sprießt	spross	gesprossen	sprösse
springen	springst; springt	sprang	gesprungen	spränge
stechen	stichst; sticht	stach	gestochen	stäche
stecken	steckst; steckt	steckte *or* stak	gesteckt	steckte *or* stäke
stehen	stehst; steht	stand	gestanden	stünde *or* stände
stehlen	stiehlst; stiehlt	stahl	gestohlen	stöhle
steigen	steigst; steigt	stieg	gestiegen	stiege
sterben	stirbst; stirbt	starb	gestorben	stürbe
stieben	stiebst; stiebt	stob *or* stiebte	gestoben *or* gestiebt	stöbe *or* stiebte
stinken	stinkst; stinkt	stank	gestunken	stänke
stoßen	stößt; stößt	stieß	gestoßen	stieße
streichen	streichst; streicht	strich	gestrichen	striche
streiten	streitest; streitet	stritt	gestritten	stritte
tragen	trägst; trägt	trug	getragen	trüge
treffen	triffst; trifft	traf	getroffen	träfe
treiben	treibst; treibt	trieb	getrieben	triebe
treten	trittst; tritt	trat	getreten	träte
triefen	triefst; trieft	troff	getrieft	tröffe
trinken	trinkst; trinkt	trank	getrunken	tränke
tun	tue tust tut; tun tut tun	tat	getan	täte
verderben	verdirbst; verdirbt	verdarb	verdorben	verdürbe
verdrießen	verdrießt, verdrießt	verdross	verdrossen	verdrösse
vergessen	vergisst; vergisst	vergaß	vergessen	vergässe
verhehlen	verhehlst; verhehlt	verhehlte	verhehlt *or* verhohlen	verhehlte
verlieren	verlierst; verliert	verlor	verloren	verlöre

INFINITIVE	PRESENT	PAST	PAST PARTICIPLE	IMPERFECT
verwirren	verwirrst; verwirrt	verwirrte	verwirrt *or* verworren (*adjective*)	verwirrte
wachsen	wächst; wächst	wuchs	gewachsen	wüchse
wägen	wägst; wägt	wog *or* wägte	gewogen	wöge *or* wägte
waschen	wäschst; wäscht	wusch	gewaschen	wüsche
weichen	weichst; weicht	wich	gewichen	wiche
weisen	weist; weist	wies	gewiesen	wiese
wenden	wendest; wendet	wandte *or* wendete	gewandt *or* gewendet	wendete
werben	wirbst; wirbt	warb	geworben	würbe
werden	wirst; wird	wurde	geworden	würde
werfen	wirfst; wirft	warf	geworfen	würfe
wiegen	wiegst; wiegt	wog	gewogen	wöge
winden	windest; windet	wand	gewunden	wände
wissen	weißt; weiß	wusste	gewusst	wüsste
wollen	willst; will	wollte	gewollt	wollte
zeihen	zeihst; zeiht	zieh	geziehen	ziehe
ziehen	ziehst; zieht	zog	gezogen	zöge
zwingen	zwingst; zwingt	zwang	gezwungen	zwänge

Some irregular verbs are used in impersonal expressions and are conjugated only with the third person:

INFINITIVE	PRESENT	PAST	PAST PARTICIPLE	IMPERFECT
dünken	dünkt *or* deucht	deuchte *or* dünkte	gedeucht *or* gedünkt	deuchte *or* dünkte
gelingen	gelingt	gelang	gelungen	gelänge
geschehen	geschieht	geschah	geschehen	geschähe
misslingen	misslingt	misslang	misslungen	misslänge
schwären	schwärt *or* schwiert	schwor	geschworen	schwöre
verschallen	verschillt	verscholl	verschollen	verschölle

Answer key

1 Determining gender and forming plurals

1·1   1. der   2. die   3. der   4. die   5. der   6. der   7. die   8. der   9. die   10. die

1·2   1. die   2. das   3. das   4. die   5. der   6. das   7. das   8. das   9. die   10. der

1·3   1. die   2. der   3. die   4. der   5. der   6. die   7. die   8. der   9. die   10. die
11. die   12. der   13. der   14. die   15. die   16. die   17. die   18. der   19. der
20. die   21. der   22. der   23. der   24. das   25. die   26. der   27. der   28. die
29. die   30. die

1·4   1. der   2. das   3. das   4. die   5. das   6. der   7. das   8. die   9. die   10. das
11. das   12. das   13. der   14. die   15. die   16. die   17. die   18. das   19. das
20. die   21. der   22. das   23. das   24. die   25. die   26. der   27. der   28. das
29. der   30. die

1·5   1. der   2. die   3. der   4. die   5. der   6. die   7. der   8. der   9. der   10. der
11. der   12. der   13. das   14. die   15. die   16. der   17. der   18. die
19. der   20. das

1·6   1. die Elefanten   2. die Jungen   3. die Wagen   4. die Lehrer   5. die Piloten
6. die Absätze   7. die Flüsse   8. die Löwen   9. die Diplomaten   10. die Tänzer
11. die Bleistifte   12. die Tische   13. die Schädel   14. die Böden   15. die Pinsel

1·7   1. die Häuser   2. die Gelächter   3. die Landungen   4. die Gewitter   5. die Väter
6. die Länder   7. die Radios   8. die Endungen   9. die Harmonien   10. die Gebiete
11. die Töchter   12. die Bücher   13. die Gefolgschaften   14. die Konstitutionen
15. die Junggesellen

2 Haben, sein, and werden

2·1
1. Wir hatten neue Bücher.
   Wir haben neue Bücher gehabt.
2. Sie war meine Freundin.
   Sie ist meine Freundin gewesen.
3. Meine Töchter waren Tänzerinnen.
   Meine Töchter sind Tänzerinnen gewesen.
4. Erik und Gudrun hatten ein Geschenk für dich.
   Erik und Gudrun haben ein Geschenk für dich gehabt.
5. Ich war kein Fußballspieler.
   Ich bin kein Fußballspieler gewesen.
6. Wart ihr in den USA?
   Seid ihr in den USA gewesen?
7. Hattest du keinen Bleistift?
   Hast du keinen Bleistift gehabt?
8. Wo waren Sie?
   Wo sind Sie gewesen?

9. Hattet ihr keine Handschuhe?
   Habt ihr keine Handschuhe gehabt?
10. Meine Geschwister waren zu Hause.
    Meine Geschwister sind zu Hause gewesen.
11. Ich hatte nur ein altes Kleid.
    Ich habe nur ein altes Kleid gehabt.
12. Du warst ein guter Freund.
    Du bist ein guter Freund gewesen.
13. Wart ihr in der Hauptstadt?
    Seid ihr in der Hauptstadt gewesen?
14. Hatten Sie eine Eintrittskarte?
    Haben Sie eine Eintrittskarte gehabt?
15. Unsere Lehrerin war freundlich.
    Unsere Lehrerin ist freundlich gewesen.

2·2   *Sample answers are provided.*
1. Sind diese Männer Ausländer?
2. Mein Bruder und ich haben keinen Regenschirm.
3. Ist der Arzt ein Freund von dir?
4. Ihre Tante war in der Bibliothek.
5. Mein Neffe hat nur zehn Euro gehabt.
6. War das Buch sehr alt?
7. Die neuen Bücher sind interessanter als die anderen Bücher.
8. Meine Freundin und ich sind in der Hauptstadt gewesen.
9. Frau Bauer hatte kein Geld.
10. Sein Großvater war ziemlich krank.
11. Das Bild ist auf dem Tisch.
12. Die Mädchen und ich hatten keine Zeit dafür.
13. Sind die Touristen im alten Dom gewesen?
14. Unsere Gäste haben vier Eintrittskarten gehabt.
15. Onkel Franz hatte meinen Regenschirm.
16. Die alte Frau ist im Krankenhaus gewesen.
17. Dieses Projekt hatte keinen Zweck.
18. Karl und ich waren Schulkameraden.
19. Die Sportler haben Durst gehabt.
20. Ist ihr Bruder Sportler gewesen?

2·3
1. Er hat einen Bleistift gebraucht.
2. Ich habe meinen Bruder gesucht.
3. Herr Schmidt hat Mathematik gelehrt.
4. Was habt ihr gelernt?
5. Die Jungen haben ein paar CDs gekauft.
6. Meine Eltern haben Radio gehört.
7. Was hat der Bürgermeister gesagt?
8. Es hat mich nicht gestört.
9. Gudrun hat die Blumen auf den Tisch gestellt.
10. Die Mädchen haben gern Schach gespielt.

2·4
1. Mein Vater hat einen Roman geschrieben.
   Mein Vater hatte einen Roman geschrieben.
2. Hast du die Zeitung gelesen?
   Hattest du die Zeitung gelesen?
3. Meine Schwester hat die alte Bluse gefunden.
   Meine Schwester hatte die alte Bluse gefunden.
4. Sonja hat ein rotes Kleid getragen.
   Sonja hatte ein rotes Kleid getragen.
5. Sie haben den Ball nicht gefangen.
   Sie hatten den Ball nicht gefangen.
6. Ich habe einen alten Freund gesehen.
   Ich hatte einen alten Freund gesehen.

7. Der Mann hat ihre Tasche gestohlen.
   Der Mann hatte ihre Tasche gestohlen.
8. Mein Sohn hat die Fahrkarten genommen.
   Mein Sohn hatte die Fahrkarten genommen.
9. Er hat ein paar Würstchen gebraten.
   Er hatte ein paar Würstchen gebraten.
10. Karl und ich haben fünfzig Euro gefunden.
    Karl und ich hatten fünfzig Euro gefunden.

2·5
1. Die Kinder sind zur Schule gegangen.
2. Die Touristen sind ins Restaurant geeilt.
3. Der junge Mann ist ins Wasser gefallen.
4. Bist du in der Schweiz geblieben?
5. Niemand ist uns gefolgt.
6. Wann sind sie nach Deutschland geflogen?
7. Wann seid ihr in Heidelberg gewesen?
8. Sonja ist so schnell gelaufen.
9. Viele Touristen sind nach Frankreich gereist.
10. Warum ist die Frau gestorben?

2·6
1. Past Es wurde ziemlich heiß.
   Pres. perf. Es ist ziemlich heiß geworden.
   Past perf. Es war ziemlich heiß geworden.
   Fut. Es wird ziemlich heiß werden.
2. Pres. Meine Eltern fahren in die Stadt.
   Pres. perf. Meine Eltern sind in die Stadt gefahren.
   Past perf. Meine Eltern waren in die Stadt gefahren.
   Fut. Meine Eltern werden in die Stadt fahren.
3. Pres. Der Diplomat fliegt nach Madrid.
   Past Der Diplomat flog nach Madrid.
   Past perf. Der Diplomat war nach Madrid geflogen.
   Fut. Der Diplomat wird nach Madrid fliegen.
4. Pres. Der Koch bäckt einen schönen Kuchen.
   Past Der Koch backte einen schönen Kuchen.
   Pres. perf. Der Koch hat einen schönen Kuchen gebacken.
   Fut. Der Koch wird einen schönen Kuchen backen.
5. Pres. Meine Familie bleibt zu Hause.
   Past Meine Familie blieb zu Hause.
   Pres. perf. Meine Familie ist zu Hause geblieben.
   Past perf. Meine Familie war zu Hause geblieben.

2·7
1. Meine Eltern werden eine Wohnung in der Stadt gekauft haben.
2. Die Ausländer werden in die Schweiz gereist sein.
3. Ich werde endlich wieder gesund geworden sein.
4. Erik und ich werden den Dieb gefangen haben.
5. Wirst du mexikanisch essen gegangen sein?

2·8
Sample answers are provided.
1. Die Sportler haben Durst.
2. Warum hast du Angst?
3. Der arme Mann hatte immer Pech.
4. Wie ist es mit einem Ausflug an den See?
5. Es wurde sehr kalt.

3 Declensions with **der**-words and **ein**-words

3·1
1. dieser junge 2. diesen netten 3. jenen blauen, jene blauen 4. der neuen 5. Welches frische
6. jedem amerikanischen 7. Der neue; diese weißen 8. dem neuen 9. die alten; dieser 10. den langen
11. Jene schöne 12. dieses kleine 13. welchem großen 14. des ganzen Winters 15. diese schöne
16. Die; jenem kleinen 17. diesen interessanten 18. jenen alten Leuten 19. diese alte 20. das neue

3·2   1. Manche schwarze   2. Manches   3. denselben   4. Dieselben   5. diejenige   6. derjenigen
7. Manchen Leuten   8. demselben   9. alle fetten   10. beiden Brüdern

3·3   1. sein armes   2. ein langes   3. seinen jüngeren   4. Ihre ausländischen   5. ihren alten
6. Unser kleiner; einem großen   7. keine süßeren   8. einer großen   9. Meine; ihre neuen
10. eines kleinen Gartens

3·4   1. Das große   2. meines toten Vaters; eine   3. jeder modernen   4. Ihren neuen, Ihre neuen
5. Ihr jüngeres   6. der nächsten   7. ihren neuen   8. Mein kranker; einem   9. euren besten
10. Welchen braunen

3·5   1. kaltes   2. Meine; einigen Nachbarn   3. keinen   4. Wenige arme   5. kranken Leuten
6. mehrere schöne   7. kalte   8. alle deutschen   9. Die neuen; sämtlicher   10. erstes   11. kalten
12. Viele neue   13. meinen alten, meine alten   14. Diese unartigen; ihrem   15. Welche deutschen

3·6   1. der schweren Arbeit   2. eines gefährlichen Gewitters   3. seiner langen Krankheit   4. des fleißigen
Schülers   5. dieses netten Mädchens   6. einer jungen Tänzerin   7. kalten Kaffee   8. warmes Bier
9. heiße Milch   10. keine amerikanische Zeitung   11. einige russische Briefmarken   12. meinen neuen
Regenmantel   13. seine gefährliche Politik   14. laute Musik   15. ihre ewigen Feinde   16. nächsten
Montag   17. mit diesem Zug   18. diesen Freitag   19. dieser großen Bibliothek   20. verschiedenen
Hörsälen   21. jenem Park   22. viele alte Leute   23. alle ausländischen Studenten   24. diese gefährliche
Lage   25. mehrere Aufstände

4   Pronoun choice by gender

4·1   1. Sie   2. Sie   3. es   4. Er   5. Er   6. Er   7. Sie   8. es   9. Er   10. Er   11. Es   12. Sie
13. es   14. er   15. Es

4·2   1. Er bekommt einen Brief.
Meine Brüder bekommen einen Brief.
Sie bekommen einen Brief.
2. Es stand auf dem Tisch.
Gläser standen auf dem Tisch.
Sie standen auf dem Tisch.
3. Sie spricht gut Deutsch.
Die Touristinnen sprechen gut Deutsch.
Sie sprechen gut Deutsch.
4. Warum ist sie zerbrochen?
Warum sind diese Flaschen zerbrochen?
Warum sind sie zerbrochen?
5. Er kommt um elf Uhr.
Die Züge kommen um elf Uhr.
Sie kommen um elf Uhr.

4·3   1. Wann ist ihre Party?
2. Willst du ihre Bluse tragen?
3. Er spricht mit seinen Eltern.
4. Er hat ihre Adresse.
5. Sie kam ohne seine Ringe.
6. Ich kaufte ihren Stoff.
7. Sie spielen in seinem Keller.
8. Er hat seine Zeitung gelesen.
9. Er erzählt von ihren Kindern.
10. Wo ist seine Bettdecke?

4·4   1. Mit wem arbeitet Thomas?
2. Was hat der Junge?
3. Was ist aus Gold?
4. Was habe ich gekauft? / hast du / haben Sie
5. Wer läuft in den kleinen Garten?
6. Wen haben wir kennen gelernt? / haben Sie / habt ihr
7. Was gibt es in dieser Straße?
8. Wessen Geschwister sind in die Schweiz gereist?

9. Wem gefällt dieser Wildwestfilm nicht?
10. Wer hat ein paar Briefe bekommen?

4·5
1. Worauf müssen wir warten?
2. Worüber freute sich Katrin?
3. Wovon weiß Erik nichts?
4. Wofür interessiert sich mein Sohn?
5. Worin habe ich den Ring gefunden? / hast du / haben Sie
6. Wonach hat Tina oft gefragt?
7. Worunter wird der Hund schlafen?
8. Worum hat der Schaffner gebeten?
9. Womit fährt Frau Benz nach Hause?
10. Wodurch lief er?

5   Special masculine nouns

5·1
1. den Matrosen, dem Matrosen, des Matrosen
2. diesen Kunden, diesem Kunden, dieses Kunden
3. jeden Jungen, jedem Jungen, jedes Jungen
4. den Knaben, dem Knaben, des Knaben

5·2
1. den neuen Kollegen, Der neue Kollege, dem neuen Kollegen, des neuen Kollegen, den neuen Kollegen
2. Dieser Riese, diesen Riesen, diesen Riesen, dieses Riesen, diesem Riesen
3. ihrem Gatten, ihren Gatten, Ihr Gatte, ihres Gatten, ihr Gatte
4. Mein Verwandter, meinen Verwandten, meinem Verwandten, meinen Verwandten, meines Verwandten
5. eines Franzosen, Ein Franzoser, einem Franzosen, einen Franzosen, einen Franzosen

5·3
1. diesen Buchstaben, dieser Buchstabe, diesen Buchstaben, dieses Buchstabens, diesem Buchstaben
2. einem Fremden, Ein Fremder, einen Fremden, einem Fremden, eines Fremden
3. Funken, Funke, Funken, Funken, Funke

5·4
1. dem großen Bären, dem großen Bären
2. ein englischer Prinz, einen englischen Prinzen
3. einen sehr guten Menschen, einen sehr guten Menschen
4. der alte Bauer, dem alten Bauern
5. unseres Nachbarn, unseren Nachbarn
6. den hübschen Fürsten, des hübschen Fürsten
7. den jungen Helden, dem jungen Helden

5·5
1. den Studenten, dem Studenten, des Studenten
2. einen Pianisten, einem Pianisten, eines Pianisten
3. unseren amerikanischen Präsidenten, unserem amerikanischen Präsidenten, unseres amerikanischen Präsidenten
4. keinen ehrlichen Diplomaten, keinem ehrlichen Diplomaten, keines ehrlichen Diplomaten

5·6
1. der Junge   2. der Matrose   3. der Mantel   4. die Lampe   5. der Mensch   6. kein Beamter
7. kein Bauer   8. kein Tourist   9. kein Name   10. kein Idiot   11. einen Herrn   12. einen Gedanken
13. einen Glauben   14. einen Aristokraten   15. einen Architekten   16. diesem Journalisten
17. dieser Lehrerin   18. diesem Nachbarn   19. diesem Dirigenten   20. diesem Deutschen
21. welches Grafen   22. welches Namens   23. welches Helden   24. welches Demokraten
25. welches Kapitalisten   26. welches Buchstabens   27. welches Jungen   28. welches Mädchens
29. welches Studenten   30. welches Herzens

6   Conjunctions and word order

6·1
1. Er versucht das Gedicht zu lernen, aber er versteht es gar nicht.
2. Du bist zwar mein Freund, aber ich kann dir nicht damit helfen.
3. Der Soldat war schwer verwundet, aber die Ärztin gab die Hoffnung nicht auf.
4. Ich will nicht wandern gehen, denn es ist zu regnerisch.
5. Mein Sohn kann nicht im Garten spielen, denn es ist sehr kalt geworden.
6. Thomas ist sehr müde, denn er hat den ganzen Tag gearbeitet.
7. Reist ihr nach Amerika, oder bleibt ihr zu Hause?

8. Lars muss gehorchen, oder er hat die Folgen selbst zu tragen.
9. Heute könnt ihr hier spielen, oder ihr könnt zum Stadtpark gehen.
10. Mein Vater spricht nicht nur Deutsch, sondern er kann auch Spanisch und Englisch.
11. Angelika spielt nicht nur Tennis, sondern sie spielt auch Fußball und Golf.
12. Wir haben nicht ferngesehen, sondern wir sind ins Kino gegangen.
13. Professor Schneider kommt morgen an und er kann bis Mittwoch bei mir bleiben.
14. Ich spiele Klavier, und mein Bruder spielt Flöte.
15. Meine Tante liest die Zeitung, und mein Onkel schläft auf dem Sofa.

6·2   *Sample answers are provided.*
1. Thomas spielt Geige
2. ich muss hier bleiben und meiner Mutter helfen
3. er ist englischer Tourist
4. seine Familie ist noch arm
5. wollen Sie einen Kombi
6. blieb hier bis neunzehn Uhr
7. es wird bald wieder gesund
8. ich möchte lieber ein Glas Wein
9. sie will ihre Tante da besuchen
10. sind sie jetzt in Heidelberg

6·3   1. seine Tochter wieder gesund ist/das kleine Kind wirklich Geige spielen kann
2. er den Fremden vor der Tür stehen sah/er das Goldstück fand
3. es wärmer im Winter in Italien ist/er jetzt viel Freizeit hat
4. er bei seiner Tante wohnte/er das Konservatorium in München besuchte
5. ich in den Bergen bin/ich den Winter in Norwegen verbringe

6·4   *Sample answers are provided.*
1. sie zu müde ist
2. das Wetter schlecht geworden ist
3. Herr Benz Diplomat ist
4. sie an der Universität studierte
5. Karl mehr Geld brauchte
6. ich in der Hauptstadt gewohnt habe
7. er in Paris war
8. meine Mutter krank ist
9. ich weiß
10. mein Mann die Fahrkarten kauft
11. der Bus kommt
12. er nicht verhungert
13. es kälter wird
14. die Kanzlerin Rom besuchen wird
15. Frau Bauer noch krank ist

6·5   1. wo seine Frau jetzt wohnt/wie lange er in der Hauptstadt bleibt/mit wem er nach Polen gefahren ist
2. wohin die Kinder gegangen sind/wessen Bücher der Mann gestohlen hat/für wen die junge Frau arbeiten musste
3. wie alt die kranke Frau ist/wie oft der Zug nach Bremen fährt/wie viele Zeitungen Sie schon verkauft haben
4. warum er so böse geworden ist/woher er diese Bilder bekommen hat/wie schnell der Rennwagen fahren kann
5. wen der Polizist verhaften wird/wie viel Geld der reiche Herr hat/von wem Gudrun dieses Geschenk bekommen hat

7   Mancher and solcher

7·1   1. acc. manchen guten Kerl
       dat. manchem guten Kerl
       gen. manches guten Kerls
2. acc. manch eine kranke Frau
       dat. manch einer kranken Frau
       gen. manch einer kranken Frau

3. acc. manch reichen Mann
   dat. manch reichem Mann
   gen. manch reichen Mannes
4. acc. manch schöne Stunden
   dat. manch schönen Stunden
   gen. manch schöner Stunden
5. acc. manche weinenden Kinder
   dat. manchen weinenden Kindern
   gen. mancher weinenden Kinder
6. acc. manches alte Haus
   dat. manchem alten Haus
   gen. manches alten Hauses
7. acc. manchen guten Film
   dat. manchem guten Film
   gen. manches guten Filmes
8. acc. manch einen Verkäufer
   dat. manch einem Verkäufer
   gen. manch eines Verkäufers
9. acc. manch starke Männer
   dat. manch starken Männern
   gen. manch starker Männer
10. acc. manche neue Lehrerin
    dat. mancher neuen Lehrerin
    gen. mancher neuen Lehrerin

7·2
1. Mancher Student liest seinen neuen Roman.
   Manche neue Angestellte liest seinen neuen Roman.
   Manches kluge Kind liest seinen neuen Roman.
   Manche ausländischen Touristen lesen seinen neuen Roman.
   Mancher Mann liest seinen neuen Roman.
2. Mit der Hilfe manches tapferen Matrosen haben wir den Mann gerettet.
   Mit der Hilfe mancher zitternden Mädchen haben wir den Mann gerettet.
   Mit der Hilfe manch eines müden Feuerwehrmannes haben wir den Mann gerettet.
   Mit der Hilfe manches Kindes haben wir den Mann gerettet.
   Mit der Hilfe manch verängstigter Leute haben wir den Mann gerettet.
   Mit der Hilfe mancher Polizisten haben wir den Mann gerettet.
3. Ich habe manch eine Studentin gefragt.
   Ich habe manchen jungen Arzt gefragt.
   Ich habe manch einen alten Herrn gefragt.
   Ich habe manche enttäuschten Diplomaten gefragt.
   Ich habe manche Professorin gefragt.
4. Erik hat es mit manchem Journalisten diskutiert.
   Erik hat es mit manchen ausländischen Akademikern diskutiert.
   Erik hat es mit manchem verwundeten Soldaten diskutiert.
   Erik hat es mit manch einer Amerikanerin diskutiert.
   Erik hat es mit manchem naiven Mädchen diskutiert.

7·3
1. acc. solchen guten Kerl
   dat. solchem guten Kerl
   gen. solches guten Kerls
2. acc. solche netten Leute
   dat. solchen netten Leuten
   gen. solcher netten Leute
3. acc. einen solchen Komponisten
   dat. einem solchen Komponisten
   gen. eines solchen Komponisten
4. acc. solch ein langes Schiff
   dat. solch einem langen Schiff
   gen. solch eines langen Schiffs

5. acc. solch dumme Sätze
  dat. solch dummen Sätzen
  gen. solch dummer Sätze
6. acc. solches interessante Buch
  dat. solchem interessanten Buch
  gen. solches interessanten Buches
7. acc. solches schlechte Problem
  dat. solchem schlechten Problem
  gen. solches schlechten Problems
8. acc. solch hübsche Tänzerin
  dat. solch hübscher Tänzerin
  gen. solch hübscher Tänzerin
9. acc. solche hübschen Tänzerinnen
  dat. solchen hübschen Tänzerinnen
  gen. solcher hübschen Tänzerinnen
10. acc. solch eine schöne Blume
  dat. solch einer schönen Blume
  gen. solch einer schönen Blume

7·4
1. Lars hat so einen großen Garten gesehen.
  Lars hat ein solches Bild gesehen.
  Lars hat so ein kleines Haus gesehen.
  Lars hat solches alte Theater gesehen.
  Lars hat solchen großen Lastwagen gesehen.
2. Alle sprechen von solch herrlichem Wetter.
  Alle sprechen von solchem dummen Roman.
  Alle sprechen von einem solchen Drama.
  Alle sprechen von solchen glücklichen Tagen.
  Alle sprechen von so einem furchtbaren Gewitter.

7·5
1. acc. welch schönen Tag
  dat. welch schönem Tag
  gen. welch schönen Tages
2. acc. welch glückliche Stunden
  dat. welch glücklichen Stunden
  gen. welch glücklicher Stunden
3. acc. was für eine Wohnung
  dat. was für einer Wohnung
  gen. was für einer Wohnung
4. acc. was für einen Esstisch
  dat. was für einem Esstisch
  gen. was für eines Esstisches
5. acc. was für ein Flugzeug
  dat. was für einem Flugzeug
  gen. was für eines Flugzeugs

7·6
1. acc. mehr heißen Kaffee
  dat. mehr heißem Kaffee
  gen. mehr heißen Kaffees
2. acc. viel schwierige Arbeit
  dat. viel schwieriger Arbeit
  gen. viel schwieriger Arbeit
3. acc. etwas warme Milch
  dat. etwas warmer Milch
  gen. etwas warmer Milch
4. acc. wenig freie Zeit
  dat. wenig freier Zeit
  gen. wenig freier Zeit
5. acc. ein paar englische Zeitungen
  dat. ein paar englischen Zeitungen
  gen. ein paar englischer Zeitungen

6. acc. zehn neue Schlipse
   dat. zehn neuen Schlipsen
   gen. zehn neuer Schlipse
7. acc. einundvierzig kleine Vögel
   dat. einundvierzig kleinen Vögeln
   gen. einundvierzig kleiner Vögel
8. acc. einen großen Koffer
   dat. einem großen Koffer
   gen. eines großen Koffers
9. acc. mehr neue Angestellte
   dat. mehr neuen Angestellten
   gen. mehr neuer Angestellte
10. acc. ein paar deutsche Briefmarken
    dat. ein paar deutschen Briefmarken
    gen. ein paar deutscher Briefmarken

7·7   1. b 2. c 3. a 4. b 5. d 6. d 7. a 8. d 9. a 10. a 11. c 12. a 13. d 14. a 15. b

8 Comparative, superlative, and irregularities

8·1   1. schlechter *worse* 2. schneller *faster* 3. langsamer *slower* 4. kleiner *smaller* 5. weiter *farther*
6. dicker *fatter, thicker* 7. bunter *more colorful* 8. praktischer *more practical* 9. künstlicher *more artificial* 10. verantwortlicher *more responsible*

8·2   1. kleineres 2. bunter 3. neueren 4. als 5. weißere 6. schneller 7. neuer 8. schwerere
9. netteren 10. kleinerer; breiteren

8·3   1. interessanter 2. stärker 3. jüngeren 4. längeren 5. kälter 6. langweiligeren 7. schwächer
8. stärkeren 9. älteres 10. langsamer

8·4   1. ärmeren 2. höher 3. eher 4. besseres 5. kränker 6. mehr; weniger 7. kürzeren
8. dunkler 9. näher 10. besser 11. netter 12. wärmer 13. größer 14. neueres 15. höheren

8·5   1. am hässlichsten *the ugliest*
   2. am kühlsten *the coolest*
   3. am weichsten *the softest*
   4. am schärfsten *the sharpest*
   5. am wenigsten *the least*
   6. am angenehmsten *the most pleasant*
   7. am tiefsten *the deepest*
   8. am wichtigsten *the most important*
   9. am gewöhnlichsten *the most usual*
  10. am schwierigsten *the most difficult*

8·6   1. das längste Gedicht
   2. dein/Ihr/euer jüngster Bruder
   3. unsere älteste Katze
   4. die kürzesten Tage
   5. die klügsten Studenten
   6. seine ärmsten Nachbarn
   7. meine reichsten Verwandten
   8. die schwächsten Birnen
   9. der schlechtesten Idee
  10. der lautesten Stimme
  11. ihrem neuesten Bild
  12. unserer angenehmsten Überraschung
  13. des wärmsten Wassers
  14. der interessantesten Geschichte
  15. des dümmsten Witzes

1. Kennen Sie den jüngeren Mann?
   Kennen Sie den jüngsten Mann?
2. Erik arbeitet mit meinem älteren Bruder.
   Erik arbeitet mit meinem ältesten Bruder.
3. Sonja hat mein größeres Zelt geborgt.
   Sonja hat mein größtes Zelt geborgt.
4. Der Vogel sitzt auf dem höheren Zaun.
   Der Vogel sitzt auf dem höchsten Zaun.
5. Hast du die längeren Bretter?
   Hast du die längsten Bretter?
6. Ist unsere Bushaltestelle näher?
   Ist unsere Bushaltestelle am nächsten?
7. Mein Vater hat immer mehr gearbeitet.
   Mein Vater hat immer am meisten gearbeitet.
8. Im Sommer ist es heißer.
   Im Sommer ist es am heißesten.
9. Meine Freundin kann weiter laufen.
   Meine Freundin kann am weitesten laufen.
10. Der Brandwein schmeckt milder.
    Der Brandwein schmeckt am mildesten.

1. b   2. a   3. d   4. a   5. b   6. a   7. d   8. b   9. c   10. b

9   Modal auxiliaries and double infinitives

1. Mein Vater muss zehn Stunden pro Tag arbeiten.
   Mein Vater will zehn Stunden pro Tage arbeiten.
2. Ich kann keine Briefe schreiben.
   Ich muss keine Briefe schreiben.
3. Die Gäste sollen tanzen und singen.
   Die Gäste dürfen tanzen und singen.
4. Sie wollen diese Fragen nicht beantworten.
   Sie mögen diese Fragen nicht beantworten.
5. Sollst du deine Freundin an der Ecke erwarten?
   Musst du deine Freundin an der Ecke erwarten?

1. Pres. Der Arzt kann diese Krankheit nicht verstehen.
   Past Der Arzt konnte diese Krankheit nicht verstehen.
   Pres. perf. Der Arzt hat diese Krankheit nicht verstehen können.
   Fut. Der Arzt wird diese Krankheit nicht verstehen können.
2. Pres. Die Schüler dürfen hereinkommen.
   Past Die Schüler durften hereinkommen.
   Pres. perf. Die Schüler haben hereinkommen dürfen.
   Fut. Die Schüler werden hereinkommen dürfen.
3. Pres. Ich muss ein paar Tage in Bonn bleiben.
   Past Ich musste ein paar Tage in Bonn bleiben.
   Pres. perf. Ich habe ein paar Tage in Bonn bleiben müssen.
   Fut. Ich werde ein paar Tage in Bonn bleiben müssen.
4. Pres. Der Wanderer will in die Berge fahren.
   Past Der Wanderer wollte in die Berge fahren.
   Pres. perf. Der Wanderer hat in die Berge fahren wollen.
   Fut. Der Wanderer wird in die Berge fahren wollen.
5. Pres. Der kranke Herr darf das Krankenhaus nicht verlassen.
   Past Der kranke Herr durfte das Krankenhaus nicht verlassen.
   Pres. perf. Der kranke Herr hat das Krankenhaus nicht verlassen dürfen.
   Fut. Der kranke Herr wird das Krankenhaus nicht verlassen dürfen.

9·3   *Sample answers are provided.*
1. Magst du meinen Onkel gern?
   Magst du die neuen Sportler gern?
   Magst du ihn gern?
2. Ich möchte in die Schweiz reisen.
   Ich möchte dieses Haus kaufen.
   Ich möchte mit Herrn Bauer sprechen.
3. Das mag wohl sein, aber es ist sowieso ungerecht.
   Das mag wohl sein, aber du wirst zu Hause bleiben.
   Das mag wohl sein, aber es ist ein Film für Erwachsene.
4. Meine Frau mochte den neuen Lehrer nicht.
   Meine Frau mochte unseren Nachbar nicht.
   Meine Frau mochte die Briefträgerin nicht.
5. Sie möchte einen Teller Suppe bestellen.
   Sie möchte ein paar Würstchen bestellen.
   Sie möchte Kartoffelsalat bestellen.

9·4   *Sample answers are provided.*
1. Kann dein Bruder Spanisch?
   Kann dein Bruder Polnisch?
   Kann dein Bruder Schwedisch?
2. Die Jungen liefen, was sie konnten.
   Der Mann lief, was er konnte.
   Ich lief, was ich konnte.
3. Können wir mit ihm Schach spielen?
   Können wir Klavier spielen?
   Können wir etwas essen?
4. Was können die Mädchen dafür?
   Was kannst du dafür?
   Was könnt ihr dafür?
5. Erik kann Chemie ziemlich gut.
   Erik kann Geschichte ziemlich gut.
   Erik kann Mathematik ziemlich gut.

9·5
1. Du hättest ihn gar nicht fragen sollen.
2. Hätten wir sie am Montag anrufen sollen?
3. Ich hätte meinen Bruder in Oldenburg besuchen sollen.
4. Ihr hättet ihn nicht um Geld bitten sollen.
5. Sie hätten es mir früher sagen sollen.
6. Der alte Mann hätte lauter sprechen können.
7. Martin hätte ihr damit helfen können.
8. Das hättest du nicht kaufen dürfen.
9. Wir hätten nicht in den Wald gehen dürfen.
10. Frau Schneider hätte sich besser ausdrücken müssen.

9·6   1. b   2. a   3. a   4. b   5. d   6. a   7. b   8. d   9. c   10. c   11. a   12. b   13. a   14. c   15. b

10   Sehen, hören, lassen, helfen, and double infinitives

10·1
1. Past Tina sah meine neue Brille.
   Pres. perf. Tina hat meine neue Brille gesehen.
   Past perf. Tina hatte meine neue Brille gesehen.
   Fut. Tina wird meine neue Brille sehen.
2. Pres. Wir hören oft Radio.
   Pres. perf. Wir haben oft Radio gehört.
   Past perf. Wir hatten oft Radio gehört.
   Fut. Wir werden oft Radio hören.
3. Pres. Erik lässt den armen Mann nicht allein.
   Past Erik ließ den armen Mann nicht allein.
   Past perf. Erik hatte den armen Mann nicht allein gelassen.
   Fut. Erik wird den armen Mann nicht allein lassen.

4. Pres. Ich helfe ihr über die Straße.
Past Ich half ihr über die Straße.
Pres. perf. Ich habe ihr über die Straße geholfen.
Fut. Ich werde ihr über die Straße helfen.

5. Pres. Er sieht schon bessere Zeiten.
Past Er sah schon bessere Zeiten.
Pres. perf. Er hat schon bessere Zeiten gesehen.
Past perf. Er hatte schon bessere Zeiten gesehen.

10·2 1. Past Sie ließ die Türglocke ertönen.
Pres. perf. Sie hat die Türglocke ertönen lassen.
Past perf. Sie hatte die Türglocke ertönen lassen.
Fut. Sie wird die Türglocke ertönen lassen.

2. Pres. Er hört seine Mutter sprechen.
Pres. perf. Er hat seine Mutter sprechen hören.
Past perf. Er hatte seine Mutter sprechen hören.
Fut. Er wird seine Mutter sprechen hören.

3. Pres. Herr Bauer sieht die Jungen spielen.
Past Herr Bauer sah die Jungen spielen.
Past perf. Herr Bauer hatte die Jungen spielen sehen.
Fut. Herr Bauer wird die Jungen spielen sehen.

4. Pres. Wie lange müssen sie arbeiten?
Past Wie lange mussten sie arbeiten?
Pres. perf. Wie lange haben sie arbeiten müssen?
Fut. Wie lange werden sie arbeiten müssen?

5. Pres. Wir helfen ihm das Gepäck tragen.
Past Wir halfen ihm das Gepäck tragen.
Pres. perf. Wir haben ihm das Gepäck tragen helfen.
Past perf. Wir hatten ihm das Gepäck tragen helfen.

6. Past Ich sah den Zug in den Bahnhof kommen.
Pres. perf. Ich habe den Zug in den Bahnhof kommen sehen.
Past perf. Ich hatte den Zug in den Bahnhof kommen sehen.
Fut. Ich werde den Zug in den Bahnhof kommen sehen.

7. Pres. Wo lässt der Kanzler seine Anzüge machen?
Pres. perf. Wo hat der Kanzler seine Anzüge machen lassen?
Past perf. Wo hatte der Kanzler seine Anzüge machen lassen?
Fut. Wo wird der Kanzler seine Anzüge machen lassen?

8. Pres. Ich höre sie flüstern.
Past Ich hörte sie flüstern.
Past perf. Ich hatte sie flüstern hören.
Fut. Ich werde sie flüstern hören.

9. Pres. Sabine hilft mir den Brief schreiben.
Past Sabine half mir den Brief schreiben.
Pres. perf. Sabine hat mir den Brief schreiben helfen.
Fut. Sabine wird mir den Brief schreiben helfen.

10. Pres. Sie will nach Italien reisen.
Past Sie wollte nach Italien reisen.
Pres. perf. Sie hat nach Italien reisen wollen.
Past perf. Sie hatte nach Italien reisen wollen.

10·3 1. Unsere Pläne lassen sich schnell ändern.
2. Es lässt sich nicht machen.
3. Die alte Uhr ließ sich leicht reparieren.
4. Die Fenster haben sich nicht leicht öffnen lassen.
5. Diese Theorie wird sich nicht beweisen lassen.

10·4 1. Er fährt heute morgen Ski laufen.
Er geht heute morgen Ski laufen.
2. Wir fuhren oft wandern.
Wir gingen oft wandern.

3. Ich fahre morgen joggen.
   Ich gehe morgen joggen.
4. Erik und Sonja werden oft schwimmen fahren.
   Erik und Sonja werden oft schwimmen gehen.
5. Er fuhr heute abend mit Tina tanzen.
   Er ging heute abend mit Tina tanzen.

10·5
1. Past Herr Benz lehrte uns rechnen.
   Pres. perf. Herr Benz hat uns rechnen gelehrt.
   Past perf. Herr Benz hatte uns rechnen gelehrt.
   Fut. Herr Benz wird uns rechnen lehren.
2. Pres. Mein Freund lernt schnell Spanisch sprechen.
   Pres. perf. Mein Freund hat schnell Spanisch sprechen gelernt.
   Past perf. Mein Freund hatte schnell Spanisch sprechen gelernt.
   Fut. Mein Freund wird schnell Spanisch sprechen lernen.
3. Pres. Sie schickt ihn sich die Hände waschen.
   Past Sie schickte ihn sich die Hände waschen.
   Past perf. Sie hatte ihn sich die Hände waschen geschickt.
   Fut. Sie wird ihn sich die Hände waschen schicken.
4. Pres. Lars geht mit Sonja mexikanisch essen.
   Past Lars ging mit Sonja mexikanisch essen.
   Pres. perf. Lars ist mit Sonja mexikanisch essen gegangen.
   Fut. Lars wird mit Sonja mexikanisch essen gehen.
5. Pres. Die Lehrerin lehrt die Schüler zeichnen.
   Past Die Lehrerin lehrte die Schüler zeichnen.
   Pres. perf. Die Lehrerin hat die Schüler zeichnen gelehrt.
   Past perf. Die Lehrerin hatte die Schüler zeichnen gelehrt.
6. Past Es ließ sich kaum glauben.
   Pres. perf. Es hat sich kaum glauben lassen.
   Past perf. Es hatte sich kaum glauben lassen.
   Fut. Es wird sich kaum glauben lassen.
7. Pres. Der Student lernt programmieren.
   Past Der Student lernte programmieren.
   Past perf. Der Student hatte programmieren gelernt.
   Fut. Der Student wird programmieren lernen.
8. Pres. Die Nachricht lässt uns erschrecken.
   Past Die Nachricht ließ uns erschrecken.
   Pres. perf. Die Nachricht hat uns erschrecken lassen.
   Fut. Die Nachricht wird uns erschrecken lassen.
9. Pres. Sie schickt die Jungen in den Garten spielen.
   Past Sie schickte die Jungen in den Garten spielen.
   Pres. perf. Sie hat die Jungen in den Garten spielen geschickt.
   Past perf. Sie hatte die Jungen in den Garten spielen geschickt.
10. Past Der Dieb hörte die Polizei kommen.
    Pres. perf. Der Dieb hat die Polizei kommen hören.
    Past perf. Der Dieb hatte die Polizei kommen hören.
    Fut. Der Dieb wird die Polizei kommen hören.

10·6 1. c 2. a 3. a 4. c 5. c 6. a 7. b 8. b 9. a 10. d 11. b 12. c 13. b 14. a 15. c

11 Prefixes

11·1
1. Pres. Ich ziehe mich um.
   Past Ich zog mich um.
   Pres. perf. Ich habe mich umgezogen.
   Fut. Ich werde mich umziehen.
2. Pres. Frau Bauer macht die Türen zu.
   Past Frau Bauer machte die Türen zu.
   Pres. perf. Frau Bauer hat die Türen zugemacht.
   Fut. Frau Bauer wird die Türen zumachen.

3. Pres. Herr Benz bringt uns Mathe bei.
   Past Herr Benz brachte uns Mathe bei.
   Pres. perf. Herr Benz hat uns Mathe beigebracht.
   Fut. Herr Benz wird uns Mathe beibringen.
4. Pres. Das Mädchen sieht sehr gut aus.
   Past Das Mädchen sah sehr gut aus.
   Pres. perf. Das Mädchen hat sehr gut ausgesehen.
   Fut. Das Mädchen wird sehr gut aussehen.
5. Pres. Mein Vater bereitet das Frühstück vor.
   Past Mein Vater bereitete das Frühstück vor.
   Pres. perf. Mein Vater hat das Frühstück vorbereitet.
   Fut. Mein Vater wird das Frühstück vorbereiten.
6. Pres. Wir gehen am Montag zurück.
   Past Wir gingen am Montag zurück.
   Pres. perf. Wir sind am Montag zurückgegangen.
   Fut. Wir werden am Montag zurückgehen.
7. Pres. Die Vorlesung fängt um elf Uhr an.
   Past Die Vorlesung fing um elf Uhr an.
   Pres. perf. Die Vorlesung hat um elf Uhr angefangen.
   Fut. Die Vorlesung wird um elf Uhr anfangen.
8. Pres. Stellen Sie Ihren Mann vor?
   Past Stellten Sie Ihren Mann vor?
   Pres. perf. Haben Sie Ihren Mann vorgestellt?
   Fut. Werden Sie Ihren Mann vorstellen?
9. Pres. Warum läufst du weg?
   Past Warum liefst du weg?
   Pres. perf. Warum bist du weggelaufen?
   Fut. Warum wirst du weglaufen?
10. Pres. Unsere Verwandten kommen nach dem Konzert vorbei.
    Past Unsere Verwandten kamen nach dem Konzert vorbei.
    Pres. perf. Unsere Verwandten sind nach dem Konzert vorbeigekommen.
    Fut. Unsere Verwandten werden nach dem Konzert vorbeikommen.

11·2
1. Hör(e) damit auf! Hört damit auf! Hören Sie damit auf!
2. Bleib(e) fort! Bleibt fort! Bleiben Sie fort!
3. Mach(e) alle Fenster auf! Macht alle Fenster auf! Machen Sie alle Fenster auf!
4. Fahr(e) um acht Uhr ab! Fahrt um acht Uhr ab! Fahren Sie um acht Uhr ab!
5. Sieh das neue Klavier an! Seht das neue Klavier an! Sehen Sie das neue Klavier an!
6. Setz(e) die Reise fort! Setzt die Reise fort! Setzen Sie die Reise fort!
7. Fahr(e) weg! Fahrt weg! Fahren Sie weg!
8. Schließ(e) ihn nicht aus! Schließt ihn nicht aus! Schließen Sie ihn nicht aus!
9. Spül(e) mit viel Wasser nach! Spült mit viel Wasser nach! Spülen Sie mit viel Wasser nach!
10. Hol(e) die Fahne nieder! Holt die Fahne nieder! Holen Sie die Fahne nieder!

11·3
1. der 2. der 3. die 4. die 5. die 6. die 7. der 8. der 9. der 10. das

11·4
Sample answers are provided.
1. Ich habe zehn Euro bekommen.
2. Welches Restaurant kannst du empfehlen?
3. Endlich entfliehen wir dem Feind.
4. Sie erwartet ein paar Freunde auf dem Bahnhof.
5. Gefallen Ihnen diese Schuhe?
6. Leider habe ich meine Bücher vergessen.
7. Der Feind will die Stadt zerstören.
8. Wir besuchten unsere Tante.
9. Was ist an der Ecke geschehen?
10. Werden wir den Zug erreichen?

11·5
1. Pres. Die Musik gefällt mir nicht.
   Past Die Musik gefiel mir nicht.
   Pres. perf. Die Musik hat mir nicht gefallen.
   Fut. Die Musik wird mir nicht gefallen.

2. Pres. Sie errötet nicht.
   Past Sie errötete nicht.
   Pres. perf. Sie hat nicht errötet.
   Fut. Sie wird nicht erröten.
3. Pres. Die alte Frau kommt nach einer Krankheit um.
   Past Die alte Frau kam nach einer Krankheit um.
   Pres. perf. Die alte Frau ist nach einer Krankheit umgekommen.
   Fut. Die alte Frau wird nach einer Krankheit umkommen.
4. Pres. Er hört nicht mit dem Unsinn auf.
   Past Er hörte nicht mit dem Unsinn auf.
   Pres. perf. Er hat nicht mit dem Unsinn aufgehört.
   Fut. Er wird nicht mit dem Unsinn aufhören.
5. Pres. Der Direktor entfernt ihn aus der Schule.
   Past Der Direktor entfernte ihn aus der Schule.
   Pres. perf. Der Direktor hat ihn aus der Schule entfernt.
   Fut. Der Direktor wird ihn aus der Schule entfernen.

11·6 1. Pres. Die Tänzerin zieht sich um.
   Past Die Tänzerin zog sich um.
   Pres. perf. Die Tänzerin hat sich umgezogen.
   Fut. Die Tänzerin wird sich umziehen.
2. Pres. Wir übersetzen das Gedicht.
   Past Wir übersetzten das Gedicht.
   Pres. perf. Wir haben das Gedicht übersetzt.
   Fut. Wir werden das Gedicht übersetzen.
3. Pres. Sie untersucht ihn ärztlich.
   Past Sie untersuchte ihn ärztlich.
   Pres. perf. Sie hat ihn ärztlich untersucht.
   Fut. Sie wird ihn ärztlich untersuchen.
4. Pres. Ich tanke in Heidelberg voll.
   Past Ich tankte in Heidelberg voll.
   Pres. perf. Ich habe in Heidelberg vollgetankt.
   Fut. Ich werde in Heidelberg volltanken.
5. Pres. Der Diplomat widerspricht sich selbst.
   Past Der Diplomat widersprach sich selbst.
   Pres. perf. Der Diplomat hat sich selbst widersprochen.
   Fut. Der Diplomat wird sich selbst widersprechen.

11·7 1. das Bücherregal 2. der Blitzkrieg 3. der Notfall 4. die Sparkasse 5. das Theaterstück
6. abhängig 7. der Lieblingsfilm 8. der Friedhof 9. das Wildpferd 10. der Schnellimbiss

12 Imperatives

12·1 1. Komm(e)! Kommt! Kommen Sie!
2. Geh(e)! Geht! Gehen Sie!
3. Schlaf(e)! Schlaft! Schlafen Sie!
4. Bring(e)! Bringt! Bringen Sie!
5. Fang(e)! Fangt! Fangen Sie!
6. Trag(e)! Tragt! Tragen Sie!
7. Hilf! Helft! Helfen Sie!
8. Schreib(e)! Schreibt! Schreiben Sie!
9. Iss! Esst! Essen Sie!
10. Brich! Brecht! Brechen Sie!
11. Halt(e)! Haltet! Halten Sie!
12. Sprich! Sprecht! Sprechen Sie!
13. Renn(e)! Rennt! Rennen Sie!
14. Sag(e)! Sagt! Sagen Sie!
15. Reinige! Reinigt! Reinigen Sie!

12·2   1. Gib aus! Gebt aus! Geben Sie aus!
        2. Beschreib(e)! Beschreibt! Beschreiben Sie!
        3. Komm(e) mit! Kommt mit! Kommen Sie mit!
        4. Entflieh! Entflieht! Entfliehen Sie!
        5. Fahr(e) ab! Fahrt ab! Fahren Sie ab!
        6. Steh auf! Steht auf! Stehen Sie auf!
        7. Erschlag(e)! Erschlagt! Erschlagen Sie!
        8. Ruf(e) an! Ruft an! Rufen Sie an!
        9. Befiehl! Befehlt! Befehlen Sie!
       10. Sprich aus! Sprecht aus! Sprechen Sie aus!
       11. Bearbeit(e)! Bearbeitet! Bearbeiten Sie!
       12. Nimm an! Nehmt an! Nehmen Sie an!
       13. Zieh(e) aus! Zieht aus! Ziehen Sie aus!
       14. Steig(e) um! Steigt um! Steigen Sie um!
       15. Wirf! Werft! Werfen Sie!

12·3   1. Spiel(e) nicht im Garten!
           Spielt nicht im Garten!
           Spielen Sie nicht im Garten!
        2. Hilf dem alten Mann!
           Helft dem alten Mann!
           Helfen Sie dem alten Mann!
        3. Fang(e) mit der Arbeit an!
           Fangt mit der Arbeit an!
           Fangen Sie mit der Arbeit an!
        4. Probier(e) den Kuchen!
           Probiert den Kuchen!
           Probieren Sie den Kuchen!
        5. Empfiehl kein Restaurant!
           Empfehlt kein Restaurant!
           Empfehlen Sie kein Restaurant!
        6. Sei mein Freund!
           Seid meine Freunde!
           Seien Sie mein Freund!
        7. Iss Pommes frites!
           Esst Pommes frites!
           Essen Sie Pommes frites!
        8. Mach(e) alle Fenster auf!
           Macht alle Fenster auf!
           Machen Sie alle Fenster auf!
        9. Beleg(e) einen Kurs in Deutsch!
           Belegt einen Kurs in Deutsch!
           Belegen Sie einen Kurs in Deutsch!
       10. Zieh(e) dich um!
           Zieht euch um!
           Ziehen Sie sich um!

12·4   1. Lernen wir das Gedicht auswendig!
        2. Gehen wir heute nachmittag schwimmen!
        3. Sprechen wir nur Russisch!
        4. Stehen wir auf!
        5. Schreiben wir ein paar Ansichtskarten!
        6. Besuchen wir das Kunstmuseum!
        7. Laufen wir zum Stadtpark!
        8. Ziehen wir uns schnell an!
        9. Lesen wir den neuen Roman!
       10. Nehmen wir einen Regenschirm mit!

12·5   1. Lass mich ihnen helfen!
           Lasst mich ihnen helfen!
           Lassen Sie mich ihnen helfen!

2. Lass ihn die Vögel fotografieren!
   Lasst ihn die Vögel fotografieren!
   Lassen Sie ihn die Vögel fotografieren!
3. Lass die Schüler über die Straße gehen!
   Lasst die Schüler über die Straße gehen!
   Lassen Sie die Schüler über die Straße gehen!
4. Lass das Konzert beginnen!
   Lasst das Konzert beginnen!
   Lassen Sie das Konzert beginnen!
5. Lass sie das Gemälde zeigen!
   Lasst sie das Gemälde zeigen!
   Lassen Sie sie das Gemälde zeigen!

12·6   1. c 2. a 3. d 4. c 5. a 6. a 7. d 8. c 9. c 10. a 11. d 12. a 13. c 14. b 15. b

13   Verbs with specific prepositions

13·1   1. auf die alte 2. an seinen 3. An der 4. auf meine 5. auf das 6. an 7. an seine neue 8. an seinem langen 9. an unserem 10. an seine 11. auf den 12. auf diese 13. an einem 14. auf den 15. an unsere

13·2   1. auf sie 2. an ihn 3. darauf 4. an sie 5. daran 6. Worauf? 7. Auf wen? 8. Woran? 9. Woran? 10. An wen?

13·3   1. um diese 2. vor jener 3. über den Zweiten 4. über Ihren 5. über jedes kleine 6. vor dem 7. über die 8. um Ihre 9. in dieses/diese 10. über Ihre

13·4   1. davor 2. in sie 3. darüber 4. darüber 5. darum 6. Über wen? 7. Worum? 8. Worüber? 9. Vor wem? 10. In wen?

13·5   1. für 2. von einem neuen 3. gegen diese gefährliche 4. dazu 5. aus 6. bei der 7. mit diesen 8. nach 9. von deinem 10. für die 11. nach dem verlorenen 12. nach meinem 13. gegen 14. bei seinen 15. nach 16. mit einem 17. zu dem/zum 18. bei der 19. für 20. von dem/vom letzten

13·6   Sample answers are provided. 1. dem alten Hund, ihrem verlorenen Bruder 2. meiner Tante, dem Gastgeber 3. Ihren Kindern, Ihrer Jugend in Italien 4. ihren Sohn, die Vergangenheit 5. die anderen Jungen, den Bus 6. ein paar Euro, Hilfe 7. dieser Gefahr, diesen Leuten 8. einer Firma in Deutschland, einem Kaufhaus 9. der Straßenbahn, der S-Bahn 10. die Ferien, meinen Geburtstag

14   Categories of irregular verbs

14·1   1. Past Wir hörten Radio.
   Pres. perf. Wir haben Radio gehört.
   Fut. Wir werden Radio hören.
2. Pres. Stefan geht nach Hause.
   Pres. perf. Stefan ist nach Hause gegangen.
   Fut. Stefan wird nach Hause gehen.
3. Pres. Wir trinken kein Bier.
   Past Wir tranken kein Bier.
   Fut. Wir werden kein Bier trinken.
4. Pres. Ich bleibe in Italien.
   Past Ich blieb in Italien.
   Pres. perf. Ich bin in Italien geblieben.
5. Past Schriebst du an deinen Vater?
   Pres. perf. Hast du an deinen Vater geschrieben?
   Fut. Wirst du an deinen Vater schreiben?
6. Pres. Die alte Dame weint vor Freude.
   Pres. perf. Die alte Dame hat vor Freude geweint.
   Fut. Die alte Dame wird vor Freude weinen.
7. Pres. Die Mädchen singen sehr gut.
   Past Die Mädchen sangen sehr gut.
   Fut. Die Mädchen werden sehr gut singen.

8. Pres. Lars sitzt auf dem Boden.
Past Lars saß auf dem Boden.
Pres. perf. Lars hat auf dem Boden gesessen.
9. Past Er schwamm einen neuen Record.
Pres. perf. Er hat einen neuen Record geschwommen.
Fut. Er wird einen neuen Record schwimmen.
10. Pres. Was kaufen Sie?
Pres. perf. Was haben Sie gekauft?
Fut. Was werden Sie kaufen?

14·2
1. breche, brach, habe gebrochen
brichst, brachst, hast gebrochen
bricht, brach, hat gebrochen
brechen, brachen, haben gebrochen
brecht, bracht, habt gebrochen
brechen, brachen, haben gebrochen
2. nehme, nahm, habe genommen
nimmst, nahmst, hast genommen
nimmt, nahm, hat genommen
nehmen, nahmen, haben genommen
nehmt, nahmt, habt genommen
nehmen, nahmen, haben genommen
3. helfe, half, habe geholfen
hilfst, halfst, hast geholfen
hilft, half, hat geholfen
helfen, halfen, haben geholfen
helft, halft, habt geholfen
helfen, halfen, haben geholfen
4. geschieht, geschah, ist geschehen
geschehen, geschahen, sind geschehen
5. spreche, sprach, habe gesprochen
sprichst, sprachst, hast gesprochen
spricht, sprach, hat gesprochen
sprechen, sprachen, haben gesprochen
sprecht, spracht, habt gesprochen
sprechen, sprachen, haben gesprochen

14·3
1. Sieht er die Elefanten?
2. Er liest ihren neuen Roman.
3. Er isst oft mexikanisch.
4. Warum stirbt er?
5. Was stiehlt er?

14·4
1. brate, briet, habe gebraten
brätst, brietst, hast gebraten
brät, briet, hat gebraten
braten, brieten, haben gebraten
bratet, brietet, habt gebraten
braten, brieten, haben gebraten
2. lasse, ließ, habe gelassen
lässt, ließest, hast gelassen
lässt, ließ, hat gelassen
lassen, ließen, haben gelassen
lasst, ließt, habt gelassen
lassen, ließen, haben gelassen
3. wachse, wuchs, bin gewachsen
wächst, wuchsest, bist gewachsen
wächst, wuchs, ist gewachsen
wachsen, wuchsen, sind gewachsen
wachst, wuchst, seid gewachsen
wachsen, wuchsen, sind gewachsen

14·5
1. Wäschst du dich?
2. Du schlägst den armen Hund.
3. Du stößt dich am Tisch.
4. Fällst du auf der Treppe?
5. Du läufst in die Apotheke

14·6
1. Past Die Lampe brannte dunkel.
   Pres. perf. Die Lampe hat dunkel gebrannt.
   Fut. Die Lampe wird dunkel brennen.
2. Pres. Der Polizist bringt eine gute Nachricht.
   Pres. perf. Der Polizist hat eine gute Nachricht gebracht.
   Fut. Der Polizist wird eine gute Nachricht bringen.
3. Pres. Ich denke wieder an meine Familie.
   Past Ich dachte wieder an meine Familie.
   Fut. Ich werde wieder an meine Familie denken.
4. Pres. Er kennt den Chef persönlich.
   Past Er kannte den Chef persönlich.
   Pres. perf. Er hat den Chef persönlich gekannt.
5. Past Wir nannten unsere Tochter Angela.
   Pres. perf. Wir haben unsere Tochter Angela genannt.
   Fut. Wir werden unsere Tochter Angela nennen.
6. Pres. Die Jungen rennen zum Sportplatz.
   Pres. perf. Die Jungen sind zum Sportplatz gerannt.
   Fut. Die Jungen werden zum Sportplatz rennen.
7. Pres. Wer sendet den Katalog zur Ansicht?
   Past Wer sandte den Katalog zur Ansicht?
   Fut. Wer wird den Katalog zur Ansicht senden?
8. Pres. Du weißt nichts.
   Past Du wusstest nichts.
   Pres. perf. Du hast nichts gewusst.

14·7
1. Past Sie diskutierten stundenlang.
   Pres. perf. Sie haben stundenlang diskutiert.
   Fut. Sie werden stundenlang diskutieren.
2. Pres. Er diszipliert sich nicht.
   Pres. perf. Er hat sich nicht diszipliniert.
   Fut. Er wird sich nicht disziplinieren.
3. Pres. Die Soldaten marschieren nach Hause.
   Past Die Soldaten marschierten nach Hause.
   Fut. Die Soldaten werden nach Hause marschieren.
4. Pres. Ich spendiere dir ein Glas Bier.
   Past Ich spendierte dir ein Glas Bier.
   Pres. perf. Ich habe dir ein Glas Bier spendiert.

14·8
1. Wo seid ihr eurem Professor begegnet?
2. Wo seid ihr meinen Verwandten begegnet?
3. Wo seid ihr dem jungen Künstler begegnet?
4. Hör mir zu!
5. Hör ihnen zu!
6. Hör der Ärztin zu!
7. Können Sie seiner Rede folgen?
8. Können Sie dieser langweiligen Vorlesung folgen?
9. Warum hast du ihm nicht geglaubt?
10. Warum hast du meinen Brüdern nicht geglaubt?

15 Passive voice versus participles as adjectives

15·1
1. Das Fenster wird von dem Jungen zerbrochen.
2. Wird der Artikel von dir geschrieben werden?
3. Ich wurde von dem Lehrer gefragt.
4. Das Bild wird von dem Maler gemalt.

5. Ein Geschenk ist von uns geschickt worden.
6. Die Stadt wurde von den Soldaten geschützt.
7. Der Ball wird von den Kindern gesucht werden.
8. Ein paar Ansichtskarten werden von mir gekauft.
9. Die Schiffe sind von dem Touristen fotografiert worden.
10. Die Bibel ist von Gutenberg gedruckt worden.
11. Die Aufgabe wird von den Schülern gelernt werden.
12. Die alten Flugzeuge werden von euch gesehen.
13. Die Schlüssel sind von ihm vergessen worden.
14. Zwei Äpfel wurden von Erik gegessen.
15. Der Ofen wird von meiner Mutter geheizt.

15·2
1. Past Die Bücher wurden in den Schrank gestellt.
   Pres. perf. Die Bücher sind in den Schrank gestellt worden.
   Fut. Die Bücher werden in den Schrank gestellt werden.
2. Pres. Von wem wird der Brief in den Briefkasten gesteckt?
   Pres. perf. Von wem ist der Brief in den Briefkasten gesteckt worden?
   Fut. Von wem wird der Brief in den Briefkasten gesteckt werden?
3. Pres. Die schönen Waren werden auf den Tisch gelegt.
   Past Die schönen Waren wurden auf den Tisch gelegt.
   Fut. Die schönen Waren werden auf den Tisch gelegt werden.
4. Pres. Hier wird Weihnachten auch gefeiert.
   Past Hier wurde Weihnachten auch gefeiert.
   Pres. perf. Hier ist Weihnachten auch gefeiert worden.
5. Past Das Wort wurde von dem Schüler buchstabiert.
   Pres. perf. Das Wort ist von dem Schüler buchstabiert worden.
   Fut. Das Wort wird von dem Schüler buchstabiert werden.

15·3
1. Die Wunde wird geheilt.
   Die Wunde ist geheilt.
2. Das Fahrrad wird verkauft.
   Das Fahrrad ist verkauft.
3. Der Laden wird eröffnet.
   Der Lade ist eröffnet.
4. Eine neue Kirche wird gebaut.
   Eine neue Kirche ist gebaut.
5. Das kleine Dorf wird zerstört.
   Das kleine Dorf ist zerstört.

15·4
1. Dem Matrosen ist von ihm für seine Hilfe gedankt worden.
2. Mir wurde von Lars nicht geglaubt.
3. Der Managerin wird von dem jungen Pianisten sehr imponiert.
4. Ihnen wird von dem Richter mit dem Todesurteil gedroht werden.
5. Von wem ist Ihnen gedient worden?
6. Ihr wurden ein paar CDs von mir zum Geburtstag geschenkt.
7. Ohrringe werden seiner Braut von dem Bräutigam gegeben werden.
8. Dir wird nicht von uns vertraut.
9. Etwas Schönes ist uns von Sabine geschickt worden.
10. Was wird eurer Schwester von euch geraten werden?

15·5
1. Diese Probleme müssen von uns gelöst werden.
2. Das Geld konnte nicht gefunden werden.
3. Der Hund hat von Thomas gewaschen werden sollen.
4. Der Dieb wird nicht verhaftet werden wollen.
5. Den Mädchen musste mit ihrer Schularbeit geholfen werden.
6. Solche Wörter dürfen nicht geschrieben werden.
7. Der Fernsehapparat hat von ihr repariert werden können.

8. Er wollte nicht von mir geraten werden.
9. Ihm soll für seine Großzügigkeit gedankt werden.
10. Das kranke Pferd hat durch einen Schuss getötet werden müssen.

15·6   1. b   2. c   3. a   4. a   5. d   6. a   7. d   8. c   9. a   10. d

16 Subjunctive mood

16·1
1. warte, warte
   wartest, wartest
   wartet, warte
   warten, warten
   wartet, wartet
   warten, warten
2. vergesse, vergesse
   vergisst, vergessest
   vergisst, vergesse
   vergessen, vergessen
   vergesst, vergesset
   vergessen, vergessen
3. schlage, schlage
   schlägst, schlagest
   schlägt, schlage
   schlagen, schlagen
   schlagt, schlaget
   schlagen, schlagen
4. gebe aus, gebe aus
   gibst aus, gebest aus
   gibt aus, gebe aus
   geben aus, geben aus
   gebt aus, gebet aus
   geben aus, geben aus
5. empfehle, empfehle
   empfiehlst, empfehlest
   empfiehlt, empfehle
   empfehlen, empfehlen
   empfehlt, empfehlet
   empfehlen, empfehlen

16·2
1. kann, könne
   kannst, könnest
   kann, könne
   können, können
   könnt, könnet
   können, können
2. mag, möge
   magst, mögest
   mag, möge
   mögen, mögen
   mögt, möget
   mögen, mögen
3. soll, solle
   sollst, sollest
   soll, solle
   sollen, sollen
   sollt, sollet
   sollen, sollen

4. darf, dürfe
darfst, dürfest
darf, dürfe
dürfen, dürfen
dürft, dürfet
dürfen, dürfen

5. bin, sei
bist, seiest
ist, sei
sind, seien
seid, seiet
sind, seien

16·3
1. mein Bruder wieder krank geworden sei.
2. unser Lehrer heute nachmittag angerufen habe.
3. Herr Bauer seinen Wagen verkaufen wolle.
4. ihre Nachbarin Schauspielerin werde.
5. niemand das Problem lösen könne.
6. der Vogel von Erik gefangen worden sei.
7. eure Schwester hier in der Küche spielen müsse.
8. sie gut singe.
9. er jetzt genug Geld habe.
10. du es verstehest.

16·4
1. der Wissenschaftler heute gestorben wäre.
2. er sich nicht daran gewöhnen könnte.
3. der Dieb von den Polizisten gesehen worden wäre.
4. man den Arzt täglich benachrichtigen sollte.
5. viele beim Unglück umgekommen wären.
6. warum die Eisenbahn nicht mehr führe.
7. ob der Fluss die Brücke fortgerissen hätte.
8. ob sie sich auf einer Insel befände.
9. wie lange die Männer wandern könnten.
10. ob Ihre Tante nach Paris reisen wollte.

16·5 *Sample answers are provided.*
1. Wenn ich mehr Geld hätte,
2. Wenn ich meinen Bruder mitgebracht hätte,
3. könnte er einen neuen Pullover kaufen.
4. hätte sie bessere Noten bekommen.
5. wenn er um Hilfe bäte.
6. wenn das Essen nicht so schlecht gewesen wäre.
7. wenn sie heute zur Arbeit gekommen wäre.
8. Ich würde mich sehr freuen,
9. Ich hätte seinen Bruder besucht,
10. Wenn wir seinen letzten Brief hätten,

16·6
1. sie in Thomas verliebt wäre.
2. sie mich gar nicht gesehen hätte.
3. wir nicht ihre Freunde gewesen wären.
4. der Film langweilig wäre.
5. ich heute abend müde wäre.
6. er eine wunderbare Stimme hätte.
7. alle Beifall klatschten.
8. er allein im Wartesaal wäre.
9. er vor einem Mikrofon stünde.
10. er Geld von uns erwartete.
11. sie krank geworden wäre.
12. sie weinen wollte.
13. sie ein Ungeheuer gesehen hätte.
14. sie nicht klar sehen könnte.
15. die Lampe zu hell gewesen wäre.

17 Numbers and numerals

17·1 *Sample answers are provided.*
1. In diesem Haus wohnt nur einer.
2. Eine ist für meinen Vater.
3. Ich kenne nur eins.
4. Unser Vater hat einen.
5. In unserer Stadt gibt es nur eine.
6. Ich kann nur eine sehen.
7. Im Hafen war nur eins.
8. Stimmt nicht! Ich habe nur einen.
9. Nein, nur eine.
10. Nein, er hat mit einer gesprochen.

17·2
1. Acht plus/und sieben ist/gleich fünfzehn.
2. Sieben mal drei ist/gleich einundzwanzig.
3. Vierzehn (geteilt) durch sieben ist/gleich zwei.
4. Neunundneunzig minus/weniger neunundfünfzig ist/gleich vierzig.
5. Achtundvierzig (geteilt) durch acht ist/gleich sechs.

17·3
1. zehnte 2. fünfzehnte 3. dreißigste 4. zweiundachtzigste 5. erste 6. dreizehnte 7. siebte
8. zweihundertste 9. siebzigste 10. dritte

17·4 *Sample answers are provided.*
1. Der Wievielte ist heute?
   Heute ist der zehnte Dezember.
   Sein Geburtstag ist am zehnten Dezember.
2. Welches Datum haben wir heute?
   Heute ist der erste Januar.
   Sie kommt am ersten Januar zu Besuch.
3. Der Wievielte ist heute?
   Heute ist der einunddreißigste Juli.
   Am einunddreißigsten Juli reisen wir nach Amerika.
4. Welches Datum haben wir heute?
   Heute ist der dritte April.
   Das Konzert ist am dritten April.
5. Der Wievielte ist heute?
   Heute ist der siebte Mai.
   Kommt er am siebten Mai nach Hause?

17·5 *Sample answers are provided.*
1. Wir haben unser Haus 1985 gekauft.
   Wir haben unser Haus im Jahre 1985 gekauft.
2. Ich reiste 2011 in die Schweiz.
   Ich reiste im Jahre 2011 in die Schweiz.
3. Die Zwillinge sind 1998 geboren.
   Die Zwillinge sind im Jahre 1998 geboren.
4. Er fing 2001 an, in Amerika zu arbeiten.
   Er fing im Jahre 2001 an, in Amerika zu arbeiten.
5. Mein Bruder hat 2009 in Afghanistan gedient.
   Mein Bruder hat im Jahre 2009 in Afghanistan gedient.

17·6
1. Die Kinder trinken mehr Milch.
2. Die Kinder trinken etwas Milch.
3. Die Kinder trinken wenig Milch.
4. Die Kinder trinken viel Milch.
5. Sie braucht wieder mehr Zeit.
6. Sie braucht wieder etwas Zeit.
7. Sie braucht wieder wenig Zeit.
8. Sie braucht wieder viel Zeit.

17·7   1. a 2. a 3. b 4. d 5. a 6. c 7. b 8. d 9. b 10. b

18 Infinitive clauses

18·1 *Sample answers are provided.*
1. meine amerikanischen Verwandten zu besuchen
2. mit dem Richter zu sprechen
3. für Frau Schneider zu arbeiten
4. die Polizei anzurufen
5. in diesem Cafe zu essen
6. den Lehrer nicht zu begrüßen
7. ihr einen Ring zu schenken
8. seiner Mutter zu danken
9. einen Regenschirm mitzubringen
10. mein Benehmen zu erklären
11. diesen Mann zu retten
12. ohne einen Reisepass zu reisen
13. so ein altes Auto zu verkaufen
14. die Kanzlerin kennen zu lernen
15. diese Ausländer zu verstehen

18·2
1. ein paar Blumen zu kaufen
2. mit der Ausländerin tanzen zu wollen
3. von ihnen zerstört worden zu sein
4. kein Eis gemocht zu haben
5. von Tina erzählt zu werden
6. das Orchester spielen zu hören
7. von dem Polizisten bestraft zu werden
8. euch bald wiederzusehen
9. mit derselben Straßenbahn gefahren zu sein
10. dem weinenden Kind geholfen zu haben

18·3 *Sample answers are provided.*
1. sofort nach Hause zu gehen
2. nicht zu lange zu schlafen
3. mehr Geld zu sparen
4. die Wahrheit gesagt zu haben
5. keinen Ring gestohlen zu haben
6. die Fragen nicht verstehen zu können
7. meine Schwester zu betrügen
8. mit Albert singen zu müssen
9. für meinen alten Chef gearbeitet zu haben
10. im Wohnzimmer zu bleiben
11. Ärztin zu werden
12. Russisch sprechen zu lernen
13. stark zu regnen
14. viel kälter zu werden
15. zu schneien

18·4 *Sample answers are provided.*
1. sein Buch zu lesen
2. einschlafen zu können
3. das Kind weinen zu hören
4. seine verstorbene Frau zu vergessen
5. seinen Bruder kommen zu sehen
6. ihnen wieder zu danken
7. mit den Streikenden zu marschieren
8. eine neue Stellung zu finden
9. den Fernsehapparat reparieren zu lassen
10. mich umzuziehen
11. Abschied von uns zu nehmen
12. vollzutanken
13. ihre Koffer mitzunehmen

14. Thomas das Geschenk zu geben
15. zu bezahlen
16. mehr Geld zu verdienen
17. ein bisschen mehr zu sparen
18. befördert zu werden
19. besser zu lernen
20. Fachmann zu werden

18·5 1. a 2. a 3. a 4. d 5. b 6. c 7. b 8. d 9. a 10. b

19 Relative clauses

19·1
1. Die Kinder, die Tina und Erik besuchen, müssen jetzt nach Hause gehen.
2. Die Kinder, die wir heute kennen gelernt haben, müssen jetzt nach Hause gehen.
3. Die Kinder, denen ich die Bücher gab, müssen jetzt nach Hause gehen.
4. Die Kinder, deren Mutter krank geworden ist, müssen jetzt nach Hause gehen.
5. Das Haus, das mehr als fünfzig Jahre alt ist, ist sehr groß.
6. Das Haus, das mein Onkel gekauft hat, ist sehr groß.
7. Das Haus, neben dem viele Bäume stehen, ist sehr groß.
8. Das Haus, dessen Farbe weiß ist, ist sehr groß.
9. Lars tanzte mit der Schauspielerin, die Französin ist.
10. Lars tanzte mit der Schauspielerin, die ich interviewen will.
11. Lars tanzte mit der Schauspielerin, von der Monika ein Geschenk bekommen hat.
12. Lars tanzte mit der Schauspielerin, deren Mann Komponist ist.
13. Sie sprechen von dem Arzt, der 100.000 Euro gewonnen hat.
14. Sie sprechen von dem Arzt, für den meine Tante arbeitet.
15. Sie sprechen von dem Arzt, nach dem der Detektiv fragt.
16. Sie sprechen von dem Arzt, dessen Praxis in der Hauptstadt ist.

19·2
1. Die Kinder, welche Tina und Erik besuchen, müssen jetzt nach Hause gehen.
2. Die Kinder, welche wir heute kennen gelernt haben, müssen jetzt nach Hause gehen.
3. Die Kinder, welchen ich die Bücher gab, müssen jetzt nach Hause gehen.
4. Die Kinder, deren Mutter krank geworden ist, müssen jetzt nach Hause gehen.
5. Das Haus, welches mehr als fünfzig Jahre alt ist, ist sehr groß.
6. Das Haus, welches mein Onkel gekauft hat, ist sehr groß.
7. Das Haus, neben welchem viele Bäume stehen, ist sehr groß.
8. Das Haus, dessen Farbe weiß ist, ist sehr groß.
9. Lars tanzte mit der Schauspielerin, welche Französin ist.
10. Lars tanzte mit der Schauspielerin, welche ich interviewen will.
11. Lars tanzte mit der Schauspielerin, von welcher Monika ein Geschenk bekommen hat.
12. Lars tanzte mit der Schauspielerin, deren Mann Komponist ist.
13. Sie sprechen von dem Arzt, welcher 100.000 Euro gewonnen hat.
14. Sie sprechen von dem Arzt, für welchen meine Tante arbeitet.
15. Sie sprechen von dem Arzt, nach welchem der Detektiv fragt.
16. Sie sprechen von dem Arzt, dessen Praxis in der Hauptstadt ist.

19·3 *Sample answers are provided.*
1. die in dem großen Haus wohnen
2. die Herr Schneider besuchen will
3. für die Martin gearbeitet hat
4. der schon kaputt ist
5. mit dem ich nach Bonn reisen will
6. dessen Farbe blau ist
7. über die Frau Benz geredet hat
8. deren Sohn im Gefängnis ist
9. in dem man viele interessante Bücher finden kann
10. in den sie eine Vase stellte

19·4
1. Ein Schimmel ist ein Pferd, dessen Farbe weiß ist.
2. Ein Russe ist ein Mann, dessen Heimat Russland ist.
3. Eine weltbekannte Sängerin ist eine Sängerin, deren Name in der ganzen Welt bekannt ist.

4. Ein Handwerker ist ein Arbeiter, dessen Beruf schwierig ist.

5. Ein Waisenkind ist ein Kind, dessen Vater und Mutter tot sind.

19·5 *Sample answers are provided.*
1. Wer nicht mein Freund ist
   Wem ich nicht trauen kann
2. der verliebt sich in sie
   den begeistert sie
3. der wird nie ein Freund
   dem ist nicht zu helfen
4. Wer immer lügt
   Wer die Unwahrheit sagt
5. der wird verhungern
   der tut mir Leid

19·6 *Sample answers are provided.*
1. sie schreibt 2. kann verdorben werden 3. wir je gehört haben 4. dir bestimmt gefallen
wird 5. Thomas erzählt 6. Sie im Geschäft haben 7. meine Frau je gesehen hat 8. auf der Straße
passiert 9. deine Mutter nicht hören darf 10. ist nicht immer das Beste

19·7 *Sample answers are provided.*
1. ein echtes Wunder war 2. Herr Bauer trinkt sehr viel Bier 3. eine Lüge ist 4. Erik hat einen teuren
Wagen gekauft 5. Sie sagt, dass Gudrun so schnell wie ein Fisch schwimmen kann 6. seine Eltern sehr
erfreute 7. eine schlechte Gewohnheit ist 8. Frau Schmidt ist jetzt die neue Managerin 9. Er berichtet
dass, der Krieg endlich vorbei ist 10. die Eltern sehr enttäuschte

19·8 1. b 2. c 3. b 4. d 5. d 6. b 7. a 8. d 9. b 10. d

20 Writing

20·1 *Sample answers are provided.*
1. Unsere ausländischen Gäste sprechen kein Deutsch.
2. Kennen Sie unsere ausländischen Gäste?
3. Tina spricht mit unseren ausländischen Gästen.
4. Sie geben unseren ausländischen Gästen Geschenke.
5. Unsere ausländischen Gäste sind von ihr eingeladen worden.
6. Er sagte, dass Martin unsere ausländischen Gäste kennen gelernt habe.
7. Das ist ein Geschenk für unsere ausländischen Gäste.
8. Wegen unserer ausländischen Gäste, mussten wir zu Hause bleiben.
9. Unsere ausländischen Gäste haben nach Berlin fahren wollen.
10. Niemand glaubte unseren ausländischen Gästen.

20·2 *Sample answers are provided.*
1. Das nette Mädchen hat uns geholfen.
2. Kennst du das nette Mädchen?
3. Wir wurden von dem netten Mädchen eingeladen.
4. Ich schicke dem netten Mädchen eine Ansichtskarte.
5. Wo wohnt das nette Mädchen, das Erik kennen lernen will?
6. Hier wohnt ein Freund, der das nette Mädchen besucht hat.
7. Er ging ohne das nette Mädchen in die Stadt.
8. Wegen des netten Mädchens, haben wir mehr Freizeit.
9. Das nette Mädchen wollte Tennis spielen.
10. Er begegnete dem netten Mädchen im Stadtpark.

20·3 *Sample answers are provided.*
1. Meine junge Nichte ist Krankenschwester.
2. Ich besuchte meine junge Nichte.
3. Außer meiner jungen Nichte ist niemand zu Hause.
4. Was gibst du meiner jungen Nichte?
5. Meine junge Nichte wurde vom Bürgermeister besucht.
6. Der Lehrer, der meiner jungen Nichte das Buch gab, ist auch Schriftsteller.
7. Tina hat gegen meine junge Nichte gespielt.

8. Ich denke oft an meine junge Nichte.
9. Meine junge Nichte hat ein Gedicht geschrieben.
10. Wer wird meiner jungen Nichte helfen?

20·4 *Sample answers are provided.*
1. Jeder amerikanische Soldat muss gesund sein.
2. Ich kann nicht jeden amerikanischen Soldaten kennen.
3. Er fragte nach jedem amerikanischen Soldaten.
4. Sie gibt jedem amerikanischen Soldaten einen Apfel.
5. Jeder amerikanische Soldat wird im Ausland dienen.
6. Er fotografiert jeden amerikanischen Soldaten, dessen Familie noch in den USA ist.
7. Er hat gegen jeden amerikanischen Soldaten gewonnen.
8. Sie versucht neben jedem amerikanischen Soldaten zu stehen.
9. Jeder amerikanische Soldat war in die Stadt gegangen.
10. Sie wurde von jedem amerikanischen Soldaten geküsst.

20·5 *Sample answers are provided.*
1. Sind diese hohen Berge höher als die Alpen?
2. Wir fotografieren diese hohen Berge.
3. Kann man zu diesen hohen Bergen laufen?
4. Diese hohen Berge sind am schönsten.
5. Diese hohen Berge konnten nicht von ihm beschrieben werden.
6. Ist das ein Bild von diesen hohen Bergen, die ich in der Ferne sehen kann?
7. Sie bauen einen Tunnel durch diese hohen Berge.
8. Niemand kann auf diese hohen Berge klettern.
9. Diese hohen Berge haben uns imponiert.
10. Anstatt dieser hohen Berge, will er den kleinen Bach fotografieren.

20·6 *Sample answers are provided.*
1. ihrem Mann gar nicht gefallen hat
2. zu teuer ist
3. sie im Einkaufszentrum gefunden hat
4. ihr nicht passt
5. das Gefängnis zu gefährlich sei
6. der Mann wirklich unschuldig sei
7. die Polizei den Verbrecher verhaften solle
8. der Verbrecher schon verhaftet worden sei
9. wo sich das Rathaus befinde
10. wann der nächste Zug komme
11. wie alt diese Kirche sei
12. ob wir Englisch verstünden
13. sie spielen Fußball
14. sie gehen mit Karl schwimmen
15. sie wollen ins Kino gehen
16. sie spielen Karten in der Garage
17. es kalt und regnerisch geworden ist
18. es am Montag ein Examen geben wird
19. das Faschingfest um 19 Uhr anfängt
20. Professor Benz eine Rede halten wird
21. mehr Geld zu verdienen
22. für ihre Operation zu bezahlen
23. eine Reise nach Polen zu machen
24. dagegen zu protestieren
25. zu versuchen ihm zu helfen

20·7 *Sample answers are provided.*
1. Meine Tochter hat wieder eine schlechte Note bekommen.
2. Nein, ich kann nicht. Ich muss Überstunden machen.
3. Er liest gern. Ich kaufe ihm einen neuen Roman.
4. Ich weiß es nicht. Die Auswahl ist so groß.
5. Wie viel brauchst du denn?

6. Nein, aber in Rom sprechen viele Englisch.
7. Ich finde sie ein bisschen zu groß für dein Gesicht.
8. Schön. Ich kaufe es. Wie viel kostet es?
9. Wir reisen mit Herrn Schukow.
10. Sie sind um sieben Uhr aufgestanden.
11. Ist er nicht von dir eingeladen worden?
12. Nein, ich habe mein Handy verloren.
13. Beim Fleischer in der Bismarckstraße.
14. Ich finde eine Seilbahn viel zu gefährlich.
15. Sie hat gestern einen neuen Blumengarten gepflanzt.

20·8 *Sample answers are provided.*

Sabine: Guten Tag, Herr Bauer. *Wohin gehen Sie?*

Herr Bauer: *Ich gehe ins Einkaufszentrum.* Ich möchte meiner Frau ein Geschenk kaufen.

Sabine: *Hat sie diese Woche Geburtstag?*

Herr Bauer: Nein, ihr Geburtstag ist im April. *Ich möchte ihr eine kleine Überraschung machen.*

Sabine: Ich gehe auch ins Einkaufszentrum. *Erik arbeitet da im Herrenkleidergeschäft.*

Herr Bauer: Ich kenne Erik nicht. *Ist er dein Verlobter?*

Sabine: Nein, er ist nur ein Freund von mir. *Mein Verlobter heißt Martin.*

Herr Bauer: Ist Martin noch Student oder *arbeitet er schon?*

Sabine: Er ist jetzt Bauingenier. *Er hat eine Stellung in Bonn bekommen.*

Herr Bauer: *Ach, es ist schon halb zwölf.* Ich muss mich beeilen. Wiedersehen!

20·9 Thomas: Ich habe Lars gestern mit einem Mädchen gesehen. *Sie sieht sehr gut aus.*

Werner: Ja, sie ist sehr schön. *Sie heißt Tina und ist seine Cousine.*

Thomas: Seine Cousine? *Vielleicht soll ich sie kennen lernen.*

Werner: Sie hat schon einen Freund und ist sogar *fast verlobt.*

Thomas: Schade. *Willst du morgen Tennis spielen gehen?*

Werner: Ich fahre morgen mit meinem Vater in die Stadt. *Er sucht ein neues Auto.*

Thomas: Was für ein Auto wird es sein? *Ein BMW ist wirklich Klasse.*

Werner: Ein BMW ist zu teuer. *Mein Vater möchte lieber einen billigeren Wagen.*

Thomas: Wenn ich ein Auto hätte, würde *ich eine Auslandsfahrt machen.*

Werner: Zuerst musst du arbeiten und *etwas Geld verdienen.*

20·10 Tante Luise: Rolf, warum hast du den Tisch noch nicht gedeckt? *Es ist schon acht Uhr.*

Rolf: Ich bin eben nach Hause gekommen. *Ich musste Brötchen beim Bäcker holen.*

Tante Luise: Frische Brötchen mit Butter! *So was mag ich gern.*

Rolf: Ich habe schon Wasser gekocht. *Möchtest du eine Tasse Kaffee?*

Tante Luise: *Nein, danke.* Ich trinke lieber Tee.

Rolf: Onkel Karl hat vor einer halben Stunde angerufen. *Er muss wieder Überstunden machen.*

Tante Luise: Der arme Mann arbeitet so viel. *Er braucht eine schöne Urlaubsreise.*

Rolf: Eine Reise? *Wohin wollt ihr denn reisen?*

Tante Luise: Ich möchte gerne nach Paris oder Madrid besuchen, aber *wir sprechen weder Französich noch Spanisch.*

Rolf: Kein Problem. In Europa *sprechen viele Leute Englisch oder Deutsch.*

Tante Luise: Hoffentlich hast du Recht. *Rolf, hast du auch eine Flasche Milch gekauft?*

Rolf: Nein, nur die Brötchen. *Soll ich zum Milchladen gehen?*

Tante Luise: Nein, die Kinder können Apfelsaft trinken. *Was willst du trinken?*

Rolf: Ich möchte Kaffee. *Und ein Brötchen mit Butter und Marmelade.*

3190105183O380